Multidimensional Functional Assessment:
The OARS Methodology

Second Edition

Duke University
Center for the Study of Aging and Human Development

MULTIDIMENSIONAL FUNCTIONAL ASSESSMENT:
THE OARS METHODOLOGY
A MANUAL

SECOND EDITION

A Publication of
The Duke University Center for the
Study of Aging and Human Development

The Center for the Study of Aging and Human Development, Duke University Medical Center, Durham, North Carolina 27710.

CONTRIBUTING AUTHORS

Dan Blazer, M.D., Assistant Professor of Psychiatry; Associate Director for Programs, Center for the Study of Aging and Human Development, Duke University Medical Center, Durham, North Carolina

Richard M. Burton, D.B.A., Associate Professor, School of Business Administration, Duke University, Durham, North Carolina

William P. Cleveland, Ph.D., Associate Professor of Community Health Sciences; Statistician, Center for the Study of Aging and Human Development, Duke University Medical Center, Durham, North Carolina

William W. Damon, Ph.D., Associate Professor of Business Administration, Vanderbilt University, Nashville, Tennessee

David C. Dellinger, Ph.D., Associate Professor, School of Business Administration, Duke University, Durham, North Carolina

Douglas J. Erickson, M.D., Resident, Vanderbilt University Medical Center, Nashville, Tennessee

Gerda G. Fillenbaum, Ph.D., Research Associate in Psychiatry; Scientific Associate, Center for the Study of Aging and Human Development, Duke University Medical Center, Durham, North Carolina

Becky Heron, B.A., Assessment Specialist, Center for the Study of Aging and Human Development, Duke University Medical Center, Durham, North Carolina

William F. Laurie, C.P.A., Project Manager, United States General Accounting Office, Cleveland, Ohio

George L. Maddox, Ph.D., Professor of Sociology, Professor of Medical Sociology, Psychiatry; Director, Center for the Study of Aging and Human Development, Duke University Medical Center, Durham, North Carolina

James T. Moore, M.D., Associate, Division of Psychosomatic Medicine, Department of Psychiatry; Director of Behavioral Sciences, Family Medicine Program, Duke University Medical Center, Durham, North Carolina

David W. Peterson, Ph.D., Professor, School of Business Administration, Duke University, Durham, North Carolina

Eric Pfeiffer, M.D., Professor of Psychiatry, Veterans Administration Hospital and the University of South Florida, Tampa, Florida

Connie Service, Research Associate, Department of Community and Family Medicine, Duke University Medical Center, Durham, North Carolina

Thomas J. Walsh, C.P.A., Supervisory Auditor, United States General Accounting Office, Cleveland, Ohio

DUKE OARS STAFF

1972 - 1978

Judy Altholz

Richard Bias

Dan Blazer

Richard M. Burton

Pamela Van Buskirk

Henry Callahan

William P. Cleveland

Charlene Connolly

William W. Damon

David C. Dellinger

Gerda G. Fillenbaum

Jeanette Franklin

Kermit Hamrick

Becky Heron

James D. Kemp

Lorraine Landy-Heil

Barbara Lawton

Don Lawton

Patti Lewis

George L. Maddox

Harry Maney

Mary Ann Matteson

Alice Myers

John B. Nowlin

Dan Peak

Dave Peterson

Eric Pfeiffer

Grace Polansky

Connie Service

Alan Whanger

Chris Woodbury

Evonne Yancey

TABLE OF CONTENTS

PART IV. TRAINING IN ADMINISTRATION OF THE OARS QUESTIONNAIRE

APPENDICES

PREFACE TO THE SECOND EDITION

At the Duke University Center for the Study of Aging and Human Development, research and training are intended to serve the aging and the aged. In the development of the Duke Older Americans Resources and Services (OARS) strategy and its related instruments, this intention is illustrated particularly well. The group at Duke who began working together to produce what was to become Duke OARS was a remarkable collection of scholars and clinicians with a wide range of multidisciplinary experience in gerontological research and practice-- physicians, social workers, nurses, sociologists, psychologists, economists, and systems analysts. They brought to the project a great deal of respect for their distinctly different but complementary expertise, and that respect has grown over the years. Duke OARS illustrates collegial relationships at their best.

Duke OARS also illustrates particularly well the operation of that invisible college of colleagues that goes far beyond Duke. The project benefitted enormously from the contributions of academic scholars, of project officers in the Administration on Aging and in various other governmental agencies, of service agency personnel, and of the participants in the various studies in which the OARS instruments were tested and refined. We owe a particular debt to scholars whose previous work is incorporated in the OARS instruments, and it is gratefully acknowledged here. We also owe a special debt to the numerous users of the OARS methodology across the country and abroad whose insights and suggestions based on their experience have been invaluable. We acknowledge with especial gratitude the contribution of colleagues at the General Accounting Office, Cleveland, Ohio, particularly that of William Laurie, Thomas Walsh, and Wilbert Ammann. The Cleveland GAO project has illustrated the logical development of Duke OARS as an information system for assessing the efficiency and effectiveness of services for older adults and for planning future services. The Cleveland project has produced a unique, valuable, and appropriate data set that, we hope, will shortly be in the public domain and available to scholars and students to explore in depth. The Cleveland data set, added to a great deal of comparable OARS data from Durham County, will provide important additions to the Center's Data Archive for Aging and Human Development, directed by Dr. Linda George.

Among the many individuals listed in this second edition as OARS staff, 1972-1978, Dr. Gerda Fillenbaum deserves a special word of thanks. Dr. Fillenbaum has been a key person in keeping contact between the Center and its growing network of OARS users. She is a living repository of the history of the project and its development.

Thanks are expressed to Deborah Coley for typing the manuscript of this edition; to Hall Ashmore for editing and producing it; to Thelma Jernigan for arranging OARS Training Sessions and to Becky Heron, who conducted the training; to Dan Blazer, Alan Whanger, Alice Myers, Kermit Hamrick, John Nowlin, Jeanette Franklin, and other members of the Center's Geriatric Evaluation and Treatment Clinic in which the OARS methodology was developed and continues to flourish; to Dietolf Ramm, William Cleveland, and their staff in the Computing and Statistical Laboratory; and to Betty Ray, Cecil Long, and Becky Tesh, who ensure that the Center operates from day to day.

George L. Maddox, Ph. D.
Center Director
August, 1978

PART I

THE MODEL

Chapter 1

Assessment of Individual Functional Status in a Program Evaluation and Resource Allocation Model*

Gerda G. Fillenbaum, David C. Dellinger, George L. Maddox, and Eric Pfeiffer

The social and political visibility of health and welfare programs has increased markedly in recent decades in the United States as numbers of participants and costs have escalated. Concomitantly, interest in the efficiency and effectiveness not only of health and welfare services but of the procedures for allocating scarce resources to these services has generated a special concern for developing and refining measures of program performance and for the impact of allocations to alternative programs (Maddox, 1972; Rivlin, 1971). This manual outlines a model designed to facilitate program evaluation and decisions regarding resource allocation. The focus of this chapter, however, will be on the first element of this model--the measurement of the functional status of individuals who compose the populations for which programs are developed and resources allocated. A brief word about how the model developed is in order.

In 1972 the Duke University Center for the Study of Aging and Human Development was asked by the Administration on Aging to structure and conceptualize an approach to understanding a persistent issue of special relevance in an aging society--alternatives to institutionalization, or better, institutionalization as an alternative in a continuum of health and welfare services. The occasion for what was presented as a rather urgent request was the juxtapositioning, in the minds of citizens and legislators, of over one million long-term care beds occupied primarily by older persons at an annual cost of over eight billion dollars in public funds and continued reports that high cost was not insuring quality care (Maddox, 1972; Shanas and Maddox, 1976). The fact that national wealth does not insure a nation's health and well-being was bad enough; the idea that public investments might decrease well-being was intolerable.

Our attempt to structure the problem of institutionalization as an option in a system of services led us to conceptualize a basic model which, we believe,

* Presented by George L. Maddox at the world conference "Aging: A Challenge to Science and Social Policy" sponsored by the INSTITUT DE LAVIE in Vichy, France, April 24-29, 1977. The research on which this chapter reports was supported by a grant from the U.S. Department of Health, Education and Welfare (93-P-75172/4). The Administration on Aging, the Social Rehabilitation Service, and the Health Resources Administration also provided support.

is not only useful in approaching the specific question of options in long-term care, but also has general applicability to program evaluation and to resource allocation decisions. This model has three critical elements:

1. A procedure for measuring the functional status of individuals and a related scheme for classifying individuals with similar status (equivalence classes).

2. The disaggregation of services into their generic elements in a way which permits comparison and costing across the particular aggregations (service packages) as they appear naturally in various programs and which permits analytic differentiation of services both from the organizational locale in which they are offered and from the particular person who provides the services. (See Burton, Damon, and Dellinger, 1976; Pfeiffer, 1975b; and Chapter 4 of this manual.)

3. A matrix which permits an analysis of the projected or actual impact of alternative service programs (service packages, or particular sets of generic services) on any identified array of individuals classified in terms of equivalent functional statuses. (See Burton, Damon, and Dellinger, 1976; and Chapter 5 of this manual.)

This chapter concentrates on the first of these three elements and will stress the logic of a measurement procedure and its related classification scheme. The details of the second and third elements of our model will be explicated in subsequent chapters, although we will indicate and illustrate briefly in this chapter how our procedure for measuring and classifying older individuals in terms of functional status relates to the other elements. We stress our focus on the functional status of individuals for a specifice reason. Program evaluation and resource allocation decisions cannot be adequately made in the absence of information about the functional status of individuals. Moreover, a review of behavioral and social scientific literature makes abundantly clear both that adequate research on the impact of programmatic interventions requires simultaneous macroanalysis of the social context of social programs and a microanalysis of individuals in those contexts and that such simultaneous analysis is extraordinarily uncommon (Hernes, 1976).

Conceptualizing the Functional Status of Individuals: The First Element

A reliable, valid, and adequate characterization of individuals which can also be accumulated to describe populations in ways simultaneously useful to clinicians familiar with older persons, to program analysts, to resource allocators, and to research scientists in a variety of disciplines is a major objective of the Duke project. Improbable as the development of such a classification procedure may seem, a failure to develop one compromises consequentially, perhaps fatally, procedures for program evaluation and resource allocation. Our interest in characterizing populations and individuals simultaneously presented, of course, some special problems in instrument development. We required an instrument that was relatively brief and easy to administer in the field as well as in clinics. It had to be satisfactory to clinicians as well as to research methodologists. Further, the data to be collected not only had to be sufficiently detailed to differentiate functioning among individuals at a point in time and within individuals over time, but also had to be reducible to a limited number of meaningful and manageable categories. The task was obviously formidable.

Our initial review of the existing literature on client classification and our experience with the first three hundred clients in the Duke Center's information, referral, and counseling service for older persons indicated that the instrument we required did not exist and suggested why this was the case. Older clients who seek help typically present multiple problems—problems which reflect various degrees of impairment in physical health, in mental health, in the capacity to carry out the self-care requirements of everyday life, and in the social resources and the economic resources which can compensate in part for personal incapacities. Limited purpose instruments were identified which addressed one or two types of impairments, but never all of them; and while issues of reliability and validity have occasionally been addressed (see, e.g., Katz and Lyerly, 1963; Gurel, Linn, and Linn, 1972; and Gurland, Yorkston, Stone, Frank, and Fleiss, 1972), such issues have not been resolved adequately for assessments across a spectrum of dimensions. Moreover, the available literature frequently concentrated on the diagnosis of particular health conditions or the identification of particular impairments rather than on assessment of functional status.

Our experience and our conceptualization of the most useful way to characterize individuals and populations for our purposes was to concentrate on a multidimensional measure of functional status. (See, e.g., Fanshel and Bush, 1970; Srole, Langner, Opler, Michael, and Rennie, 1962.) This approach appeared to be appropriately flexible and to focus on the summary of individual and population characteristics of paramount common interest to clinicians, research scientists, program analysts, and resource allocators—that is, it focused on the functional capacity of individuals to carry out usual social roles in a competent and personally staisfying way.

The demanding task we set for ourselves necessarily involved some strategic compromises. Experts in our research group with experience in assessing physical and mental health, economic resources, social resources, and activities of daily living inevitably wanted more detail than was in fact possible. Defensible compromises and accommodations were made in the interest of developing a manageable assessment instrument which could produce a reliable, valid classification of functioning in five dimensions and which could do so in about thirty minutes.

The instrument we developed and have used in our assessment clinic and in community surveys includes, in addition to certain demographic information, a Part A, which concentrates on functioning in the five dimensions of interest, and a Part B, which concentrates on the perception of needed services and a report on services used. The total instrument requires about forty-five minutes to administer. Additional details describing the instrument are provided in the Appendix to this chapter.

Measuring Five Dimensions of Individual Functioning

Our pilot studies took us through numerous iterations of questions designed to assess five dimensions of functioning: social resources, economic resources, mental health, physical health, and activities of daily living (ADL). Although our experience suggested that these were descrete and importantly different dimensions of functioning, their independence was seriously challenged. We were pragmatic rather than doctrinaire on this issue and elected to await the evidence.

As can be seen in Table 1, we now have relevant data from an appropriate study population of 997 randomly selected community-dwelling persons sixty-five years of age and older. The intercorrelations among the various dimensions are modest, with the highest correlations being between mental health and ADL (+ .55) and between those two dimensions and physical health (+ .55 and + .54, respectively). Our consultants and colleagues have occasionally argued that the various dimensions contribute differently to overall functioning and/or that economic resources and social resources are contextual factors which are conceptually different from the other three dimensions. (See, e.g, Williams, 1974.) Perhaps this is so. But the issue should be resolved by evidence and theoretical perspecitve. Our strategy has been to conceptualize and to store our data in ways which maximize our options for subsequent analysis of data.

Table 1

Product Moment Correlations Among the Five Dimensions of Functioning

	Economic Resources	Mental Health	Physical Health	ADL
Social Resources	.30	.38	.21	.16
Economic Resources		.39	.29	.26
Mental Health			.53	.55
Physical Health				.54

Information based on 997 randomly selected community residents aged sixty-five and over.

In developing questions which would tap essential aspects of each of the five dimensions, we drew as often as possible on a wide variety of previously reported items. The various iterations of our pilot questionnaire provided data which permitted assessment of the discriminant value of each question. The result--the Multidimensional Functional Assessment Questionnaire (MFAQ)-- provides a reasonably reliable and valid assessment instrument which can double adequately as a clinical intake procedure and as an epidemiologic survey questionnaire that can be administered and scored by a minimally trained individual and that is economical and flexible from the point of view of data management. The basic structure of the MFAQ is described briefly in the Appendix to this chapter. Information on the data sources is provided in Chapter 2, and the questionnaire itself is reproduced in Appendix A of this manual.

As we have noted, the MFAQ is divided essentially into two parts; our attention here focuses only on Part A (functional status). We assessed level of functioning in each of five dimensions, with the final assessment being made for each dimension by the interviewer on a six-point scale precisely defined by criteria for each of the six points. The continuum ranges from unimpaired functioning (1) to total dysfunction (6).

Reliability. We had considerably more than a ritualistic interest in establishing the reliability of functional assessment based on the MFAQ. This was the case particularly since our experience in policy analysis convinced us that research purporting to be applicable to significant societal issues should not only be reliable but also have a high probability of being effectively challenged and disqualified when evidence of unknown reliability is introduced (Maddox and Karasik, 1976, pp. 1-10). In the case of the MFAQ, interrater reliability tests made during the development of the instrument were acceptably high for all five dimensions. Not only did raters agree closely in assessing the relative severity of impairment of selected individuals (rank order agreement measured by Kendall's coefficient of concordance ranged from .74 for mental health to .88 for physical health), but they also assigned highly similar ratings (identical on 70 percent of the occasions examined, differing by as much as 2 points only 2 percent of the time). Recent independent testing shows rating agreement to be identical on 86 percent of rating occasions. The disciplines of the raters (we compared, for example, social workers, psychiatrists, and research personnel) had minimal effect on reliability of assessment.

Validity. The procedure used to evolve the MFAQ provides some assurance of its content and consensual validity. The team which developed the questionnaire included research investigators and a variety of clinicians who had had considerable exposure to both the relevant literature on client assessment and to older persons in community, clinical, and long-term care settings. Further, and more importantly, functional status assessed solely on the basis of questionnaire responses agrees well with functional status assigned independently and after extensive personal examination by an appropriate criterion group of clinicians (social workers, psychiatrists, and physicians' assistants). The only significant difference is found in the ADL dimension, where clinical interviews produced a significantly lower ADL assessment. Finally, the questionnaire is sufficiently sensitive that it can discriminate appropriately among groups of persons whose functional status can be expected to differ in certain anticipatable ways. On the average, for example, we would expect that the elderly living in the community would have a better functional level than out-patients at a geriatric assessment clinic, who, in turn, we would expect to function better on the average than the institutionalized. This, in fact, is what we found. (Details of the findings are provided in Chapter 3.)

As we have noted above and will note again below, the reliable, valid assessment of individual functional status is but the first essential element in our model. The third element, a transition matrix, conceptualizes the ultimate issue with respect to the validity of measurement--the capacity to estimate the probabilities of predicted stability and orderly change in individual functional status over time under specified conditions. We are currently at work on the issue of predictive validity of the MFAQ.

The Functional Classification Scheme

Our attention now shifts to problems of data reduction. As noted above, initial reduction involves translating reliably from multiple questions regarding each dimension into five summary measures on six-point scales. That further reduction is required is suggested by the number of different functional profiles which are potentially possible from these observations alone--7,776 (6^5). This number is clearly impractical for purposes of analysis. We have settled, in the short run, for a manageable scheme which dichotomizes the six-point scale as *unimpaired* (1-3) and *impaired* (4-6) for each of the five dimensions, resulting in 32 (2^5) profiles, or equivalence classes. Thus, an individual who is assessed to be *unimpaired* on all dimensions falls into equivalence class 1, and an individual who is *impaired* in all dimensions falls into class 32; the other thirty combinations range in between these extremes. For purposes of follow-up in any defined population we have added an additional category to indicate death.

On the basis of the evidence currently available to us, we are not at this time prepared to specify the normative distributions of older populations among our equivalence classes or to demonstrate the significance of the observed combinations of impairments. However, we do know that, in two populations which have been studied, 30 of the 32 equivalence classes have entries and that individuals are not randomly distributed among the classes. We are, thus, in a position to concentrate on the second element of our model--the generic services and their aggregation as service packages--and, eventually, on the third element--the outcomes which are expected or observed when persons of known equivalence classes are exposed to identified service packages.

In the short run we are in a position to use the observed distribution of functional impairments in each of the five dimensions to characterize populations and subpopulations of older persons differentiated by age, ethnicity, and rural-urban residence. We know already, for example, that, of the random sample of Durham County, North Carolina, elderly described in Chapter 9, 9 percent are impaired in social resources, 13 percent in mental health, 14 percent in economic resources, 22 percent in ADL, and 26 percent in physical health. In addition, from preliminary data in a comparable study of a random sample of 1,609 elderly persons in Cleveland, Ohio, described in Chapter 10, we know that the use of the MFAQ produced an almost identical distribution of impairments.

Another procedure for data reduction that we have found useful is the Cumulative Impairment Score (CIS). This score sums the position of an individual on the six-point scale for each of the five dimensions. Thus, the CIS can range from 5 (unimpaired) to 30 (totally impaired), with a midpoint of 17.5. The use of the CIS to describe the distribution of, for example, a community-dwelling sample and a sample of long-term care residents has been found to produce significantly different mean CIS scores and little overlap in the distribution. (See Chapter 9 for a more detailed discussion.) With such information it is possible to explore whether or not individuals in the overlap category (low CIS scores for institutional residents and high CIS scores for community-dwellers) can be explained by the different equivalence classes.

Some Current and Potential Developments of the Model

Although our ultimate interest is in articulating the role of the MFAQ in our program evaluation and resource allocation model, it is worth noting that the instrument has been immediately useful in several ways. It is currently being used, for example, as an initial screening and intake instrument in the Duke Center's Geriatric Evaluation and Treatment Clinic, an affiliate of the county community mental health clinic. In addition, the MFAQ is similarly used at intake for all patients over sixty-five years of age in the ambulatory clinic of Duke's Family Medicine Program. In this instance, the instrument is part of a research-demonstration project designed to assess the impact of information about patient functioning on chart entries and management plans made by family medicine residents who have functional status profiles of their older patients at the time those patients are first seen. Finally, since the MFAQ has been used in clinics and in epidemiologic surveys of random samples of community-dwelling and institutionalized older populations, the profiles of these various populations can be usefully compared in terms of observed distributions of functional impairment. Specifically, MFAQ survey data can provide information on the distribution of impairments, which, when compared with known participants in existing programs, can identify untreated impairment.

We must hasten to add that we do not consider the MFAQ as a "needs survey" instrument. *Need* is a second-order construct, a judgment made by someone evaluating what we consider to be a first-order construct, *impairment*. We do not think it is useful to interchange casually *impairment* and *need*, because the perception of an impairment as a need is a complex judgment. Indeed, the decision to translate a *need* into a condition warranting social intervention involves social preferences. Consider, for example, the problem of a policy analyst or resource allocator who, given that some impairment is inevitable, must determine a desirable--or preferred--distribution of individuals among equivalence classes as we have conceptualized them. If a preferred distribution is identified, our classification scheme suggests options for programmatic intervention directed toward changing the population profile in a preferred way. Our strategy of conceptualizing the problem makes it clear that social preferences involve political *and* economic considerations. Both considerations are involved in resource allocation, and our procedure is designed to provide relevant information without prejudging what those social preferences should be.

Although we are still a considerable distance from the routine application of our model, some significant advances have been made. A reliable, valid instrument for measuring and classifying individuals in terms of functional status exists. In addition to this first element of our model, preliminary work at Duke and by colleagues in the U.S. Government Accounting Office in Cleveland, Ohio (see Chapter 4; and Comptroller General, 1977a; 1977b), indicates that our strategy for conceptualizing generic services can be reliably applied in disaggregating the services offered by a variety of organizations serving older persons and then reaggregated to describe the services being offered to individuals whose functional status is known. We therefore have the essential elements to proceed to the third step in our model--the impact of defined service packages on individuals whose functional status is known or on equivalence classes of individuals (Burton, Damon, and Dellinger, 1976).

Of immediate interest is the important research now underway under the direction of William Laurie of the Cleveland, Ohio, branch of the U.S. Government Accounting Office (Comptroller General, 1977a; 1977b). Using the Duke MFAQ and the related generic services classification, Laurie and his associates have been able to combine in the same data file: (1) the initial functional status of a sample of a defined population (N = 1,609), (2) the generic services offered to this defined population over a period of a year by essentially every health and welfare organization (including Medicare and the Veterans Administration) in the relevant geographic area, and (3) the functional status of the defined population one year later. A pertinent illustration of the utility of our transition matrix—point three of our model—is therefore imminent. This illustration from Cleveland is most accurately described as an exercise in program evaluation. That is, it is an exercise in demonstrating the impact of current allocations for service programs. But, with such information, the next possible step would be an exercise in deliberate alternative resource allocation in the interest of modifying a population's functional status profile in preferred directions. We do not minimize the problems inherent in deciding what constitutes a *preferred* direction. That decision is fundamentally a political, not just a professional, decision. We argue here only that our model suggests a useful way of structuring the decisions and providing relevant information.

Summary

The necessity to evaluate alternatives to institutionalization and the lack of a useful means of doing this led us to design and develop a model which not only would address the specific issue of institutionalization, but also would facilitate program evaluation and resource allocation more generally. Three critical elements constitute this model: (1) assessment of individual functional status so that classes of functionally equivalent persons can be formed, (2) disaggregation of services and reaggregation according to actual usage, and (3) a matrix tying these together and permitting a prediction of future outcome as a result of specific intervention.

In this chapter we have focused on the first of these three elements—the assessment of functional status. By means of a simple and fairly brief multidimensional assessment questionnaire which we have developed, the validity and reliability of which have been established, personal level of functioning on each of five dimensions (social resources, economic resources, mental health, physical health, activities of daily living) can be determined. The resulting information permits placement of individuals in functional equivalence classes and thus operationalizes one of the three critical elements of the model. The Multidimensional Functional Assessment Questionnaire, however, has application beyond the model, for it has also been designed to be appropriate for population surveys, clinical intake, and follow-up and has proved its usefulness in each of these areas.

REFERENCES

Burton, R. M., Damon, W. W., and Dellinger, D. C. Estimating the impact of health services in a community. *Behavioral Science*, 1976, *21*, 478-489.

Comptroller General of the United States. Report to Congress on the well-being of older people in Cleveland, Ohio. U.S. General Accounting Office, HRD-77-70. Washington, D.C.: U.S. General Accounting Office, 1977a.

Comptroller General of the United States. Report to Congress on home health--the need for a national policy to better provide for the elderly. U.S. General Accounting Office, HRD-78-19. Washington, D.C.: U.S. General Accounting Office, 1977b.

Fanshel, S. and Bush, J. W. A health-status index and its application to health-services outcomes. *Operations Research*, 1970, *18*, 1021-1066.

Gurel, L., Linn, M. W., and Linn, B. S. Physical and mental impairment of function evaluation in the aged: The PAMIE scale. *Journal of Gerontology*, 1972, *27*, 83-90.

Gurland, B. J., Yorkston, N. J., Stone, A. R., Frank, J. D., and Fleiss, J. L. The structured and scaled interview to assess maladjustment (SSIAM): I description, rationale, and development. *Archives of General Psychiatry*, 1972, *27*, 259-264.

Hernes, G. Structural change in social resources. *American Journal of Sociology*, 1976, *82*, 513-547.

Katz, M. M. and Lyerly, S. B. Methods for measuring adjustment and social behavior in the community: I rationale, description, discriminative validity and scale development. *Psychological Reports*, 1963, *13*, 503-535.

Maddox, G. L. Intervention and outcomes: Notes on designing and implementing an experiment in health care. *International Journal of Epidemiology*, 1972, *1*, 339-345.

Maddox, G. L. and Karasik, R. B. (Eds.), *Planning services for older people.* Durham, N.C.: Duke University Center for the Study of Aging and Human Development, 1976.

Pfeiffer, E. A short, portable mental status questionnaire for the assessment of organic brain deficit in elderly patients. *Journal of the American Geriatrics Society*, 1975a, *23*, 433-441.

Pfeiffer, E. (Ed.), *Multidimensional functional assessment: The OARS methodology--a manual.* Durham, N.C.: Duke University Center for the Study of Aging and Human Development, 1975b.

Rivlin, A. *Systematic thinking for social action.* Washington, D.C.: The Brookings Institution, 1971.

Shanas, E. and Maddox, G. L. Aging, health, and the organization of health resources. In R. Binstock and E. Shanas (Eds.), *Handbook of aging and the social sciences*. New York: Van Nostrand Reinhold, 1976.

Srole, L., Langner, T. S., Michael, S. T., Opler, M. K., and Rennie, T. A. C. *Mental health in the metropolis: The midtown Manhattan study*. Vol. 1, New York: McGraw Hill, 1962.

Williams, A. Measuring the effectiveness of health care systems. *British Journal of Preventive & Social Medicine*, 1974, *28*, 196-202.

In addition to basic demographic and interview specific information, the MFAQ includes two sections: Part A, Assessment of Individual Functioning, and Part B, Assessment of Services Utilization.

Part A: Assessment of Individual Functioning.

Part A is divided into seven major sections. These sections, in order, with a listing of the number of primary questions (some questions include several items) and a descriptions of their content are:

Section	No. of questions	Content
Basic Demographic	11	Address; date; interviewer; informant; place of interview; duration; sex; race; age; education; telephone number.
Social Resources	9	Marital status; resident companions; extent and type of contact with others; availability of confidante; perception of loneliness; availability, duration, and source of help.
Economic Resources	15	Employment status; major occupation of self (and of spouse, if married); source and amount of income; number of dependents; home ownership or rental, and cost; source and adequacy of financial resources; health insurance; subjectively assessed adequacy of income.
Mental Health	6	Short Portable Mental Status Questionnaire (SPMSQ), a ten-item test of organicity (Pfeiffer, 1975a); extent of worry, satisfaction, and interest in life; assessment of present mental status and change in the past five years; fifteen-item Short Psychiatric Evaluation Schedule.
Physical Health	16	Physician visits, days sick, in hospital and/or nursing home in past six months; medications in past month; current illnesses and their extent of interference; physical, visual, and hearing disabilities; alcoholism; participation in vigorous exercise; self-assessment of health.

Activities of Daily Living	15	Extent of capacity to: telephone, travel, shop, cook, do housework, take medicine, handle money, feed self, dress, groom, walk, transfer, bathe, and control bladder and bowels. Also, presence of another to help with ADL tasks.
Informant Assessments	10	Information on the focal person's level of functioning on each of the five dimensions is sought from a knowledgeable informant. Specifically:
		Social: Capacity to get along with others; availability, duration, and source of help in time of need.
		Economic: Extent to which income meets basic self-maintenance requirements.
		Mental: Ability to make sound judgements, cope; interest in life; comparison with peers; change in past five years.
		Physical: Assessment of health; extent of interference of health problems.
Interviewer Section (a) interview specific	4	Sources of Information; reliability of responses.
(b) interview assessments	15	Social: Availability and duration of help when needed; adequacy of social relationships.
		Economic: Assessed adequacy of income; presence of reserves; extent to which basic needs are met.
		Mental: Ability to make sound judgements, cope; interest in life; behavior during interview.
		Physical: Whether obese or malnourished.
		Rating Scales: Five six-point scales, one for each dimension.

Part B: Services Assessment.

For each of the twenty-four nonoverlapping services named below, enquiry is made into (a) utilization in the past six months, (b) intensity of present utilization (e.g., frequency), (c) service provider (e.g., self, family and friends, agency), and (d) perceived current need for service.

1. Transportation
2. Social/Recreational
3. Employment
4. Sheltered Employment
5. Educational Services, employment related
6. Remedial Training
7. Mental Health

8. Psychotropic Drugs
9. Personal Care
10. Nursing Care
11. Medical Services
12. Supportive Services and Prostheses
13. Physical Therapy
14. Continuous Supervision

15. Checking
16. Relocation and Placement
17. Homemaker-Household
18. Meal Preparation
19. Administrative, Legal, and Protective
20. Systematic Multidimensional Evaluation

21. Financial Assistance
22. Food, Groceries
23. Living Quarters (Housing)
24. Coordination, Information, and Referral

Order of Administration

Specific information on administration is given in Chapter 15. However, the general order of administration follows the section order given above, except that the SPMSQ is given first, and acts as a screener, so that the interviewer can determine whether or not to continue interviewing the focal person—that is, whether or not an informant will be required.

When information is desired from both Parts A and B, Part B is administered immediately following the ADL section. Total administration time is approximately forty-five minutes, the time required for Part A being about thirty minutes.

Assigning Ratings on the Basis of Questionnaire Data

The information gathered is intended to be condensed into level of function ratings, one rating being assigned in each of the five dimensions (social resources, economic resources, mental health, physical health, and ADL). In classifying individuals, trained interviewers or raters read through the material in the relevant sections and then assign a rating. Interrater reliability is facilitated by having both an adjectival marker for each point of the scale of functioning (1 = excellent, 2 = good, 3 = mildly impaired, 4 = moderately impaired, 5 = severely impaired, and 6 = totally impaired) and a descriptive paragraph detailing the conditions which have to be met before a particular value can be assigned. These conditions are tied to specific responses in the questionnaire.

CHAPTER 2

CONCEPTUALIZATION AND DEVELOPMENT OF THE MULTIDIMENSIONAL
FUNCTIONAL ASSESSMENT QUESTIONNAIRE

GERDA G. FILLENBAUM

In order to apply a classification system based on functional status it is necessary to be able to measure functional status. A survey of the literature and extensive clinical experience with elderly clients suffering from age-related problems indicated that information was necessary on five dimensions—social resources, economic resources, mental health, physical health, and activities of daily living (ADL)—to obtain a comprehensive overview of individual functioning. However, although several existing and excellent measures covered a narrower range of dimensions, we could not locate any questionnaire which covered this breadth of personal functioning. Specifically, a host of investigators had been concerned with the assessment of mental and physical health (see, e.g., Gurel, Linn, and Linn, 1972; Gurland, Yorkston, Stone, Frank, and Fleiss, 1972; Kahn, Goldfarb, Pollack, and Peck, 1960; Leighton, Harding, Macklin, McMillan, and Leighton, 1963; Lowenthal, 1964; Srole, Langner, Michael, Opler, and Rennie, 1962); many other investigators had been concerned with social and self-care aspects (see, e.g., Katz and Lyerly, 1963; Katz, Ford, Moskowitz, Jackson, and Jaffe, 1963; Lawton and Brody, 1969); and, more broadly, the socioeconomic, physical health, and self-care dimensions had also been investigated (see, e.g., Jones, 1974). Many additional and more recent references are available in Murnaghan (1976). None of these, however, provided a measure which paid similar attention to all the dimensions we considered important, and a summary assessment of functional status on the dimensions being considered in these studies was not always available. Consequently, it was necessary for us to develop our own measure.

In developing our own measure we imposed certain constraints and desired certain standards. First, the questionnaire had not only to be valid and reliable (information on these aspects is reported on in Chapter 3), but it also had to be sufficiently detailed to be clinically useful—the entire range of functioning from excellent to totally impaired had to be covered—and sufficiently brief to permit rapid data gathering in survey work. The questionnaire also had to be readily understood by those for whom it was intended and sufficiently straightforward that it would be easy to administer. Finally, the information obtained for each of the five dimensions covered by the questionnaire had to be readily summarizable on a brief scale, with the meanings of the points of the scale being uniform across the dimensions. In addition, in each dimension, certain information was considered basic to a determination of level of functioning:

Social Resources: Quantity and quality of relationships with friends
                     and family; availability of care in time of need.

Economic Resources: Adequacy of income and resources.

Mental Health: Extent of psychiatric well-being; presence of organicity.

Physical Health: Presence of physical disorders; participation in physical activities.

ADL: Capacity to perform various instrumental and physical (or bodily care) tasks which permit individuals to live independently.

The literature was scanned for relevant scales and items. Some were found to be appropriate without change or were standard items, and others required modifications. Some we had to devise. In addition to meeting the requirement of relevance, the items selected also had to meet at least one of five additional criteria:

1. Reliability and validity were already known.

2. We were willing to determine reliability and validity.

3. Local or national comparison standards were available.

4. The item was relevant to present theory and findings.

5. The item was required because of accepted professional standards.

While objective data were preferred, subjective items were included when they seemed appropriate.

Since severely impaired persons might not be capable of answering questions, and since there might be serious doubts regarding the reliability of some persons' answers, the questionnaire was so designed that assessment of functional status could be based either on the responses of the focal person or on those of an appropriate informant. Furthermore, such assessments could be made either by the interviewer or by an independent rater using questionnaire data only. The summary ratings of functional status on each of the five dimensions were made on six-point scales, not only because our experience indicated that this was the maximum number of points for which it was still possible to obtain rating agreement, but also because the absence of a specific numerical midpoint ensured that individuals would not be placed in a catch-all category. The points of the scale are uniform across dimensions: 1 = excellent functioning, 2 = good, 3 = mildly impaired, 4 = moderately impaired, 5 = severely impaired, 6 = totally impaired. Descriptive paragraphs in the questionnaire amplify these adjectival markers and tie the items of the questionnaire to the scales.

The original questionnaire which was drawn up was pretested, consequently modified, and administered to ninety-eight clinic clients. As a result, further modifications were made, and a rudimentary question concerned with services desired and received was added. This revised questionnaire (which is generally referred to as the Community Survey Questionnaire, the validity and reliability of which have been closely examined, details being given in Chapter 3) was used in a survey of a 10 percent random sample of community residents aged sixty-five and over (N = 997). (See Chapters 7 and 9 for a more detailed report on this sample.) The data so obtained were subject to an analysis which indicated the extent to which each item discriminated between excellent functioning (a rating of 1) and totally impaired functioning (a rating of 6) on each of the five dimensions (Woodbury and Clive, 1975). Using this information, we selected those items with maximum discriminatory power and those items which clinical judgment indicated to be important, and, after appropriate pretesting, they formed the functional assessment section, or Part A, of the Multidimensional Functional Assessment Questionnaire. In addition, the services section was also revised. Specifically, for each of twenty-four essentially nonoverlapping and mutually exhaustive generic services, information is sought on receipt of service within the past six months, current receipt, and amount, source, and present desire for service. This constitutes Part B, the services assessment section, of the questionnaire.

The present questionnaire therefore consists of two parts which can be used independently: Part A, functional assessment, and Part B, services assessment. The first item administered is a screening device on the basis of which the interviewer can determine whether or not the focal person can give reliable answers, that is, whether or not information must be obtained from an informant. Information is then requested in the following order: (1) demographic characteristics, (2) Part A, (3) Part B, (4) informant-supplied information on the five dimensions, (5) interviewer records and impressions, (6) ratings of functional status on each of the five dimensions.

All items in Part B (services assessment) were developed specifically for this questionnaire. The items in Part A were derived from a variety of sources, as indicated in Table 1. The total questionnaire takes about forty-five minutes to administer.

Table 1

Multidimensional Functional Assessment Questionnaire:
A Brief Description and Source of Items

Item	Dimension	Description, Source, and Purpose
Cover sheet		Interview specific information.
Preliminary Questionnaire	M	Adapted for use with a community sample from Mental Status Questionnaire (MSQ) which was standardized on institutionalized persons. MSQ information is found in Kahn, Goldfarb, Pollack, and Peck (1960); Preliminary Questionnaire standardization is found in Pfeiffer (1975a). Here, the Preliminary Questionnaire is used as (a) a screening device, with a minimum of 4 errors information required from an informant, and (b) a quick assessment of organicity.
1-5	S	Basic demographic characteristics. Standard items.
6, 7	S	Marital status, living arrangements. Standard items.
8-12	S	Objective and subjective social items. From North Carolina Governor's Coordinating Council on Aging (n.d.), questions 1-4, with 2, 4 modified.
13, 14	S	Unique. Items 11-13 are also similar to some items on the Chicago Activity Inventory, B, Friends section, Havighurst and Albrecht (1953) and on the Cumming and Henry Morale Index (1961).
15	E	Employment status. Standard item.
16, 17	E	Major lifetime occupation of self and spouse. This may be unique.
18	E	Income sources and amount. Common to such major surveys as Social Security Administration Longitudinal Retirement History Survey (SSA LRHS, 1969 questionnaire) Irelan (1972), and the "Parnes" study (1969 questionnaire), Parnes et al., (1975).
19	E	Number of persons supported financially. Required for determining income adequacy.

19

Item	Dimension	Description, Source, and Purpose
20	E	Home ownership/rental. Standard in assessing economic status.
21-23	E	Adequacy of assets, expenses. Probably unique as phrased here.
24	E	Receipt of services: food. Comparable item in "Parnes" (1969), question (q.) 67.
25	E	Need for food stamps. Probably unique.
26	E	Presence of health/medical insurance. Standard item; see, e.g., SSA LRHS, Irelan (1972).
27-30	E	Subjective assessment of economic well-being. North Carolina Governor's Coordinating Council on Aging (n.d.), questions 1-4, with 2 modified.
31-33	M	Life satisfaction. North Carolina Governor's Coordinating Council on Aging (n.d.), questions 3, 6, 8.
34	M	Short Psychiatric Evaluation Schedule. Adapted from Kincannon's Mini-Mult (1968) by Pfeiffer (1975b).
35, 36	M	Self-assessment of mental health. Probably unique.
37-40	P	Extent of disabling illness and receipt of medical care in past six months. Standard items.
41	P	Receipt of services: medical care. Standard item; used in unique way here.
42, 43	P	Medications taken in past month. Standard item.
44	P	Current illnesses, extent of interference with activities. Illness list probably standard; interference assessment is probably not standard.
45-48	P	Presence of physical disabilities and other physical problems. Phrasing may be unique, but general concept is standard.

20

Item	Dimension	Description, Source, and Purpose
49, 50		Use and need for supportive devices and prostheses. Primarily a services item, but has physical health implications.
51	P	Indirect measure of alcoholism. Modification of standard item.
52	P	Participation in sports. Unique.
53-55	P	Subjective health assessment. From North Carolina Governor's Coordinating Council on Aging (n.d.), items 1, 3 modified. Similar items on Duke University's First Longitudinal Study (Palmore, 1970); on "Parnes" questionnaires: q. 38a, 1967; q. 40, 1969; q. 67, 1971 (see Parnes et al., 1975); and on Social Security LRHS, 1969 questionnaire, Irelan (1975).
56-69	A	Instrumental and physical aspects of ADL. Derived from Lawton and Brody (1969).
71		Part B. Services Assessment. Unique.
73, 74	S	Informant items (comparable to questions 13, 14). Unique.
75	E	Informant item. Unique.
76, 77	M	Informant items. Unique.
78-80	M	Informant items. Adaptation of questions 32, 35, 36.
81, 82	P	Informant items. Adaptation of questions 53, 55.
83-86		Interviewer items, interview specific. Standard.
87, 88	S	Interviewer assessments. Adaptation of q. 14a. Unique.
89-91	E	Interviewer assessments. Unique.
92-95	M	Interviewer assessments. Items 92-94 are adaptation of questions 76-78.
96	P	Interviewer assessment.

Item	Dimension	Description, Source, and Purpose
97-101		S, E, M, P, A rating scales.

S = Social Resources; E = Economic Resources; M = Mental Health; P = Physical Health; A = ADL

REFERENCES

Cumming, E. and Henry, W. H. *Growing Old: The process of disengagement.* New York: Basic Books, 1961.

Gurel, L., Linn, M. W., and Linn, B. S. Physical and mental impairment of function evaluation in the aged: The PAMIE scale. *Journal of Gerontology*, 1972, *27*, 83-90.

Gurland, B. J., Yorkston, N. J., Stone, A. R., Frank, J. D., and Fleiss, J. L. The structured and scaled interview to assess maladjustment (SSIAM): I description, rationale, and development. *Archives of General Psychiatry*, 1972, *27*, 259-264.

Havighurst, R. J. and Albrecht, R. *Older people.* New York: Longmans, Green and Company, 1953.

Irelan, L. M. Retirement history study: Introduction. *Social Security Bulletin*, 1972, *55*, No. 11, 3-8.

Jones, E. W. Patient classification for long-term care: Users manual. DHEW Publication No. (HRA) 75-3107. Washington, D.C.: U.S. Government Printing Office, 1974.

Kahn, R. H., Goldfarb, A. I., Pollack, M., and Peck, A. Brief objective measures for the determination of mental status in the aged. *American Journal of Psychiatry*, 1960, *107*, 326-328.

Katz, M. M. and Lyerly, S. B. Methods for measuring adjustment and social behavior in the community: I rationale, description, discriminative validity and scale development. *Psychological Reports*, 1963, *13*, 503-535.

Katz, S., Ford, A. B., Moskowitz, R. W., Jackson, B. A., and Jaffe, M. W. Studies in illness in the aged. The index of ADL: A standardized measure of biological and psychosocial function. *Journal of American Medical Association*, 1963, *185*, 914-919.

Kincannon, J. C. Prediction of the standard MMPI scale scores from 71 items: The mini-mult. *Journal of Consulting and Clinical Psychology*, 1968, *32*, 319-325.

Lawton, M. P. and Brody, E. M. Assessment of older people: Self-maintaining and instrumental activities of daily living. *Gerontologist*, 1969, *9*, 179-186.

Leighton, D. C., Harding, J. P. S., Macklin, D. B., MacMillan, A. M., and Leighton, A. H. *The character of danger.* New York: Basic Books, 1963.

Lowenthal, M. F. *Lives in distress.* New York: Basic Books, 1964.

Murnaghan, J. H. (Ed.), *Long-term care data*. Report of the conference on long-term health care data. Tucson, Arizona, May 12-16, 1975. Supplement to *Medical Care*, 1976, *14*, No. 5.

North Carolina Governor's Coordinating Council on Aging. *Social indicators for the aged. A report of the survey of needs, 1971-1972*. Raleigh, N.C.: N.C. Department of Human Resources, n.d.

Palmore, E. *Normal aging I*. Durham: Duke University Press, 1970.

Parnes, H. S., Adams, A. V., Andrisani, P. J., Kohen, A. I., and Nestel, G. *The pre-retirement years*. Vol. 4: *A longitudinal study of the labor experience of men*. Manpower R & D Monograph 15. Washington, D.C.: U.S. Department of Labor, Manpower Administration, 1975.

Pfeiffer, E. A short, portable mental status questionnaire for the assessment of organic brain deficit in elderly patients. *Journal of the American Geriatrics Society*, 1975a, *23*, 433-441.

Pfeiffer, E. A short psychiatric evaluation schedule. Paper presented at the 28th Annual Meeting, Gerontological Society, Louisville, Kentucky, October 26-30, 1975b.

Srole, L., Langner, T. S., Michael, S. T., Opler, M. K., and Rennie, T. A. C. *Mental health in the metropolis: The midtown Manhattan study*. Vol. 1. New York: McGraw Hill, 1962.

Woodbury, M. A. and Clive, J. An application of mathematical typology to assessing degree of impairment of elderly persons in the OARS data base. Manuscript. Durham, N.C.: Department of Community Health Sciences, Duke University Medical Center, June, 1975.

Chapter 3

Validity and Reliability of the Multidimensional Functional Assessment Questionnaire

Gerda G. Fillenbaum

With adults--and particularly the elderly--in mind we have developed a simple, inexpensive, accurate means of assessing personal level of functioning on five dimensions: social resources, economic resources, mental health, physical health, and activities of daily living (ADL). While such an assessment is basic to the OARS Program evaluation and resource allocation model (see Chapter 1), the Multidimensional Functional Assessment Questionnaire was developed so that it could also be used independently. It is suitable--and presently being used--for clinical intake, population surveys, and longitudinal studies.

Basically, the questionnaire seeks to determine functional status on the major dimensions of functioning and is as concerned with measuring adequacy of functioning as it is with measuring inadequacy. This questionnaire, therefore, covers both a broader area (more dimensions) and a broader range (excellent to totally impaired) of functioning than do most assessment instruments. Further, the final assessments that are made can be uniformly understood across the five dimensions, for a particular rating carries the same implication regardless of which dimension is being rated. Thus, a rating of 1, for example, always indicates excellent functioning, and a rating of 6 always indicates totally impaired functioning.

The questionnaire consists of two parts: Part A, which is concerned with assessment of functional level, and Part B, which is concerned with assessment of service use and the recipient's perceived need for specific services. Studies of validity and reliability, however, refer solely to Part A. Part A is divided into a number of sections--one section for each of the dimensions of personal functioning, one for the informant's and one for the interviewer's view of the focal person, and a basic demographic section.

With the exception of ADL, where only factual information is sought, both factual information and subjective assessments are requested from the focal person; but when the focal person does not seem to understand the questions an informant is asked to supply factual data. The information obtained permits an assessment of level of functioning on a six-point scale ranging from excellent to totally impaired for each of the five dimensions. Total administration time (for both Part A and Part B) averages forty-five minutes.

The current questionnaire, the Multidimensional Functional Assessment Questionnaire (MFAQ), is reproduced in Appendix A and has been empirically derived from an earlier multidimensional assessment instrument, the Community Survey Questionnaire (CSQ), the validity and reliability of which had been established and will be reported on in detail below. The CSQ had been administered to 997 randomly selected community residents aged sixty-five and over. Using the data so obtained, Woodbury and Clive (1975) developed a program which indicated the extent to which each CSQ item discriminated between excellent and totally impaired functioning on each of five dimensions--social resources, economic resources, mental health, physical health, and ADL. Based on these data, items with maximum discriminatory power were selected, the final item selection being modified where necessary on the basis of clinical experience and subject response. Because of external supporting evidence, and because of the manner in which Part A of the MFAQ has been constructed, we may presume that the validity and reliability of the parent instrument have been retained.

Validity

The manner in which both the CSQ and MFAQ were constructed ensured consensual validity since only those items which experts agreed should be present were included. This, however, is a fairly weak form of validity, and since level of functioning ratings made solely on the basis of OARS questionnaire data are intended to be comparable to ratings on level of functioning made by acknowledged professionals after personal examination, results of professional examination were used as the standard against which to validate OARS level of functioning ratings.

Comparison with Clinic Interview Data

An early form of the CSQ, identical in relevant aspects to the MFAQ, was administered by a research technician to twenty-two clients with whom there was to be no continued contact. These clients were then seen in clinical interviews and evaluated by seven clinicians (psychiatrists and social workers), four of whom saw four cases each and the rest of whom saw one, two, and three cases each. After identifying information had been removed from the questionnaires, these clients were later rated by the clinicians, who rated not only their own clients, but their clients embedded in a set of sixteen cases to reduce further the possibility of client identification. Each of the five dimensions was examined separately. Ratings based on clinical interview were compared with ratings based on questionnaire data by means of paired t-tests. Statistically significant differences were found for only one dimension--ADL--where ratings based on clinical interview indicated a poorer level of functioning than ratings based on intake form data (t = 2.25, d.f. = 21, p < .05). These data suggest that, with the possible exception of ADL, questionnaires and clinical interviews yield similar ratings.

Comparison with Professional Examination

With the use of the CSQ, data had been obtained from nearly 1,000 community residents. (See Chapters 7 and 9.) A year later 120 of these community residents were selected such that all combinations of impairment on each of the five dimensions were represented. Four of the original group had died, and, of the 116 remaining, all answered the CSQ again and were invited to participate in a health examination--i.e., an examination of mental health by a psychiatrist and an examination of physical health by a physician's assistant. Of the 110 who were available for this aspect of the study, 26 refused completely to participate, and data on only mental health was obtained for one person and only on physical health for another. The remaining 82 completed both examinations. Of the participants, 53 were white, 31 black, 34 male, and 50 female; 34 were married, 41 widowed, and 9 were single (i.e., had never married, divorced, or separated). Those who participated fully did not differ in terms of sex, race, age, marital status, occupational level, or level of impairment from those who refused to participate.

For the examination of mental health, subjects were randomly assigned to one of ten psychiatrists, precautions being taken to ensure that one of these psychiatrists, who had rated some of the questionnaires answered by this group, did not see in examination any person whose CSQ he had rated. Subjects were seen privately and were interviewed for the length of time necessary to come to a decision regarding mental state and to complete the Overall and Gorham Brief Psychiatric Rating Scale and a symptoms check list. Diagnosis was formulated where appropriate, a narrative summary written, and a rating made on the six-point mental health scale.

Physical examinations were performed by four physician's assistants to whom subjects were randomly assigned. Again, all the examiners used a similar procedure--a short medical history, an electrocardiogram, a measure of height, weight, and blood pressure, and further examination as required. In addition, a ten-point performance status scale was completed, on which a rating of 1 = normal, no complaints, no evidence of disease, able to carry out normal activity, and on which 10 = moribund, unable to care for self. Finally, subjects received a rating on the six-point physical health scale. None of these examiners was ever permitted access to information on the questionnaire, and all had received some instruction in the use of the relevant rating scale.

In order to determine whether relative level of functioning derived from these two procedures was in agreement, participants were ranked on the basis of each of these ratings, and the rankings were compared using Spearman rank order correlation. On mental health, the Spearman rank order correlation was .62 (p < .001), and on physical health it was .70 (p < .001). While these results indicate that there is good agreement between the professional assessment and the questionnaire-based estimate on relative severity of impairment, the correlations are not substantial. In part this may be attributable to: (1) a difference in methods--that is, that questionnaire-based information is being compared with professional examination (Fiske, 1971)--(2) not uncommon intraprofessional differences in interpretation of level of functioning (Haberman, 1967), or (3) differences in the use of the six-point rating scale.

To examine the latter possibilities, Spearman rank order correlations between the professional rating and the CSQ rating were calculated separately for the cases examined by each professional. Although questionnaire-based ratings indicated that the professionals had been allocated similar subjects, wide differences among both psychiatrists (r_s = .28 to .92) and among physician's assistants (r_s = -.24 to .80) were found, indicating that intraprofessional differences were present. To minimize problems due to rating differences, the psychiatrists were asked to rank the persons they had seen. Since two of the physician's assistants had examined more persons than they could rank, the ten-point performance status scale was used as the basis for ranking on the physical health dimension. In addition, rating differences among trained staff raters were taken into account.

The original analyses were then repeated for each psychiatrist and physician's assistant, and agreement between professional examination and questionnaire-based assessment was found to be closer than it was previously, although some differences did remain evident: the psychiatrists' r_s ranged from .49 to 1.00, and the physician's assistants' r_s ranged from .61 to .81. This suggests that the initial finding of a Spearman rank order correlation of .62 for mental health and of .70 for physical health underestimates the actual amount of agreement present between the professional assessment and the questionnaire-based assessment of level of functioning in these areas.

These studies, one looking at all five dimensions of functioning in a clinical setting and the other concentrating on personal examinations of mental and physical health by psychiatrists and physician's assistants, indicate that the CSQ does measure level of functioning for social resources, economic resources, mental health and physical health. On ADL, however, the questionnaire tends to give too rosy a picture, for clinicians in personal contact with clients notice difficulties which are not so evident from questionnaire data alone. Questionnaire users, therefore, should not underestimate reported ADL difficulties.

Discriminability

In order to be useful, a questionnaire must be able to discriminate appropriately among groups which differ in known ways. We have information on three populations living in the same geographical area: (1) a random sample of 997 community residents aged sixty-five and over; (2) 98 consecutive clients aged fifty and over referred to a clinic because of age-related problems (most live in the community); and (3) a random sample of 102 persons aged sixty-five and over living in institutions. While considerable variation in level of functioning may be present in each of these groups, we would expect, on average, that the community sample would be the healthiest, that the institutionalized would be the sickest, and that the clinic clients would fall in between. In addition, since this particular clinic specializes in treatment of the mentally impaired aged, we would expect its clients to have a mental health rating only slightly better than that of those in institutions.

As can be seen in Table 1, the findings are in agreement with expectations. While the range is wide--with rare exceptions all levels of functioning are represented in each of the three groups--those living in the community, on average, have the best level of functioning on each of the five dimensions, the institutionalized are the most impaired, and the clinic group falls in between. And, on the mental health dimension, the clinic group does indeed function only slightly better than the institutional group (mental health rating, clinic mean = 4.13, SD = .87; institutional mean = 4.53, SD = 1.22). Thus, the questionnaire discriminates appropriately among populations known to be different.

28

Table 1

Table 1

Comparison of Ratings on Five Dimensions for
Community, Clinic, and Institutionalized Subjects

	Community		Clinic		Institution	
	Mean	SD	Mean	SD	Mean	SD
Social Resources	2.24	1.00	3.26	1.18	4.20	1.13
Economic Resources	2.79	1.08	2.91	1.02	3.26	.84
Mental Health	2.79	1.06	4.13	.87	4.53	1.22
Physical Health	3.04	1.02	3.60	.91	3.74	.98
ADL	2.36	1.42	3.64	1.48	5.31	.91
N	997[a]		98		102	

[a] Due to insufficient data some subjects did not receive ratings. The number receiving ratings was: Social--980; Economic--971; Mental--970; Physical--994; ADL--996.

Reliability

Pretesting indicated that the CSQ and the MFAQ could be readily understood and responded to appropriately by persons similar to those for whom it was intended and that the questionnaire yielded information which could be rated. These matters are crucial to obtaining reliable data (Rose and Bell, 1971). Beyond that, however, we were concerned with test-retest reliability (the extent to which a person would give the same response on a second testing occasion), inter-rater reliability (the extent of agreement among different raters), and intra-rater reliability (self-consistency in rating).

Test-retest reliability. After an interval averaging five weeks (it ranged from three to eight weeks), the CSQ was readministered to thirty community residents who were representative of those aged sixty-five and over in the local area. On being seen again, these subjects were also asked whether certain major life events had occurred since the first administration of the CSQ so that these changes could be taken into account in examining the data. One third of the community resident population had experienced personal injury or sickness or the death of a close friend or family member. Response given the first time was compared with response given the second time. In all, 240 pairs of discrete items were examined. Not included among these were items concerned with the previous month (a time period not common to the two testing occasions) and ADL items beginning, "Could you do. . . ." (These were asked of very few subjects.) When only the final score of a scale was legitimate, the individual items comprising the scale were not examined; otherwise, individual scale items and final score were considered.

Certain differences in response on the two occasions were considered acceptable. Differences of one point were disregarded for all items which had to be answered on a scale of three or more points and in which the distinction between adjacent items was not clear (e.g., "quite often"/"sometimes"/"almost never"). Where distinctions between adjacent items were very clear (e.g., "without any help at all"/"with some help"/"completely unable"), no difference was acceptable.

Overall, 95.3 percent of the items were answered on both occasions, 91.7 percent of the responses being identical by our definition. Items concerned with subjective matters were the most likely to alter, with 11.4 percent of the subjective items and 7.3 percent of the objective items changing. In addition, while, as can be seen in Table 2, all but one of the test-retest correlations of the scores of combined items were statistically significant, correlations tended to be lower for groups of subjective items than they were for objective items.

Table 2

Community Survey Questionnaire
Test-Retest Correlations of Combined Scores

	r
Social Resources	
Objective	.71**
Subjective	.53**
Economic Resources	
Subjective	.79**
Mental Health	
(both subjective)	
Life Satisfaction	.42*
Mental Health	.32
Physical Health	
Subjective	.59**
ADL	
(both objective)	
Instrumental	.71**
Physical	.82**

*p < .05
**p < .001

The changes typically indicated a better level of functioning at the first interview than at the second, and responses were internally consistent, the initial higher objectively determined level of functioning being accompanied by a subjectively determined good state of feeling, and the poorer objective level on re-interview being accompanied by a lower subjective self-assessment.

Although subjects differed widely in basic demographic characteristics, all answered most of the questions (range unanswered = 0.7, mean = 3.46, SD = 1.87). The number of items answered differently on the two occasions ranged from 9 to 43 (mean = 19, SD = 8.38), with little obvious difference between high and low response changers.

In summary, rate of response was high and there was some variability in consistency of response, with changes being greatest for subjective matters. The latter is not unique (see, e.g., USNCHS, No. 45; Zubin, 1969). Level of functioning was poorer on the second occasion than on the first. This may reflect the actual situation, for, as mentioned earlier, a third of the subjects had experienced some untoward event since first being seen. But it may also reflect the impact of good interviewers and of increased accuracy in reporting symptoms and chronic conditions on re-interview (USNCHS, Nos. 26, 45), matters which are typically underreported (USNCHS, No. 23).

Inter-rater agreement. Following a training session, each of eight CSQs, labelled "initial" questionnaires, were rated by ten raters, and an additional nine questionnaires, called "in-common" questionnaires, were rated over a period of time by eight raters. These nine questionnaires were dispersed among groups of twenty questionnaires which were only rated by one individual.

Inter-rater agreement was calculated separately for each dimension for the "initial" and "in-common" sets of questionnaires. Intra-class correlation coefficients (Haggard, 1958) were statistically significant for all dimensions, but were low for the economic dimension. Figures, first, for the "initial" questionnaires and, second, for the "in-common" questionnaires on each of the five dimensions are: Social Resources .73, .79; Economic Resources .69, .18; Mental Health .68, .55; Physical Health .83, .67; and ADL .93, .86. (These figures tend to be underestimates of extent of agreement since the available computer program could make assessments only when some disagreement was present; questionnaires on which there was complete agreement among raters had to be excluded.) The economic dimension was the only dimension on which discipline of rater seemed to have an effect.

As can be seen in Table 3, the results of Kendall's coefficient of concordance, W (Siegel, 1956), were in agreement and showed that raters agreed with each other regarding the relative severity of those assessed.

Examination of the specific ratings assigned indicated that on at least 70 percent of the occasions identical ratings were assigned, that differences were rarely greater than one point (two-point differences occurred only 2 percent of the time), and that disagreement on placement in an impaired category (ratings of 4-6) or unimpaired category (ratings of 1-3) occurred about 7 percent of the time. An independent examination of inter-rater agreement on the MFAQ, in which ratings made by interviewers were compared with those of an independent rater, showed that, for sixty-nine randomly selected questionnaires (from a set of 3,345), identical ratings occurred on 86 percent of all possible rating occasions, with differences of one, two, and three points occurring 7 percent, 5 percent, and 2 percent of the time, respectively (Laurie, 1977).

31

Table 3

Community Survey Questionnaire
Inter-Rater Agreement and Intra-Discipline Agreement for Each Dimension
(Kendall's coefficient of concordance, W)

	Social Resources	Economic Recources	Mental Health	Physical Health	ADL	No. of Raters
Inter-Rater Agreement						
"Initial" (8 questionnaires)	.79***	.82***	.74***	.88***	.76***	10
"In-Common" (9 questionnaires)	.87***	.38**	.65***	.77***	.74***	8
Intra-Disciplinary Agreement on "Initial" Questionnaires						
Social Workers	.89**	.84*	.77*	.93**	.86*	3
Psychiatrists	.89**	.82*	.87*	.89**	.79*	3
Researchers	.87**	.85**	.70**	.89***	.70**	4

*p < .05
**p < .01
***p < .001

Two other questionnaires similar in certain respects to our instruments but concentrating more heavily on assessing mental health have been reported: the interview schedule used in the Midtown Study (Langner and Michael, 1963; Srole, Langner, Michael, Opler, and Rennie, 1962) and the Structured and Scaled Interview to Assess Maladjustment (SSIAM) (Gurland, Yorkston, Stone, Frank, and Fleiss, 1972; Gurland, Yorkston, Goldberg, Fleiss, Sloane, and Cristol, 1972). In the Midtown Study, the two psychiatrists who made mental health ratings--like OARS, on a six-point scale--were in perfect agreement only 43 percent of the time, but within one point of each other 87 percent of the time--a percentage agreement somewhat lower than that obtained on the CSQ or the MFAQ. In the second study, four of the five areas of maladjustment measured by the SSIAM were subjected to factor analysis. Inter-rater agreement among three raters for fifteen subjects on the six factors obtained indicated high agreement on rank ordering of subjects, but perhaps not such high agreement on the numerical rating assigned, for raters differed significantly on two factors. The data from these two well-designed studies suggest that trained raters using our instruments compare favorably with other trained raters using different instruments to measure similar phenomena.

Intra-rater agreement. In order to assess self-consistency of rating, the CSQs rated in the studies examining inter-rater agreement were rated again twelve to eighteen months later by the seven raters (of the original ten) who remained.

In view of the extended time period between rating and re-rating, the substantial intra-rater reliability seen in Table 4 (where Pearson product moment correlations range from .47 to 1.00 and are typically significant at the .1 percent level) indicates that rating standards remain stable over a considerable period of time. The lowest correlation of .47 for rater D on mental health may reflect D's change in knowledge of the area, for while D worked as a social worker, his entry into the program had been from a different discipline.

Table 4

Community Survey Questionnaire
Intra-Rater Reliability[a]

Rater	Social Resources	Economic Resources	Mental Health	Physical Health	ADL
A	.86[b]	.90	.76	.92	.97
B	.87	.80	.96	.87	.90
C	.87	.72**	.87	.78	.97
D	.95	.87	.47*	.82	.98
E	.82	.91	.83	.83	.88
F	.93	.79	.83	.92	1.00
G	.91	.67**	.89	.90	.97

[a] Pearson product moment correlations

[b] All unstarred correlations are significant at $p < .001$

* $p < .05$
** $p < .01$

The data indicate that trained raters, even when drawn from different disciplinary backgrounds, rate in a similar manner and maintain their style of rating for a substantial period of time.

Summary

Part A of the Multidimensional Functional Assessment Questionnaire is designed to assess personal level of functioning on five dimensions: social resources, economic resources, mental health, physical health, and ADL. Raters read the answers given to each of the structured items on the questionnaire and, on the basis of these responses, assign a level of functioning rating on a six-point scale (1 = level of functioning excellent, 6 = totally impaired) on each of the five dimensions. Examination indicates that assessments of four of these dimensions (social resources, economic resources, mental health, and physical health) are comparable to assessments of the same individuals made by appropriate professionals but that the questionnaire may underestimate impairment on the fifth dimension, ADL.

The items on the questionnaire are readily understood, and people do not object to repeated administration. The information yielded is adequate to assess level of functioning, and raters from different disciplines use the questionnaire equally effectively and maintain their standards of rating for a considerable period of time.

REFERENCES

Fiske, D. W. *Measuring the concepts of personality*. Chicago: Aldine Publishing Company, 1971.

Gurland, B. J., Yorkston, N. J., Stone, A. R., Frank, J. D., and Fleiss, J. L. The structured and scaled interview to assess maladjustment (SSIAM): I description, rationale, and development. *Archives of General Psychiatry*, 1972, *27*, 259-264.

Gurland, B. J., Yorkston, N. J., Goldberg, K., Fleiss, J. L., Sloane, R. B., and Cristol, A. H. The structured and scaled interview to assess maladjustment (SSIAM): II factor analysis, reliability, and validity. *Archives of General Psychiatry*, 1972, *27*, 264-267.

Haberman, P. W. Appendix. The reliability and validity of the data. In Kosa, J., Antonovsky, A., and Zola, I. K. (Eds.), *Poverty and health*. Cambridge: Harvard University Press, 1969.

Haggard, E. A. *Intra-class correlation and the analysis of variance*. New York: Dryden Press, 1958.

Langner, T. S. and Michael, S. T. *Life stress and mental health: The midtown Manhatten study*. Vol. 2. New York: Free Press of Glencoe, 1963.

Laurie, W. Personal communication, 1977.

Rose, C. L. and Bell, B. *Predicting longevity*. Lexington, Massachusetts: Heath Lexington Books, 1971.

Siegel, S. *Non-parametric statistics for the behavioral sciences*. New York: McGraw Hill, 1956.

Srole, L., Langner, T. S., Michael, S. T., Opler, M. K., and Rennie, T. A. C. *Mental health in the metropolis: The midtown Manhattan study*. Vol. 1. New York: McGraw Hill, 1962.

U.S. National Center for Health Statistics. Interview data on chronic conditions compared with information derived from medical records. *Vital and Health Statistics*. P.H.S. Publication No. 1000, Series 2, No. 23. Washington, D.C.: U.S. Government Publication Office, 1967.

U.S. National Center for Health Statistics. The influence of interviewer and respondent psychological and behavioral variables on the reporting in household interviews. *Vital and Health Statistics*. P.H.S. Publication No. 1000, Series 2, No. 26. Washington, D.C.: U.S. Government Publication Office, 1968.

U.S. National Center for Health Statistics. Reporting health events in household interviews: Effects of reinforcement, question length, and reinterviews. *Vital and Health Statistics*. Series 2, No. 45. DHEW Publication No. (HSM) 72-1028. Washington, D.C.: U.S. Government Publication Office, 1972.

Woodbury, M. and Clive, T. An application of mathematical typology to assessing degree of impairment of elderly persons in the OARS data base. Report to the Project Director, Older Americans Resources and Services Project, The Center for the Study of Aging and Human Development, Duke University Medical Center, Durham, N.C., 1975.

Zubin, J. Cross-national study of diagnosis of the mental disorders: Methodology and planning. *American Journal of Psychiatry*. 1969, *125*, No. 10, Supplement.

Chapter 4

The Concept of a Service Package: Prescribing, Measuring, and Costing Services

David C. Dellinger

The ultimate purpose of assessing the functional status of individuals is to decide how the projected status of those individuals might be improved. This is obviously true in the case of diagnostic assessments, but it is just as true when functional assessments are used in the evaluation of service programs or in the assessment of the general needs of a community.

The means utilized for improving the projected status of individuals is most often the provision of services. However, if an appropriate set of services is to be provided for an individual, there must be some unambiguous method of specifying what those services are, and, moreover, there must be a method of making appropriate changes in service programs to assure that the specified services are actually made available. The former involves the prescription of services for an individual; the latter involves the planning and budgeting processes through which service programs are established and supported.

The Multidimensional Functional Assessment Questionnaire (MFAQ) was developed within a conceptual framework which includes the concept of the *service package,* a particular set of services assigned to a particular individual which can be specified both in terms of the types and in terms of the quantities of the services it includes. Analytically, the service package serves as a critical link between the providers of services--mental health clinics, nursing homes, or home help organizations, for example--and the individuals who receive their services. Operationally, the service package could provide a link between the prescribers and the providers of services in much the same way that a physician's instructions provide the link between himself and a hospital staff. In this role, the service package could also be the key to the coordination of the sets of services prescribed for individuals. Finally, the service package is the key to meaningful program evaluation and resource allocation.

The concept of a service package is not a new one. Indeed, we are quite accustomed to using single descriptive terms--*nursing home services, hospital services,* or *home services*, for example--to refer to what really are sets of services. The primary difficulty with using these common terms, however, is that they do not define unique sets of services but, rather, describe the settings in which they are received. The individuals in nursing homes, for example, often receive vastly different sets of services, all of which are collectively termed *nursing home services*, and, moreover, many of the service packages received by patients in nursing homes are quite often also received by people living in other settings. Hence, these terms do not define sets of services at all; they fail to identify specifically the kinds of services actually being provided.

This general semantic problem led to, among other things, the recognition of the need for a set of generic services, carefully defined in terms of the services actually involved, which could be used as building blocks for uniquely defined service packages. Appendix B of this manual is an attempt to fulfill this need and contains the definitions of twenty-four generic services which provide a *core* of specifically defined services, or service definitions, useful in many different applications. (Some modifications or additions may, of course, be necessary for particular applications.) These service definitions were derived by the disaggregation of the services normally provided under the general headings of, for example, *nursing home services* and *home care services* and by a reaggregation of those services into these twenty-four more specifically defined and identifiable generic services. In addition, Part B of the MFAQ contains a set of questions designed to determine the services actually being received by an individual so that his service package can be uniquely defined.

These service definitions were tested by service providers, administrators, and clinicians and found to identify adequately the actual service provided. They have also been used in a number of studies (see Chapters 9, 10, and 11 of this manual and Comptroller General, 1977a; 1977b) and found to identify effectively the actual service packages individual patients were receiving. In a recent survey reported on in more detail in Chapter 11, for example, one patient in a nursing home was found to be receiving each week 1.2 hours of personal care, 2.3 hours of nursing care, and 7.5 hours of social/recreation service while, at the same time, another patient was receiving 11.4 hours of nursing care, 2.3 hours of personal care, no social/recreation service, and 5 hours of coordination and referral services. A person living at home could, of course, receive either of these two service packages.

A major role envisioned for applying the service package concept lies in the evaluation of service programs. Specifically, it has long been recognized that the impact of a single isolated service on an individual's functional status is practically impossible to determine and that it is the total set of services acting together which makes the impact. Nutritional programs, for example, are not independent of medical programs in their impact on an individual. Significantly, however, the service package concept--primarily because its generic services can be so clearly defined--provides a convenient device for investigating not only which service packages are related to the greatest changes in individuals' functional status, but also which services are actually included in those service packages. The United States General Accounting Office (GAO), for example, recently conducted a study (Comptroller General, 1977a) designed to evaluate the government sponsored service programs for a group of elderly citizens in Cleveland, Ohio, using the service package concept and was able to determine not only which service package was being provided for each of approximately sixteen hundred elderly individuals and to identify the providers of the individual services in the packages, but also to determine the functional status of each of the individuals in the study. In particular, the GAO was able to confirm (1) that, generally, the more impaired elderly were receiving those service packages containing more types and higher quantities of services, (2) that the costs of 70 percent of the services received by the extremely impaired elderly living in the community were borne by the family or friends of the recipient, and (3) that the service packages received by the extremely impaired elderly were similar regardless of whether the recipient resided in an institutional or in a home setting. A follow-up study is being conducted in which individual functional status changes over time can be observed and related to the service packages received by the individual in order to evaluate more directly the impact of services on their recipients.

In addition, the GAO's Cleveland study also addressed the problem of estimating the costs of services packages. The cost to the government of providing individual services was estimated by the service providers and used, in turn, as a basis for estimating the costs of complete service packages. Specifically, it was confirmed that the cost to the government of providing the service packages for the severely impaired elderly was, in general, lower if the service packages were provided in an institutional setting rather than in a community setting. Apparently, the reason so many of the severely impaired elderly can continue to function in the community is that such a large portion of the services received by them is provided by friends and family.

The primary purpose for which the service package concept was developed was planning and resource allocation. Essential to effective planning and resource allocation is a method for comparing the costs of alternative ways of providing services. While good planning should not seek the least expensive set of services, it should seek the least expensive ways of providing the services planned. The service package concept provides a means for investigating the costs of alternative ways of producing the same service package. A study referred to earlier (Chapter 11 of this manual), for example, went beyond identifying the service packages received by the patients in a nursing home; it included finding estimates of the costs of providing those same service packages in alternative settings. Not surprisingly, some service packages could be provided at less cost in the nursing home while others would cost less in other settings. A more recent GAO study (Comptroller General, 1977b) utilized the service package concept to compare the costs of two alternative forms of care for the elderly: home care and institutional care. (See Chapter 12.)

Ultimately, with the three principle components of the OARS Model, planning and resource allocation--or budgeting--at the community level could be based on analyses of the impact alternative sets of service packages might have on the functional status of individuals in the community. (See, e.g., Chapter 5 of this manual.) Based on such analyses, the decision makers would select the set of service packages expected to produce what they viewed as the most favorable change in the functional status of the individuals in the community for the investment required. By adding up the quantities of services of each type contained in the selected set of service packages, the total quantity of each type of service required could be determined and service programs adjusted to meet those requirements. The information required for this sort of analysis is not available at present, but, as indicated earlier, partial analysis using only the service package concept can greatly improve planning and resource allocation decisions.

Reliability and Validity

Assessment of service utilization is relatively new in its application to programs for the elderly, and experience with both service definitions and Part B of the MFAQ is limited. However, while formal validity and reliability testing have not been completed, our experience to date has been encouraging. The key issues in validity and reliability are:

1. Are the definitions reliable and valid in the sense (a) that different people identify the same activities by the same service title and quantity and (b) that the activities are properly classified and measured?

2. Do the questions in Part B of the MFAQ lead to the *proper* identification and measurement of the services received?

Experience to date in working with service providers such as nursing home administrators, nurses, clinical social workers, community service program administrators, and county social service directors, nurses, and social workers has been good. And while, in earlier versions of the definitions, these service providers had difficulty with some of the units of measure, the definitions have since been modified to clarify such issues, and only rarely do service providers have difficulty in identifying the appropriate service definitions for the activities in which they are engaged. In addition, in the GAO study in Cleveland, Ohio (Comptroller General, 1977a), the 118 agencies who used these definitions (with minor modifications) to identify all the services they provided to the elderly also reported no difficulty. The modifications to the service definitions for the GAO study in Cleveland included changing units of measure on several services and the addition of four services. The agencies were able to identify both the types and quantities of services they provided and to make an estimate of the average cost of providing a unit of each service.

Part B of the MFAQ has been used in a large number of interviews, and interviewers with proper training have had no difficulty in helping service recipients report both the types and quantities of services received. At this time we do not know the extent to which the responses are accurate, but, based on available information from studies of medical reporting, we would, in general, expect that individuals would underreport on items which have no obvious significant impact. In addition, in the Cleveland study, reports on the services received by individuals were available from the recipient as well as from the agency providing the services, and, except for special cases--where subsidized meals were paid for partially by the recipient, for example--the GAO found satisfactory agreement between them.

The set of services defined by the OARS project is not expected to be either complete or entirely appropriate for all purposes. However, it has been shown to provide a standardized *core* of services for all applications thus far, and it does permit cross-study comparisons for many purposes. In some applications, in fact, it may be necessary to disaggregate further the services for special purposes, but the disaggregated services can be reaggregated for cross-study comparisons. Medical services, for example, are highly aggregated, even at the generic level, and it may be necessary to disaggregate further in terms of medical speciality or in terms of primary, secondary, or tertiary care. Such further disaggregation can be accomplished without destroying the usefulness of standardized definitions.

Examinations of the reliability and validity of the service definitions and of Part B of the MFAQ are now in progress. In the meantime, the Center for the Study of Aging and Human Development would appreciate reports of user experience and problems with this component of the OARS model.

REFERENCES

Comptroller General of the United States. Report to Congress on the well-being of older people in Cleveland, Ohio. U.S. General Accounting Office, HRD-77-70. Washington, D.C.: U.S. General Accounting Office, 1977a.

Comptroller General of the United States. Report to Congress on home health--the need for a national policy to better provide for the elderly. U.S. General Accounting Office, HRD-78-19. Washington, D.C.: U.S. General Accounting Office, 1977b.

CHAPTER 5

A CONCEPTUAL MODEL FOR RESOURCE ALLOCATION: THE OARS MODEL

RICHARD M. BURTON, WILLIAM W. DAMON, AND DAVID C. DELLINGER

In a previous chapter, the general nature of the problem which motivated the development of the Multidimensional Functional Assessment Questionnaire (MFAQ) was described. (See Chapter 1.) The purpose of this chapter is to describe more formally the resource allocation model implicit in much of the OARS work and to discuss its prospects for future applications.

The problem, as it was initially put to the Center for the Study of Aging and Human Development at Duke University, was to devise a method for evaluating alternatives to institutionalization for the elderly (Maddox, 1972). There was a general feeling among those responsible for programs that too many elderly persons were being relegated to institutional care and that other more effective ways of caring for the elderly were being neglected. It was felt, in fact, that we were not getting our money's worth out of programs for the elderly and that a method was needed for evaluating alternatives.

A number of innovative proposals for providing care for the elderly had been made. Among them were nutritional programs, Meals on Wheels programs, mental health programs, and homemaker service programs. In addition, there were already many programs in existence which provided care for the elderly, including Medicare, Welfare, legal aid clinics, counseling programs, housing programs, and several volunteer programs. In short, while there were many alternative ways of caring for the elderly, there were, unfortunately, no obvious ways to evaluate those alternatives comparatively.

The problem was obviously complex. The alternatives included a wide array of services individually aimed at helping the elderly in a number of single dimensions--that is, for example, in their mental *or* physical health, in their social *or* economic welfare, *or* in simply assisting them perform the routine activities of daily living--but it was generally recognized that the problems were not *uni*dimensional and that the impact of services, in fact, was *multi*dimensional. Moreover, technical knowledge regarding the delivery and the effects of the various services provided for the elderly was dispersed among a number of professions, and little information other than demographic data was available on the status of the members of the elderly populations who were the intended beneficiaries of the programs.

Early on it became apparent that the problem could be formulated in a classic cost-benefit format. Unfortunately, however, it also became apparent that such a formulation was fraught with difficulties. Little information was available on the cost of providing such a wide variety of proposed services, for example, and there did not exist a common way of defining and measuring the benefits expected from them. A purposeful decision was made, therefore, to deal with these difficult problems of measurement and definition, thereby creating the three key building blocks out of which to construct a complete resource allocation system based on cost-benefit analysis: functional assessment, service packages, and a method for predicting impact.

It was clear that a project of this nature would require an interdisciplinary team and that a great deal of effort would be necessary to coordinate the work of its participants. Not only was an analytical structure necessary to integrate the relevant technical knowledge dispersed among a large number of different professionals, but an empirical component was required to test the theoretical concepts as they were developed and to provide immediate feedback to guide further theoretical developments. Hence, an interdisciplinary team was formed which included, among others, psychiatrists, social workers, economists, operations researchers, nurses, social scientists, and lawyers; a clinic was established to permit the clinicians on the interdisciplinary team to perform the empirical work; Durham County, North Carolina, was selected as a "laboratory"; the program was dubbed the Older American Resources and Services (OARS) Project; and finally, a conceptual model was developed to guide it.

The Conceptual Model

The cost-benefit framework selected for the problem required that a system be devised for linking the costs of alternative programs for the elderly to the benefits expected to be produced by those programs. The costs of the programs were to reflect social costs, most of which could be measured in terms of the resources consumed and converted into dollars, and the benefits were to be measured in terms of the impact the programs would have on the population which was to be served.

In the general mathematical version of the conceptual model we maximize a utility measure, U, on the final state of the population subject to a budget constraint. That is, we:

Maximize $U (m_1, m_2, \ldots, m_n)$

subject to $\sum_{\ell} c_\ell \, y_\ell \leq B$

and $\quad H (x_1, x_2, \ldots, x_n, m_1, m_2, \ldots, m_n, y_1, y_2, \ldots, y_k) = 0$

where $\quad x_h$ is the number of individuals initially in state h, h = 1, 2, $\ldots$, n

m_h is the number of individuals expected to be in state h after receiving the services, h = 1, 2, $\ldots$, n

c_ℓ is the cost of a service facility of type ℓ

y_ℓ is the number of service facilities of type ℓ planned

B is the total budget

and $\quad$ H is a complex function relating the planned facilities and the current status of the population to the expected status of the population.

However, while this form is conceptually complete, it is not very operational. We must be able concretely to relate cost to facilities, facilities to services, services to service packages, and service packages to individuals, and we must be able accurately to measure the effect of service packages upon the individuals in the target population. This suggests the development of a sequence of relationships which relates facilities to services and, in turn, services to changes in functional status. This kind of sequential relationship was employed in the OARS model in Durham County and is represented here by the schematic diagram in Figure 1. Beginning in block 1 with a list of "Resources," Figure 1's scheme concludes in block 8 by relating those resources to the changes they bring about in the target population. In between blocks 1 and 8 are diagramed the model's various component parts, including those concerned with the generation, the provision and measurement, the combination, and the assignment of various services. First, each of these components and their interrelations in forming the whole model will be briefly described, and then will follow a more detailed discussion of the technology, or transition, matrix.

In the first block of Figure 1 we show a sample of the more than twenty-five different organizations which constitute the service generation system for the elderly in Durham County. These organizations both consume resources and generate services; thus, it is possible to state the relationship between the costs and the services produced. Stating this relationship, however, requires that the services be defined in such a way that they can be measured, as, for example, in numbers of trips (for transportation services) or in numbers of hours (for personal care, nursing care, continuous supervision, homemaker-household, and coordination, information, and referral services). A sample of the twenty-four generic services, and their respective units of measure, defined for the OARS model is given in the third block of Figure 1.

As seen in the fourth block of Figure 1, the total set of twenty-four services produced for the Durham County elderly is allocated among the individual members of the target population by means of "service packages," or particular sets of services specifically designed for and assigned to particular persons according to their individual needs. The service package received by one individual, for example, may consist of three trips and five hours of nursing care each week, while that received by another individual may consist of only one trip and three hours of nursing care in the same time period. Conceptually, of course, a large number of service packages are possible, but indications thus far are that a relatively small number of service packages are actually used.

The fifth, sixth, and seventh blocks of Figure 1 depict the concept for estimating the impact a particular set of services will have on the target population. Specifically, the size of the target population and the functional status of its individual members having already been determined (block 5), the available service packages are assigned to particular individuals (block 6). The "technology matrix" indicated by block 7 is modeled on a matrix of transition probabilities in a Markov chain and is, in fact, a set of probabilities each of which indicates the probability that an individual member of the target population will change to a particular functional status, given his current functional status and a specific

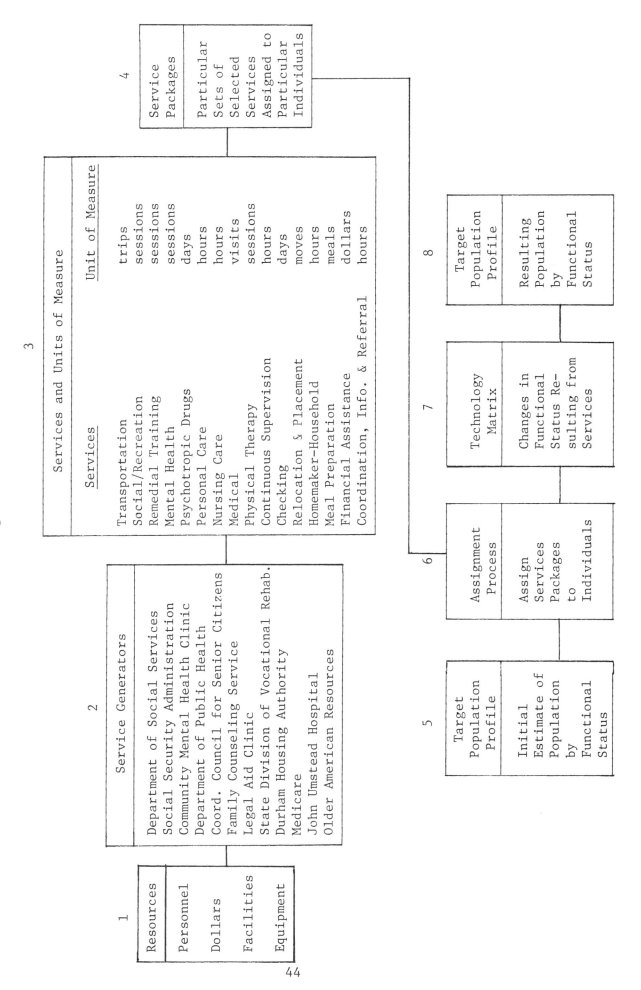

Figure 1

Schematic Diagram of the OARS Model

service package. Thus, the changes in the target population denoted by block 8 can be described as a function of the service packages available, which, in turn, are a function of the service generation system chosen and, ultimately, of the costs of producing the services.

The conceptual model diagramed in Figure 1, then, links the *cost* of producing services to the estimated *impact* of those services on the target population, and it shows how the model's component parts could eventually be integrated to produce the information needed for resource allocation. In addition, the model also contains the two components essential for program evaluation--functional status assessment and service packages. Both these components are discussed in detail elsewhere in this manual (see Chapters 1, 2, and 4), but the third component--the technology, or transition, matrix--is not.

The Technology Matrix

The fundamental idea underlying the technology matrix is quite simple and is used by most of us informally. Specifically, we learn by experience and analysis that particular actions produce particular outcomes and that when a particular outcome is desired we must take an appropriate action. When we have cold symptoms, for example, we adopt a form of treatment which we have learned will usually--but not always--relieve the symptoms. The technology matrix is a device for formalizing this kind of learning so as to permit the prediction of the future functional status of individuals. It explicitly recognizes that such predictions are uncertain--that is, that the future functional status of an individual cannot be predicted exactly--but it also recognizes that the approximate distribution of a large number of persons initially assigned the same functional status and provided with the same service package *can* be predicted. For example, if a hundred persons with the same cold symptoms were given the same treatment, one could, by means of a technology matrix, predict not only the approximate number of them who would recover immediately, but also the number of them who would have a mild cold and the number who would have a severe cold. Such estimates are most often stated in the form of probabilities, of course, but when these probabilities are placed in a table the rows of which represent initial functional status and the columns of which represent predicted functional status, there results the matrix of transition probabilities we refer to as the technology matrix. A procedure for estimating transition probabilities was developed and tested as a part of the OARS project (Burton, Damon, and Dellinger, 1975), and formal mathematical procedures exist for estimating transition probabilities from empirical observation (Anderson and Goodman, 1957).

Obviously, the transition probabilities in the technology matrix can be obtained only as a result of careful collection of the data concerned with the changes in functional status which can be related to particular service packages. At present, the only set of observations suitable for beginning the monumental task of estimating transition probabilities has been collected by the U.S. General Accounting Office in Cleveland, Ohio (Comptroller General, 1977a; 1977b), and until many more sets of data are collected in a suitable form--that is, in a form which includes data not only on the functional status of individuals at two points in time, but also on the package of services received by those individuals in the intervening period--a generally useful technology matrix will not be developed.

Even without the technology matrix, however, it is still possible to make planning and resource allocation decisions by basing them on information concerned with the functional status of the target populations and with the generic services provided to it. And, significantly, while the results obtained by using this less-sophisticated method may, themselves, be less sophisticated than those which are potentially available through the use of the technology matrix, they clearly are superior to those which can be obtained without the use of functional status and service production information. Employing only the initial functional status information collected by it's survey in Cleveland, Ohio, for example, the U.S. General Accounting Office (GAO) was able to spot not only maldistributions of services, but also gross mismatches between the services being provided and those that were needed according to their data (Comptroller General, 1977a). In addition, the GAO, again using only a combination of functional status data and service production data, was also able to estimate the cost of home-delivered services, as an alternative to institutionalization, for the elderly in several different classes of functional status (Comptroller General, 1977b). Similarly, the Duke OARS team has utilized data on functional status and services to investigate alternatives to institutionalization (see Chapter 11 of this manual), and, in the planning for a mental health clinic in Durham County, functional status information on the elderly in the county have provided the basis for estimating the potential need for the services of the clinic. Of especial interest, perhaps, is that M. P. Lawton, R. J. Newcomer, and T. O. Byerts, coeditors of *Community Planning for an Aging Society* (London: Dowden, Hutchinson, Ross, Inc., 1977), have detailed procedures for planning based only on functional status.

The examples cited above indicate not only that great improvement in planning and resource allocation can be made, but also--and more importantly--that this improvement can be made using only partial analyses made within the correct overall conceptual framework. Hence, we need not wait for the complete development of the technology matrix to implement the OARS model.

REFERENCES

Anderson, T. W. and Goodman, Leo A. Statistical inference about Markov chains. *Annals of Mathematical Statistics*, 1957, *28*, 89-110.

Burton, R. M., Damon, W. W., and Dellinger, D. C. Patient states and the technology matrix. *Interfaces*, 1975, *5*, 43-53.

Comptroller General of the United States. Report to Congress on the well-being of older people in Cleveland, Ohio. U.S. General Accounting Office, HRD-77-70. Washington, D.C.: U.S. General Accounting Office, 1977a.

Comptroller General of the United States. Report to Congress on home health--the need for a national policy to better provide for the elderly. U.S. General Accounting Office, HRD-78-19. Washington, D.C.: General Accounting Office, 1977b.

Lawton, M. P., Newcomer, R. J., and Byerts, T. O, (Eds.), *Community planning for an aging society*. London: Dowden, Hutchinson, Ross, Inc., 1977.

Maddox, G. L. Intervention and outcome: Notes on designing and implementing an experiment in health care. *International Journal of Epidemiology*, 1972, *1*, 339–345.

PART II

DATA GATHERING, PROCESSING,
AND MANAGEMENT

Chapter 6

Interviewing: Hints and Helpful Approaches

William F. Laurie and Thomas J. Walsh

Having lived through interviewing a sample of 1,609 older people in Cleveland, Ohio, using the OARS Multidimensional Functional Assessment Questionnaire (Comptroller General, 1977), we have learned much about what to do and what not to do. The following hints and helpful approaches might make your interviewing easier.

Many of our hints and approaches sound like common sense. They are. However, in the hectic rush of controlling interviews, what seems to be commonsense often is not. Accordingly, we believe that relaying these hints and approaches may help others avoid the pitfalls we encountered in our interviewing experience.

Our comments are divided into three categories: (1) managing the interview process, (2) validating interviewers' work, and (3) keeping the nonresponse rate low. We singled out the latter two subjects because of their importance in ensuring accuracy and completeness of data.

Managing the Interview Process

Interviewer characteristics. Interviewers should be selected according to two kinds of characteristics: (1) those which will keep the nonresponse rate down, and (2) those which will make for objectivity in asking questions and recording answers. In addition, interviewers generally should be warm and friendly, but businesslike enough to elicit true responses.

It is important to select interviewers who are compatible with the target population. We interviewed people over sixty-five who primarily were female and apprehensive about strangers, for example, so we primarily selected females who would minimize the older individuals' apprehensions.

It is also important to consider the racial mix of the interviewers relative to that of the target population. We were advised at the start of our study, for example, that it was better to have interviewers of the race of those being interviewed. Our experience showed that this was not always necessary, but in some cases it did help. Another factor to consider is where the interviewers live. If interviewing throughout a large city, for example, you should employ interviewers from each part of the city.

With respect to objectivity, it is important to have interviewers who will record what the individuals being interviewed say rather than what the interviewer thinks they *should* say. There really are no guidelines for selecting those interviewers with more objectivity, but it should be dealt with during training. Also during interviewing, it is important to look for inconsistencies in answers and to point out any problems in this area to the interviewer. In addition, any similarity in the responses recorded by the same interviewer could identify possible biases on his or her part.

Other factors can also be considered, such as availability and age. In our study, for example, many of the interviewers were married women who found time to interview while their children were in school, and most of our interviewers were over thirty years old. However, there was no consistent indication that age made a difference in the number of interviews completed. As can be seen in Table 1, which shows the average number of interviews completed by each of four age groups, interviewers in their thirties averaged more in the first phase while those over fifty averaged more in the second phase.

Table 1

Average Numbers of Interviews Completed by Interviewer Age Groups

| Age group | Average Numbers of Interviews Completed | |
	First phase	Second phase
21-30	48	32
31-40	70	46
41-50	34	58
Over 50	62	67

In general, the following broad guidelines should be considered in selecting interviewers:

1. The racial balance of the interviewers should approximate the expected ratio of races among the target population.

2. The interviewer should have a pleasant but firm personality.

3. Interviewers should be able to establish themseleves as people to be trusted.

4. Interviewers can be of varying ages, depending on the target population.

5. Previous interviewing experience is very helpful.

6. Interviewers should have the use of an automobile.

7. Interviewers should be available on at least a half-time basis and have few outside pressures.

One possible source of experienced interviewers is the Census Bureau. We found that the Census Bureau had a group of experienced interviewers who worked from time to time on special surveys. Fortunately, we were able to tap this source at a time when these interviewers were between special surveys and obtained some good, experienced interviewers.

We cannot stress enough the importance of having good interviewers. They not only will collect accurate data but will play an important role in keeping the nonresponse rate down. A good interviewer can nearly always get the interview.

Assigning interviews. In making assignments, the convenience of the interviewer should be kept in mind whenever possible. One might ask, for example:

1. What side of town does the interviewer live on?

2. Does the interviewer want to work in a racially mixed neighborhood?

3. Does the interviewer prefer the low, middle, or higher income neighborhoods?

The chart in Figure 1 shows the matters we considered when assigning names of persons to be interviewed to the interviewers in our survey.

Having the interviewers keep a record of their visits to individual homes is helpful to:

1. The interviewer, for call-backs when the respondent was not home on earlier visits.

2. Another interviewer, who might be asked to convert a refusal.

3. The project office, when the respondent has moved.

4. The interviewers who will be asked to reinterview at a later date.

In addition, interviewers should record any pertinent comments respondents may make along with their own impressions which may help future interviewers. Comments such as these, for example, are often especially helpful:

1. No one was home at various times and days of the week.

2. Respondent was adamant about not being interviewed.

3. No one answered the door, but noises indicated someone was home.

4. Daughter refused to allow mother to be interviewed.

5. Interview was completed, but respondent asked not to be bothered again.

If a survey calls for interviewing the same respondent more than once, the data from the first interview and from the interviewer's records can be used to make subsequent interviews easier. Information that would be helpful to future interviewers might include:

Figure 1

Matters To Consider When Assigning Names of Those To Be Interviewed

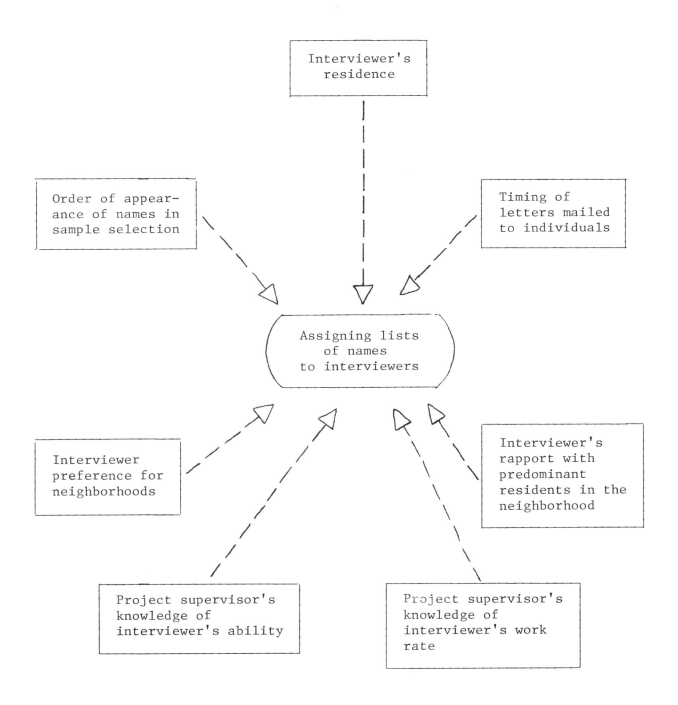

1. Name of interviewer who completed the first interview. (If rehiring some interviewers, for example, you may want to assign the same respondents to them; some respondents welcome back the interviewer as an old friend.)

2. Foreign language required, if any.

3. Circumstances surrounding and reason for first refusal if the respondent was converted from a refusal to a participant.

4. Any helpful notes recorded by the first interviewer.

5. Names of people obtained during first interview who would know whereabouts of respondent.

Interviewer performance records. We kept a daily log showing which interviewers came to the office, the number of completed interviews each submitted on that day, and the number each had completed to date. This enabled us to see which interviewers were not coming in weekly, as requested, and meeting their quota of five completions per week. This figure was purely an arbitrary number and judged to be a fair quota based on the amount of time required to complete one interview—forty-five minutes for our study. Occasionally, we had to call interviewers and ask them to come to the office to report on their assignments.

We maintained another logbook with a separate page which showed the following information for each interviewer:

1. Interviewer's name.

2. Page number of assignment received.

3. Date assignment was received.

4. Number of names on assignment page.

5. Number of names outstanding.

By keeping a running tally of the names outstanding, we were able to tell at a glance whether an interviewer needed another assignment or had enough names to work with. This judgement was based on our knowledge of the interviewer's ability and performance rate. If a slow-working interviewer had too many names outstanding, we would ask for some to be turned in and then assign the work to an interviewer needing more names.

It is a good idea to establish a quota of how many interviews are to be completed each week so that the interviewers will know what is expected of them. The quota depends on the length of the interview, travel requirements, and what an interviewer must do to find an eligible respondent. Some interviewers will exceed the quota; a few will not meet it.

In addition, interviewers should be required to complete a certain number of interviews before being paid the agreed amount for the training session. This will avoid investing time and money into training someone who quits after only a few interviews.

Completed interviews. Whether the interviewing is done in-house or by a contractor, all completed questionnaires must be edited and coded. Editing is needed to guarantee completeness, consistency, and accuracy in the responses, and coding is necessary to transfer the responses into data processing form. The editing and coding also can be accomplished in-house or by a contractor, but, either way, we recommend strict controls to maintain reliability and accuracy. Even if the contractor is noted for reliability, you are responsible for the end product and must maintain quality controls. The added cost will assure success.

Editing and coding can be accomplished separately or simultaneously because only one person need go through the questionnaire in detail and because, by it-self, coding is a boring process and can lead to errors. From time to time you should check the work of the editors to see that quality work is being maintained.

For a questionnaire containing about 100 items--some with multiple answers--and a predetermined coding pattern, we estimate that the average person can edit and code fifteen to twenty questionnaires per eight-hour working day. Using this criterion for a 2,000-interview survey, we estimate that you would need one person full-time for four months and one person half-time for two months. If the inter-views come in at a faster rate in the beginning, the part-time person should work full-time in order to avoid a large backlog. (The questionnaires should be re-turned to the interviewers for correction as soon as possible.) Then, as the work tapers off toward the end of the survey, one or both of the editors can work only part-time.

As stated previously, every questionnaire must be edited. The editors should have specific procedures to follow in order that their work is done ef-ficiently and systematically. Following are some guidelines:

1. Observe the first-in-first-out method; that is, edit the questionnaires as they are received.

2. There should be an answer for each question. If not, the editor must know:

   a. why the respondent refused to answer the question,

   b. why the question did not apply to the respondent,

   c. why the respondent did not know the answer, or

   d. why the question wasn't asked.

3. If a respondent refused to answer too many questions or didn't know the answer, the editor must judge whether or not to accept the entire ques-tionnaire as valid.

4. The answers must be consistent and reasonable. For example, if a re-spondent has not completed high school, the editor would not expect to

see "Doctor" or "Teacher" listed as an occupation for the respondent.

5. Questionnaires containing missing or erroneous data should be returned to the appropriate interviewers as soon as possible for corrections so they can then return to or call the appropriate respondents to obtain the correct or missing data.

6. All answers must be legible.

To minimize errors and returned questionnaires, the interviewers should be trained to edit their own work prior to submitting it. Nevertheless, the editors will find some questionnaires with problems; these should be returned to the appropriate interviewers during their weekly visits.

At the beginning of the survey you will probably find many questionnaires being returned because of missing and incomplete answers. This will occur less often after the interviewers become accustomed to the questionnaires and learn how to complete them properly. Any interviewers who continue to submit work with the same type of errors should be asked to resign; otherwise, the accuracy of the data will suffer greatly.

As part of the editing process in our study we checked the consistency of the ratings given by our interviewers. (At the completion of each interview, our interviewers were required to rate the person's status in each of five dimensions: (1) social resources, (2) economic resources, (3) mental health, (4) physical health, and (5) activities of daily living.) Specifically, we performed a consistency check on the ratings in which we determined whether or not the ratings given by the interviewer generally agreed with the participant's responses to the questionnaire and with the editor's rating. If the editor disagreed with a particular rating, he would question the interviewer about it. Most of the time the interviewer had supplemental information which was not shown on the questionnaire but which supported the rating. For example, in conversation with the participant's spouse, the interviewer might have obtained information which would affect the participant's mental health or social resources ratings, or, by observing the living conditions or the participant, the interviewer might have seen something that would affect the economic resources or physical health ratings. Sometimes the interviewer acknowledged rating the participant too low or too high and would then change the rating.

To check the consistency of the interviewers' ratings, we selected 2 percent of the questionnaires at random and rated the individuals based only on the responses shown in the questionnaires. In Phase I our ratings agreed with 85 percent of the interviewers' ratings. In Phase II we were 88 percent in agreement. In those cases where ours and the interviewers' ratings disagreed, the difference was never more than one point.

Validating Interviewers' Work

To show that the responses on the questionnaire are authentic and to convince others that the data base is supported by genuine responses, the work of the interviewers must be validated. Specifically, you must prove that the interviewer talked to the correct person and that the answers recorded are those the respondent gave. The necessity of this task cannot be stressed enough. During routine validation, for example, we found that one interviewer had fabricated all or part of thirty-seven interviews. In many cases the interviewer invented answers because the respondent had refused the interview. We validated the interviewer's work and reconducted those interviews.

Depending on the amount of time available and the number of validations to be made, you can validate either in person or by telephone. Personal validations are more costly because more time is required for travel and because you must pay travel costs in addition to an hourly rate, but you can have telephone validations made from the home or the office, paying only the hourly wage. In most cases, telephone validations should suffice.

To conduct the validation process, you should select at random some work from all of the interviewers that is representative of the number they have turned in. In addition, you should select interviews from different time periods for two reasons: (1) you want to catch any fabrication early in the study, and (2) fabrication is more likely to appear late in the study because interviewers may get tired of interviewing. In addition, select some converted refusals for validation, particularly if you are paying more for them.

It is not necessary to ask every question during the validation process, but ask enough questions to determine the following:

    1. Was the person named on the questionnaire interviewed?

    2. Was that person interviewed in the manner prescribed (face-to-face or by telephone)?

    3. Are the responses on the questionnaire the responses given to the interviewer?

In addition, select four or five key questions to which the respondent would normally give the same replies at a later data:

    1. How much education do you have?

    2. What is your marital status?

    3. What is your occupation?

    4. What is your spouse's occupation?

    5. Do you own your home or rent?

You may also include opinion questions about how the person felt about the interview or the interviewer. This information could be used to redesign the questionnaire for future use and to identify characteristics of good interviewers.

It may happen that there will be validation replies which are not the same as those on the questionnaire. The validator, however, should not be hasty in judging an interview invalid. Some responses may change; the validator may not be talking with the person interviewed; and some people become annoyed about being bothered again and deliberately give different answers.

If the validator finds a questionnaire with several discrepancies, more questionnaires of that interviewer should be checked. If the rest are valid, the interviewer should be confronted and an acceptable explanation obtained. If the validator finds other questionnaires which do not validate, and if an acceptable explanation cannot be obtained, that interviewer's data should be discarded and the interviewer removed from the project. All of the interviewer's work must be validated or not be used.

Keeping Nonresponse Low

A *nonrespondent* is defined as a person in your sample who is not interviewed. It is very important to keep nonrespondents at a minimum in order to have complete data, for each nonrespondent represents the voices of several people in your universe that will not be heard in the data. Too many nonrespondents, in fact, will result in a smaller universe, may bias the data, and may limit the conclusions you make in your report.

Regardless of how many nonrespondents you have, look for any characteristics which differentiate them from those subjects who did respond. For example, were men more likely to be nonrespondents? Were upper income people? Were older people? Were blacks? Were whites? Hopefully, there will be no biases in your nonresponse so that you can assume that the voices of the nonrespondents will be heard through the voices of other similar people who did respond.

You should expect to have some nonrespondents. When you are dealing with a diverse population and an equally diverse group of interviewers, you must expect it. Some people will not be willing to talk to the interviewers; some interviewers will not be skilled or persistent enough to complete the interview; and people not at home, on vacation, or in the hospital, for example, will account for some nonrespondents. In our study we tried to keep our nonresponse rate under 20 percent. Here are some guidelines to use to keep the nonresponse rate low:

1. Consider the timing of the interviews. Holiday periods are bad because many people are busy, have visitors, and might not want to be bothered. Late spring and summer are good because the weather is warmer and daylight is longer. (However, one disadvantage of summer is that both respondents and interviewers will want to take some vacation time.)

2. Interviewers should understand the purpose and importance of your survey. This is important for two reasons. The interviewers will try harder to complete each interview and convey the importance of the survey to the person being interviewed.

3. Try to locate anyone in your sample who has moved to determine if he is still eligible to be in your sample. Because not all are complete, we

used many different sources to locate people. Some possible sources include: telephone company listings, forwarding addresses from the Post Office, the Polk Directory, obituary columns from public libraries or newspapers, and neighbors. One of the best ways to locate somebody is to have the interviewer go to the original address and talk to the neighbors.

There are certain techniques to be employed in attempting interviews with those people who have already refused once. Some of the techniques we found useful are:

1. Selecting those interviewers who had good results with the regular work.

2. Sending a different interviewer from the one who was refused the first time. Interviewers affect people differently.

3. Sending a letter which appeals to the person for help and which explains the benefits of participation.

4. Paying a higher rate to the interviewers for interviews with people who refused once.

5. Considering any notes made by the first interviewer which describe the circumstances of the refusal. The second interviewer may find these useful.

However, before attempting to interview people who refused once, use the first interviewer's notes to identify circumstances where a second attempt would be of no use. For example, we did not try again if the notes indicated the person had been outwardly hostile or was seriously ill.

We have found that a commonsense approach which starts with appropriate selection and training of interviewers and which continues through careful work assignment, up-to-date record-keeping, and prompt editing, validating, and coding of questionnaires results in useful, reliable information--information crucial to the outcome of a study.

REFERENCES

Comptroller General of the United States. Report to Congress on the well-being of older people in Cleveland, Ohio. U.S. General Accounting Office, HRD-77-70. Washington, D.C.: U.S. General Accounting Office, 1977.

Chapter 7

Sample Design, Data Management, and Data Analysis: Illustrating Some Basic Issues

William P. Cleveland

In this chapter the Duke OARS sampling and data management procedures are used as an illustration of a standard approach to such issues. Specifically, basic procedures for acquiring data, checking them, making them computer ready, and generating summary tabulations are described. While those thoroughly familiar with such operations will find little new here, this information will neverthe-less be useful as a reference for those individuals involved with a project of this kind for the first time and, perhaps, as a review for more experienced individuals.

The Duke OARS Samples

The OARS program at the Duke University Center for the Study of Aging and Human Development has administered the Multidimensional Functional Assessment Questionnaire to three groups of older persons in the local area--community residents, the institutionalized, and clinic clients--and it was found that sampling procedures are critical when the investigator must be able to justify generaliza-tions to populations and subpopulations. Following are brief descriptions of the manner in which each of the three samples was selected, the manner in which data were gathered, and the procedures for preparing data for analysis.

The community survey. In Durham County, North Carolina, a stratified random probability sampling procedure was used to select 10 percent of the community residents aged sixty-five and over. Areas which, according to census tract data, contained approximately equal populations of persons sixty-five and over were used as sampling units. These sampling units were stratified by race ($\geq$ 91 per-cent black vs. $\leq$ 90 percent black), by location of residence (rural vs. urban), and by a specially generated socioeconomic index based on selected housing char-acteristics to ensure that there was appropriate proportional representation of all segments of the community resident population.

The design was self-weighting, the size of the sample from each stratum be-ing proportional to the population in that stratum. (In this case, approximately 10 percent of each stratum was selected.) When this strategy is used, the pro-portion of the sample with a given characteristic is a correct estimate of the proportion of the population having that characteristic. The variances within the different strata were sufficiently similar that overall sample variances were used rather than weighted ones. By means of this sampling procedure 1,138 persons were selected, of whom 997, or 87.7 percent, completed acceptable inter-views in the winter of 1972-1973. This is the community sample to which refer-ence is made in other chapters of this manual.

The institutional survey. Durham County, North Carolina, is served both by small care facilities having five or fewer occupants and by large facilities where the number of occupants may range from six to several hundred. This survey, however, was restricted to persons aged sixty-five and over who had lived in Durham County for twelve months before entering an institution. Information for the institutional survey was gathered in the late summer of 1973 by means of two sampling procedures. In the small facilities, a one-in-five sample of the institutions was drawn, and every person over sixty-five in the chosen facilities was eligible for an interview. In the large facilities, the names of residents aged sixty-five and over were alphabetized and every fifth name selected. Substitutions were made for those persons who were selected but subsequently found not to meet age or residential requirements. Of the 112 persons selected by means of the two sampling procedures, 102, or 91.1 percent, completed the interviews, six refused, and four died before being contacted.

The clinic survey. The OARS Clinic offers service to persons aged fifty and over referred because of age-related problems. All new clients seen consecutively between 1 July 1972 and 30 June 1973 were included in the sample. Of the 100 persons seen, 98 gave useful information. Unlike in the community and institutional samples, some of the clients in the clinic sample (20 percent) were between the ages of fifty and sixty-four.

Accuracy of Information

The OARS instrument is designed to be as unambiguous and as easy to complete as possible. Nevertheless, errors occur, and a compulsive and dedicated data technician is required to check over all the questionnaires as soon as they are available. Because of carelessness or lack of diligence, for example, interviewers may not ask each item on the questionnaire or mark all answers clearly. Such errors must be caught immediately after the questionnaire is turned in so that the interviewer--or the respondent, if necessary--can be recontacted speedily and corrections made. In particular, individual items should be scanned and the overall consistency of the responses checked; by the time inconsistencies are found by a computer it may be too late for corrective action. Finally, while such issues as these apply primarily to survey situations rather than to clinic settings, it is well to have a technician check the forms to ensure their having valid, interpretable, and consistent entries even if they were administered in a clinic.

In a large survey where the reliability of the interviewers is not known, a certain fraction, perhaps 5 percent, of each interviewer's subjects should be contacted by the field supervisor to ensure that information has not been manufactured. In addition, in order to improve the response rate, it may be necessary to approach some subjects several times. Some interviewers are better than others in encouraging subject participation, and they can, in some instances, persuade reluctant subjects to respond where other interviewers have failed. Such interviewers are worth identifying.

Coding the Data in Machine-Readable Form

Data coding is largely mechanical, but it is important that it be done with

a high degree of accuracy. The object is to transfer the data on the questionnaire to computer cards or directly to disk storage for later computer analysis.
Before any keypunching is attempted, all ambiguities on the questionnaires
should have been eliminated and all coding decisions made. Since the card number
and card columns for each entry are marked on the questionnaire, a keypuncher can
work directly from it. This eliminates the possibility of transcription errors
which can occur when intermediate forms are used. The data for each subject oc-
cupy six cards.

   At least two options are available to ensure accurate keypunching. The
first is to have a person punch all the data from the questionnaire onto the
cards and then to have this process repeated using an interpreting keypunch.
The interpreter reads the previous cards as a new set is being punched, compares the old set with the new one, and signals discrepancies. The questionnaire
is then checked and correct entry made on the new set of cards.

   At Duke, a second method was used in which two different persons punched the
data on the cards independently. A computer program was then used to compare the
two sets of cards and to print out both cards in cases where it found discrepancies. Both decks were corrected and rerun until all inconsistencies were removed.
This system minimizes the chance that a person will simply accept someone else's
previous interpretation of an ambiguous entry without thoroughly checking the
questionnaire. Either of these systems can be used in a key-to-disk operation
in which data are entered directly into computer storage without the use of cards.
A key-to-disk system offers the additional possibility of range checks on data
as they are entered. This notifies the keypunch operator immediately of an out-
of-range or inappropriate entry.

Generating Data Summaries and Analyses

   Once the data have been punched, a computer program is required to read them
and generate the information desired for reports. While special programs in a
general purpose language can be written to analyze data, it is generally expensive
and unwise to have this done. Most computers of moderate size (i.e., those with
at least 300K bytes of core memory) have sets of data analysis programs available.
These have been used many times and are either error free or contain known errors
with known remedies. To repeat the effort of generating such programs is folly.

   The best known of these sets of programs, or program packages, are *SPSS
(Statistical Package for the Social Sciences*, Nie et al., 1975), *SAS (Statistical
Analysis System*, Barr et al., 1976), and *BMDP (Biomedical Computer Programs*,
Dixon, 1975). The technical staff of any computer operation will be familiar
with these programs and know their use. Some special programming is still required, but it consists mostly of spelling out the format in which the data were
keypunched, naming the different items on the questionnaire, and requesting the
information desired in terms of these names. Such requests are particularly
simple if the response frequencies of the answers to each item are all that is
wanted. Card numbers and columns can be incorporated into the item names for
easy reference to the questionnaires. Regardless of the specific analyses desired, response frequencies for each item should be generated to catch any errors which might have slipped past previous stages and because such basic information is invariably required.

Summary

With the OARS Multidimensional Functional Assessment Questionnaire used as an example, the basic steps involved in acquiring data and in getting it into a computer have been described. These steps involve close supervision of interviewers, careful keypunching, and the generation or selection of some kind of program to read the data once they have been keypunched. Once these steps have been taken, a computer data base is available from which any number of further analyses can be carried out. The program packages described not only can generate marginal tabulations of each item, but can also do analyses of variance, cross tabulations, regressions, and other procedures necessary to more complicated kinds of analyses related to even more complicated questions about the data. All of the analyses contained in this manual were generated by such a package. The technical expertise required to carry out these steps is not great, but a person with sufficient experience and administrative ability is needed to coordinate operations and get them to run smoothly.

REFERENCES

Barr, A. J., Goodnight, J. H., Sall, J. P., and Helwig, J. T. *A user's guide to SAS-76*. SAS Institute Inc., P.O. Box 10066, Raleigh, N.C. 27605, 1976.

Dixon, W. J. (Ed.), *BMDP: Biomedical computer programs*. Berkeley: University of California Press, 1975.

Nie, N. H., Hull, C. H., Jenkins, J. G., Steinbrenner, K., and Bent, D. H. *SPSS: Statistical packages for the social sciences*. 2nd ed. New York: McGraw Hill, 1975.

CHAPTER 8

WAYS OF COMBINING FUNCTIONAL ASSESSMENT DATA

ERIC PFEIFFER

The OARS Multidimensional Functional Assessment Questionnaire (MFAQ) is a present state assessment instrument designed for use with individuals and/or populations. It measures a subject's functional level, at the time of administration, in each of the following areas, or dimensions: social resources (S), economic resources (E), mental health (M), physical health (P), and capacity for self-care, or activities of daily living (A).

The OARS questionnaire systematically gathers subjective and objective information regarding the functioning of an individual in such a way that information in each of the five areas evaluated can be compressed or summarized into a single summary functional rating. In this summary rating schema, described in more detail in the interviewer's instruction manual, a rating of 1 = outstanding functioning, 2 = good functioning, 3 = mild impairment, 4 = moderate impairment, 5 = severe impairment, and 6 = complete impairment.

The same schema applies to each of the five areas evaluated. Thus, a rating of 5 on social resources means "severely socially impaired," a rating of 5 on economic resources means that "economic resources are severely impaired," a rating of 5 on mental health means "severely mentally impaired," and so on. Each person receives a rating in each area. The individual's overall functioning can then be further summarized by four different methods which can be used to categorize individuals or groups of like individuals, using the basic OARS SEMPA ratings. These methods of summarizing will be illustrated using two case examples, Cases 1 and 2:

	S	E	M	P	A
Case 1	2	5	3	5	5

	S	E	M	P	A
Case 2	1	1	2	2	1

After each of these summarizing methods has been illustrated, there will follow a discussion of (1) each of the five areas, or dimensions, of functioning selected for assessment, and (2) the utilization of generic services.

Summarizing Functional Data

The OARS profile. An OARS SEMPA profile is a simple summary statement of an individual's functioning on each of the five dimensions selected for assessment.

Thus, Case 1, with a SEMPA functional rating of 2-5-3-5-5, represents an individual with good social functioning, severe economic impairment, mild mental impairment, severe physical impairment, and severe impairment in capacity for self-care. Similarly, Case 2, with a SEMPA functional rating of 1-1-2-2-1, represents an individual with excellent social resources, excellent economic resources, good mental and physical health, and excellent self-care capacity.

While the profile method still contains a large amount of detail about an individual and is, therefore, very useful for clinical application, it is less useful for describing populations in as much as 7,776 (6^5) different profiles can exist. For purpose of describing and classifying populations, therefore, still more compacted methods of summarizing data need to be employed.

The Cumulative Impairment Score (CIS). A second way of summarizing the information obtained from the OARS interview schedule, with substantially fewer resulting categories, is to *add* the functional rating on each dimension to form a single numerical Cumulative Impairment Score (CIS). Thus, the CIS for Case 1 is 20 (2 + 5 + 3 + 5 + 5 = 20), and the CIS for Case 2 is 7 (1 + 1 + 2 + 2 + 1 = 7). In general, CIS ratings below 10 indicate excellent overall functioning while CIS scores greater than 18 indicate that significant impairments exist in several areas of functioning. Scores in the range from 14 to 17 indicate impairments of lesser severity or impairments in only a very few areas of functioning.

The CIS permits the subdivision of a population into twenty-six distinct classes, a more manageable number of categories than the 7,776 different profiles which result when the OARS profile method is used. These classes can also be further collapsed at will (e.g., CIS of 5-17 vs. CIS of 18-30), resulting in a still smaller, still more manageable number of categories.

Number of significant impairments. Still another method of summarizing the OARS questionnaire information is to indicate the number of significant impairments, defined by a functional rating of 4 or greater, which are manifested by an individual. In this method, Case 1 would be described as having "three impairments"--economic resources, physical health, and self-care capacity--while Case 2 would be described as having "no impairments." In using this method, only six categories are possible. It should be clear that the smaller the number of resulting categories, the greater the loss of detailed information.

Functional equivalence classes. Another more complex, and hence more informative, way of summarizing functional state information is the creation of a series of functional equivalence classes, that is, classes within which individuals share the same functional status. Specifically, by means of a simple dichotomy between "not impaired" (ratings of 1-3) and "impaired" (ratings of 4-6), a series of functionally equivalent classes is created which encompasses all possible combinations of "impaired"/"not impaired" on each of the five dimensions evaluated. The number of such functional equivalence classes is 32 (2^5), and they are depicted in Table 1. Here, class 0 represents that class of persons having no impairments on any of the five dimensions, while class 31 represents those persons characterized by impairment on all five dimensions. For purposes of follow-up, an additional category, Death, has been added as a possible outcome.

Which of the above summary methods for classifying individuals--or groups

Table 1

Composition of the Thirty-Two Functionally Equivalent Classes

Functionally Equivalent Classes

Dimensions of functioning	0	1	2	3	4	5	6	7	8	9	10	11	12	13	14	15	16	17	18	19	20	21	22	23	24	25	26	27	28	29	30	31	Death
Physical health		X					X	X	X	X							X	X	X	X	X	X					X	X	X	X		X	
Mental health			X				X				X	X	X				X	X	X				X	X	X		X	X	X		X	X	
Social resources				X				X			X			X	X		X			X	X		X	X		X	X	X		X	X	X	
Economic resources					X				X			X		X		X		X		X		X	X		X	X	X		X	X	X	X	
Activities of daily living						X				X			X		X	X			X		X	X		X	X	X		X	X	X	X	X	

X = impaired (ratings of 4 – 6)

Blank = not impaired (ratings of 1 – 3)

of like individuals--should be used in a specific program, survey, or planning effort depends, of course, on the specific objectives sought. But this flexibility with respect to methods of classifying individuals or populations is one of the most desirable features of the OARS methodology, for the same basic set of data can be analyzed in several different ways to meet the needs of its many different users.

Substantive Areas for Functional Assessment

Based on the judgment of experienced clinicians and on the previous work of researchers in the health and social services field, five major areas of human functioning were selected for systematic evaluations in the OARS methodology: social resources, economic resources, mental health, physical health, and activities of daily living (ADL). Following are brief discussions of each of these areas.

Social resources. In regard to social resources, systematic inquiry is made into the extent, quality, and availability of social interactions. This includes a focus on marital status, on living arrangements, (specifically, on whether individuals live alone or with someone else), on the availability of a confidant whom individuals can trust and confide in, and, finally, on the presence, availability, and willingness of someone in the environment to provide some kind of on-going care in case of illness or disability. This information is then evaluated and summarized into an overall social resources rating, or a social functioning rating, on a six-point scale.

The rating process allows for a weighting of subjective and objective data by the interviewer or by a professional person rating the entire set of data on an individual. For instance, individuals who are married, who have many friends and many social contacts, and who have someone available who could take care of them indefinitely in case of disability would be viewed as having either good or excellent social resources. On the other hand, individuals currently separated or divorced, living alone, with few friends or other social contacts, with no one to trust and confide in, with feelings of loneliness and dissatisfaction over the amount of social contacts they have, and who, in addition, have no one who could give them even temporary help in case of illness or disability would be regarded as severely socially impaired. Individuals with intermediate responses to these items, or a scattering of positive and negative responses, would be given intermediate ratings.

Economic resources. An assessment of economic resources is important not only because the presence of economic resources can make available needed services to ameliorate other conditions or impairments, but also because financial deprivation can be a barrier to obtaining adequate services and, in addition, can impair social, mental, and physical functioning.

To arrive at a rating of an individual's economic functioning, employment status and current earnings, amount and sources of income, home ownership, and subjective financial evaluations are all taken into consideration. Thus, individuals who are employed, who have a good annual income either from earnings or from investments, who own their own homes, who are able to meet all of their basic needs, and who consider themselves reasonably well-off financially would be rated as being in good or excellent economic health. On the other hand, individuals who are currently unemployed, who receive no income or only income of a public assistance nature, who do not own any real estate property, whose basic needs for food, shelter, and clothing, as well as for small luxuries, are not being adequately met, and who see themselves as financially worse off than other people would be rated as severely financially impaired. Again, intermediate responses would lead to an intermediate functional rating on economic resources.

Mental health. In regard to mental health, a number of factors are considered. The first of these is concerned with intellectual intactness, for which the Short Portable Mental Status Questionnaire (Pfeiffer, 1975a)--a ten-item test of orientation, recent memory, long-term memory, and capacity for serial calculation--is administered to indicate the present level of intellectual intactness or deterioration. The second area evaluated in the mental health section is concerned with the presence or absence of functional psychiatric symptomatology. For this area, the Short Psychiatric Evaluation Schedule (Pfeiffer, 1975b)--a fifteen-item "yes-no" questionnaire measuring the presence of symptoms of anxiety, depression, suspiciousness, hypochondriacal complaints, and other physical manifestations of emotional disturbances--is included among the basic information gathered regarding mental health. Additional information collected concerns itself with self-assessed present life satisfaction and with individuals' subjective evaluations of their own mental health, particularly any perceived changes in mental health functioning over the past five years. In addition, information regarding individuals' mental functioning is obtained from interviewer observation with respect to the presence or absence of a number of behavioral traits and, where available, from standardized reports made by reliable informants.

With respect to the rating of mental functioning, individuals, for example, who exhibit marked intellectual deterioration, who exhibit significant symptoms of anxiety, depression, paranoia, or hypochondriasis, who are not satisfied with life, who regard their own mental health as declining, and who also are observed by the interviewer to be manifesting a number of psychiatric symptoms would be rated as severely mentally impaired. On the other hand, individuals with intact mental functioning, a lack of specific psychiatric symptomatology, good life satisfaction, and a positive subjective view of their own mental health corroborated by a positive view of their mental health on the part of an informant as well as by positive behavioral observations on the part of the interviewer would be considered to have good or outstanding mental health functioning. Again, intermediate responses or a mixture of positive and negative responses would lead to intermediate levels of mental health ratings.

Physical health. In the area of physical health, information is obtained on number of doctor visits, on number of days of disability at home, and on length of stay in hospital or nursing home. Information is also obtained regarding the receipt of a broad range of medical prescription drugs as well as the presence or absence of a variety of significant illnesses and the extent to which individual subjects find these disabling. The presence or absence of specific physical handicaps and the use of prosthetic devises is also determined. Finally, individuals are asked for an overall assessment of their own physical health. Again, all this information is summarized into a single functional rating on the physical health rating scale which follows a rating schema identical to that employed in the other functional areas.

Activities of daily living. Information in the area of self-care capacity, or the activities of daily living, is divided into two segments. The first of these is concerned with information regarding individuals' capacity for the performance of a variety of activities necessary in maintaining an independent household. These include the independent use of the telephone, the capacity to use public transportation, to go shopping, to prepare meals, to do routine housework, to take one's own medication, and to handle one's own money. The second area of functioning assessed is concerned with the individuals' capacity to take care of their own bodily functions. This includes an assessment of individuals' capacity to eat by themselves, to dress and undress themselves, to take care of their own appearance, to walk, to get in and out of bed, to take a shower or bath, and to be continent of bowel and bladder.

Again, all this information is summarized into a single functional rating regarding ADL capacity For example, individuals who require some help with shopping, heavy housework, and laundry would be rated as mildly impaired on ADL, and individuals who are confused and disoriented and who regularly require assistance with eating and dressing would be rated as severely impaired on ADL.

Utilization of Services

Part B of the MFAQ seeks information about a variety of services which aging or impaired individuals might require. A simple listing of the varieties of services covered in the questionnaire appears below. In addition, Appendix B of this manual contains a complete set of definitions of these services, including definitions of the purpose of each service, the activities it involves, the relevant personnel used for the delivery of each service, as well as some indication of the usual quantitative measures used in the delivery of each service.

List of Generic Services

1. Transportation
2. Social/Recreational Services
3. Employment Services
4. Sheltered Employment
5. Educational Services, Employment Related
6. Remedial Training
7. Mental Health Services
8. Psychotropic Drugs
9. Personal Care Services
10. Nursing Care
11. Medical Services
12. Supportive Devices and Prostheses
13. Physical Therapy
14. Continuous Supervision
15. Checking Services
16. Relocation and Placement Services
17. Homemaker-Household Services
18. Meal Preparation
19. Administrative, Legal, and Protective Services
20. Systematic Multidimensional Evaluation
21. Financial Assistance
22. Food, Groceries
23. Living Quarters (Housing)
24. Coordination, Information, and Referral Services

In the OARS questionnaire, information is systematically obtained regarding services subjects are currently receiving and also those services they feel they currently need. Thus, it is possible to obtain information regarding the "service package"--the set of services--which individuals are currently receiving as well as information regarding the set of services which they feel they currently need. The information thus obtained provides the building blocks utilized either by clinicians working with individual patients or by program planners working with populations to design service programs for those individuals or populations. Defining what constitutes an "appropriate service package" for individuals or populations also requires taking into consideration the functional status of the individuals or populations as assessed by the earlier substantive part of the OARS questionnaire.

REFERENCES

Pfeiffer, E. A short, portable mental status questionnaire for the assessment of organic brain deficit in elderly patients. *Journal of the American Geriatrics Society*, 1975a, *23*, 433-441.

Pfeiffer, E. A short psychiatric evaluation schedule. Paper presented at the 28th Annual Meeting, Gerontological Society, Louisville, Kentucky, October 26-30, 1975b.

PART III

ILLUSTRATIONS AND APPLICATIONS
OF THE OARS STRATEGY

Chapter 9

The OARS Durham Surveys: Description and Application

Dan Blazer

As has been seen in earlier chapters, the OARS model consists of three primary elements: (1) a classification of individuals according to functional status, (2) a disaggregation of services into generic components and a reaggregation according to actual utilization, and (3) a means of assessing the impact of a particular intervention on a particular functional class. The OARS surveys in Durham, North Carolina, however, have focused primarily upon the first of these three elements--individual functional status; and while some data on services have been gathered which, in fact, led to the development of the present service items, they were obtained at an early stage of our conceptualization of services and are, therefore, not as complete as those which can now be obtained. Hence, the Durham surveys are primarily an illustration of some of the uses of functional status information.

As has also been seen in other chapters, three surveys were conducted in Durham County, North Carolina, to obtain information on the functional status of its elderly population: (1) a random sample of 10 percent of the community resident elderly aged sixty-five and over (N = 997), (2) a stratified random sample of 20 percent of the elderly aged sixty-five and over in institutions (N = 102), and (3) all consecutive new clients coming to the OARS clinic within a twelve-month period (N = 98). It is important to note here that the clinic accepts clients aged fifty and over and that, unlike the community and institutional samples, 20 percent of the clients in the clinic sample are between the ages of fifty and sixty-four. The initial information from the elderly in the community and from those in institutions together indicates the status of the elderly in Durham County. In addition, the clinic group provides information on a subsample of particular interest--persons seeking help because of problems with aging.

In this chapter, the demographic characteristics of these three sample groups will first be outlined. A description of the initial functional status of the three groups and of the changes that occurred over the period of about a year will follow, along with an indication of the factors related to institutionalization and death. Finally, the relationship between functional status and need for services, particularly as it is perceived by care-givers in a clinic setting, will be reported.

Demographic Characteristics

The demographic characteristics of each of the three populations studied are presented in Table 1.

Table 1

Percentage Distribution of Demographic Characteristics*

	Community (N = 997)	Clinic (N = 98)[a]	Institutions (N = 102)
Age			
50-64		20	
65-74	68	48	32
75+	32	32	68
Mean Age	72.6	70.4	79.3
Standard Deviation	6.2	7.9	8.2
Sex			
Male	37	38	29
Female	63	62	71
Race			
White	66	67	76
Black	34	33	24
Marital Status			
Single	5	3	18
Married	44	40	11
Widowed	46	44	64
Divorced	2	10	3
Separated	3	3	5

a Twenty percent of the individuals were less than 65 years old.

* Because of rounding, percentages may not total 100.

The mean age of the institutionalized population was significantly greater than that of the community resident elderly (79.3 years vs. 72.6 years). The proportion of females was substantially greater, and the proportion of blacks was smaller, in the institutionalized than in the community population. The community and clinic populations were similar in marital status, but differed strikingly in this regard from the institutionalized. Among the institutionalized, 64 percent were widowed (vs. 46 percent in the community and 44 percent in the clinic), only 11 percent were married (vs. 44 percent in the community and 40 percent in the clinic), and 18 percent had never been married (vs. 5 percent in the community and 3 percent in the clinic). The proportions of persons separated or divorced were roughly comparable across the three populations.

The examination of the living arrangements of those in the community and clinic surveys (see Table 2, where living arrangement is displayed by marital status) indicates that roughly a quarter of each group lived alone, that about 5 percent lived only with non-kin, and that the rest lived with members of the family (typically a spouse), except for 15 percent of the clinic group, who lived in institutions.

Table 2

Living Arrangements of Community and Clinic Populations
by Marital Status (as Percentage of Each Marital Status)

	Alone	Spouse Only	Spouse and Kin	Kin Only	Non-Kin	Institutions	N
Community Population							
Single	44	---	---	35	21	---	48
Married	1	78	20	1	1	---	440
Widowed	50	---	---	45	6	---	462
Divorced and Separated	49	---	---	36	15	---	47
Total %	28	35	9	24	5	---	
N	276	345	88	243	45	---	997
Clinic Population							
Single	---	---	---	68	---	33	3
Married	5	72	18	---	---	5	39
Widowed	35	---	---	33	7	26	43
Divorced and Separated	21	---	---	39	23	8	13
Total %	21	29	7	21	6	15	
N	21	28	7	21	6	15	98

Functional Status

After having completed the OARS questionnaire, each subject was rated by
the interviewer on a six-point rating scale with respect to each of five dimensions of functioning: social resources, economic resources, mental health, physical health, and activities of daily living (ADL). For logistic reasons, impairment was distinguished from nonimpairment by means of a numerical rating.
Specifically, if individuals received a rating of 1-3 on a dimension, they were
considered to be functioning adequately on that dimension. If individuals received a rating of 4-6, they were considered to be impaired on that dimension.

Table 3 presents a summary of the initial level of functioning on each of
the five dimensions for each of the three populations surveyed. The majority of
the community-based elderly were found to be relatively intact, the percentage
impaired ranging from a low of 9 percent on social resources to a high of 26
percent on physical health. Additionally, those subjects categorized as impaired
in the community population were primarily among those who were "moderately impaired," that is, those with a rating of 4.

In the clinic population, a much more even distribution between "impaired"
and "not impaired" subjects occurred. While over 80 percent had impaired mental
health (the clinic specialized in this area), roughly half were impaired on each

of the other dimensions. The number of persons in the clinic population assigned a rating of 6, "completely impaired," remained relatively small, however.

Table 3

Functional Status by Dimension for Community, Clinic, and Institutional Populations--Initial Status

Community Population
(N = 997)

	Rating						Mean Rating	Percentage Not Impaired	Percentage Impaired
Dimension	1	2	3	4	5	6			
Social resources	37	36	18	6	2	1	2.0	91	9
Economic resources	13	31	42	12	2	0	2.6	86	14
Mental health	19	45	23	9	3	1	2.3	87	13
Physical health	12	31	31	17	7	2	2.8	74	26
ADL	33	30	16	11	6	5	2.4	78	22

Clinic Population
(N = 98)

Social resources	8	21	30	29	11	1	3.2	59	41
Economic resources	10	20	24	36	9	0	3.1	55	45
Mental health	2	7	10	42	29	10	4.2	19	81
Physical health	3	14	34	32	15	2	3.5	51	49
ADL	14	12	13	20	28	12	3.7	39	61

Institutional Population
(N = 102)

Social resources	5	10	20	28	21	17	4.0	35	65
Economic resources	4	16	32	48	0	0	3.2	52	48
Mental health	3	11	16	23	27	21	4.2	30	70
Physical health	0	10	30	23	11	26	4.1	40	60
ADL	0	3	4	20	28	45	5.1	7	93

Based on Interviewer Ratings

The institutional population presents a strikingly different picture. Impairment ranged from a low of 48 percent on economic resources to a high of 93 percent on ADL. Ratings of "excellent" functioning were rare and did not occur at all in the areas of physical health and activities of daily living. In this population, ratings of "complete impairment" were quite common, with the highest proportion of "complete impairment" occurring in ADL. Of some additional interest is the relative clustering around the ratings of 3 and 4 with respect to economic resouces. It appears that once individuals were institutionalized a minimum of financial resources were mobilized on their behalf. On the other hand, very few of the institutionalized subjects were rated "well off financially."

Table 4

Community Population
Mean Level of Functioning by
Age, Race, Sex, and Marital Status

	N*	65-74 yrs.	75+	White	Black	Married Male	Married Female	Widowed Male	Widowed Female	Other Male	Other Female	80+
Social	972	2.0	2.0	1.9	2.3	1.7	1.9	2.5	2.0	2.5	2.2	2.0
Econ.	972	2.5	2.7	2.3	3.1	2.3	2.3	2.6	2.6	2.7	2.7	2.7
Mental	972	2.2	2.5	2.2	2.7	2.1	2.3	2.6	2.2	3.1	2.3	2.7
Phys.	972	2.7	3.1	2.7	3.0	2.6	2.7	3.1	2.8	3.3	2.7	3.4
ADL	972	2.1	3.0	2.2	2.6	2.1	2.2	2.6	2.2	2.9	2.2	3.6
N		660	312	644	328	269	164	69	376	28	66	152

* Complete information present for only 972 of the 997 subjects.

Based on Interviewer Ratings

Table 4 presents the mean level of functioning for the community population broken down by age, race, sex, and marital status. For some dimensions (e.g., social resources), age, race, sex, and marital status do not make a difference in the ratings. As expected, levels of physical health and ADL functioning decrease with age.

Cumulative Impairment Score

In addition to being considered separately, the ratings on each of the five dimensions can be summed, yielding a Cumulative Impairment Score (CIS) which can range from 5 (no impairment on any dimension) to 30 (all dimensions totally impaired). A CIS was obtained for each subject interviewed in the community, clinic, and institutional populations.

When the CISs of each of the three populations are graphed (see Figure 1), each population can be seen to have its own distinct distribution of impairment. The numerical midpoint of the CIS range (18) appears to be a significant cutoff point. Approximately 12 percent of the community population is distributed beyond this point on the impaired side, and 14 percent of the institutionalized population falls on the healthy side of this midpoint. The clinic population falls in between the community and institutionalized elderly. Thus, there is a definite overlap between the three populations.

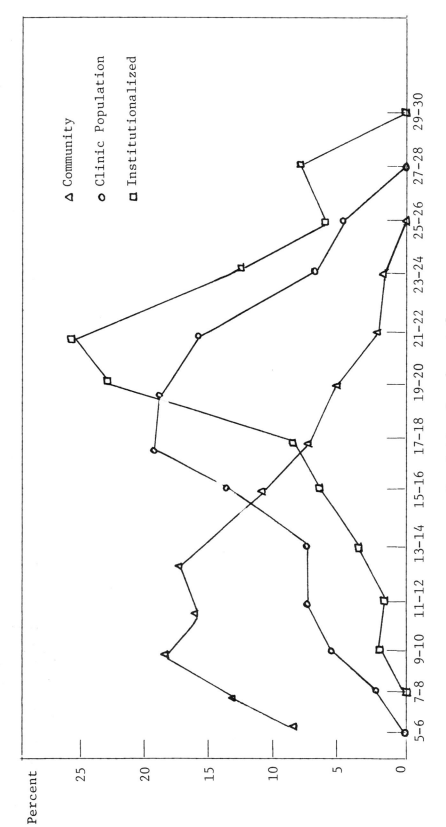

Figure 1

Distribution (in percentages) of Cumulative Impairment
Scores in the Three Populations

CIS Means

Community = 12.2
Clinic = 17.7
Institutionalized = 20.7

It is clear from Figure 1 that there were individuals still residing in the community who, according to their CISs, were as impaired as most of the people residing in institutions. The absolute number of people is actually quite large-- between 1200 and 1400 in Durham County--even though their proportion is relatively small. At the same time, a small but significant proportion of the individuals residing in institutions have impairment scores similar to those of the majority of the community residents. In this regard it should be noted that some institutions serving Durham County residents are intended for the healthy elderly.

Thus, there is significant overlap between the clinic and institutionalized populations. And while this may be due, in part, to the fact that 15 percent of the clinic clients already lived in institutions, it may also indicate that individuals referred to such a clinic are at risk for institutionalization.

Correlations Among the Five Dimensions

Table 5 presents a summary of the correlations among the five dimensions for each of the three populations. The extent of correlation varies widely across the five dimensions and also across the populations. The largest correlation (0.72) is observed between ADL and physical health in the community population. This is closely followed by quite high correlations between ADL and mental health in both the institutional and the community populations (0.62 and 0.61, respectively). On the other hand, most of the correlations with social resources and economic resources are relatively low, suggesting that these function more independently. One interesting finding is the low correlation between physical health and mental health in the clinic and institutional populations. This is probably a statistical artifact due to the reduction in the range of the ratings. There is a significant correlation in the community population, however. One clinical implication is the need to consider the "whole person" (i.e., multidimensional functioning) in any treatment or service program.

Table 5

Correlations Among the Five Dimensions for the Community,
Clinic, and Institutional Populations--Initial Status

Correlations Among the Five Dimensions

	Community (N = 997)				Clinic (N = 98)				Institution (N = 102)			
	ER	MH	PH	ADL	ER	MH	PH	ADL	ER	MH	PH	ADL
Social	.31	.42	.25	.24	.27	.42	.35	.37	.63	.30	.03	.31
Economic		.42	.33	.30		.24	.41	.34		.15	-.04	.15
Mental			.55	.61			.08	.55			.18	.62
Physical				.72				.34				.59

ER = Economic resources, MH = Mental health, PH = Physical health, ADL = Activities of daily living

Based on Interviewer Ratings

Outcome Studies of Three Populations of the Elderly

Information from the Durham surveys has also been used to assess change (improvement or decline) in functional status on each of the five dimensions over time and to examine factors predicting institutionalization (applicable only in the community and clinic populations) and death. The information necessary to do this is available from a number of follow-up studies.

The community population. In-person follow-up was conducted with 120 selected subjects fifteen months after the initial contact. Of these 120, 30 had a CIS of 5-9, 30 had a CIS of 10-13, but with only one dimension impaired, 30 had a CIS of 14-17, and 30 had a CIS of 18 or more. In addition, a telephone survey which focused on death, institutionalization, and current social resources, economic resources, and ADL status was carried out on a random sample of 331 subjects, one-third of the original community sample, thirty months after the initial contact. This subsample of 331 is the basis of the death and institutionalization data. The subsample of 120 provides information on functional status change.

The clinic population. All available clients (76) were reinterviewed seven to twenty months after the initial data was obtained.

The institutional population. All survivors (72 persons) were contacted after approximately fifteen months.

Change in Functional Status

Based on interviewer ratings, Table 6 presents the initial and follow-up mean functional ratings on each of the five dimensions for the three populations studied. In all three populations, mean levels were calculated only for those subjects for whom both initial and follow-up data were available. Note that individuals who died between the initial interview and the follow-up interview were not included. This fact is of greatest significance in the institutional population, where thirty subjects, 29 percent of the original sample, died. Thus, those surviving were an elite group when compared to the overall population to which they belonged. Another methodological difficulty is that individuals with a rating of 1 could not improve and that individuals with a rating of 6 could not decline. (They could die, but in that case they were not included in Table 6.) Thus, stability or actual improvement in mean level of functioning on follow-up, in the institutional population especially, was likely to be due to a combination of natural history, deletion of the dead, and regression towards the mean.

We may be able to develop a more realistic picture by introducing a somewhat arbitrary convention: All persons dying during the follow-up interval could be automatically assigned to the category indicating deterioration in each dimension measured. The findings of such an analysis are presented in Table 7. Here, the institutional sample still shows a marked improvement in mental health (although it should be noted that most clients remain impaired) but also shows declines in social resources, economic resources, physical health, and ADL.

Table 6

Comparison of Mean Levels of Functioning at Initial Interview and One Year Follow-up for Survivors of Community Subgroup, Clinic, and Institutional Populations

| | Community N = 116[a] | | Clinic N = 76[b] | | Institution N = 70[c] | |
	Initial	Follow-up	Initial	Follow-up	Initial	Follow-up
Social resources						
Mean	2.08	2.08	2.30	2.86**	3.90	3.37**
SD	1.11	1.20	1.21	1.14	1.41	1.58
Economic resources						
Mean	2.54	2.62	3.22	2.95**	3.26	3.27
SD	1.05	.82	1.13	.94	.88	1.07
Mental health						
Mean	2.41	2.68**	4.22	4.03	4.10	3.43***
SD	1.13	1.16	1.14	1.20	1.50	1.37
Physical health						
Mean	2.98	2.96	3.47	3.50	3.77	3.44*
SD	1.22	1.29	1.11	1.15	1.32	1.18
ADL						
Mean	2.62	2.85*	3.62	3.70	4.86	4.89
SD	1.50	1.54	1.62	1.77	1.13	1.08
CIS						
Mean	12.63	13.22*	17.74	17.01*	19.89	18.40***
SD	4.73	4.47	4.29	4.44	4.09	4.65

Based on Interviewer Ratings

Significance levels of paired t-tests between initial and follow-up data:
*p = < .05
**p = < .01
***p = < .001

Reasons for absence from follow-up:
[a] Deceased – 4
[b] Deceased – 13; Refused – 6; Not located – 3
[c] Deceased – 30

Examination of the clinic population shows a trend toward improvement in the economic resources and mental health dimensions (as compared to the institution and community groups) and in the social resources dimension (as compared to the community group). These improvements were perhaps the result of service interventions which may have facilitated receipt of income, effectively helped mental health, and promoted social resources.

Table 7

Percentages of Community, Clinic, and Institutional Subjects Changing
Level of Functioning by Type of Change and Dimension

Group	N	Social			Economic			Mental health			Physical health			ADL		
		+	–	0	+	–	0	+	–	0	+	–	0	+	–	0
Community	120	30	32	38	17	27	56	19	40	41	30	32	38	18	38	44
Clinic	89[a]	35	31	34	30	26	44	30	36	34	24	38	38	19	42	39
Inst.	100[b]	40	46	14	15	43	42	40	34	26	29	41	30	17	52	31

Based on Interviewer Ratings

```
+ = improved
– = declined (includes died)
0 = no change
```

[a] Information absent on 6 persons who refused to participate and 3 who could not be located.

[b] Information absent on 2 persons who refused to participate.

Outcome Measures: Institutionalization and Death

Institutionalization. A total of 10 out of 331 persons (or 3 percent of the community sample) became institutionalized within twelve months of the initial interview. Age, sex, and, race were relevant demographic factors predicting institutionalization, white males aged seventy-five and over being at a greater risk. In fact, individuals who were institutionalized were more impaired on all dimensions of functioning except economic resources.

Death. Based on their age, sex, and race, 5 percent of the community sample, 4 percent of those in the clinic, and 8 percent of the institutionalized could be expected to die within twelve months of the initial interview. The actual percentages dying were 4 percent, 13 percent, and 29 percent, respectively. This probably reflects the greater amount and range of initial impairment among the clinic clients and the institutionalized. Further analyses have shown that age and sex influence the mortality experience in the three groups studied. The levels of social resources and economic resources functioning do not predict death, but ADL (in all three populations), physical health (in the community and institution populations) and mental health (in the community population) do contribute to the prediction of mortality.

Functional Status and Need for Services: The Application of Survey Data to Service Planning

The OARS questionnaire systematically obtains information regarding services (i.e., "service packages") which subjects are currently receiving as well as those services which they perceive themselves as needing. The information thus obtained provides the building blocks utilized either by clinicians working with individual patients or by program planners working with populations to design service programs for individuals or populations.

The OARS Clinic population provides a unique opportunity to consider the relationship between functional status and the need for services in a clinic population. Since decisions on the need for services are more likely to be made by care-givers than by care-receivers, data from the OARS Clinic can provide useful information on the assignment of services to clients.

In accordance with clinic procedure, recommendations for services were made by a clinician and were based on data collected from the OARS questionnaire and on a clinical evaluation. The services most frequently recommended by the clinicians after evaluation of referred individuals are presented in Table 8.

Table 8

OARS Clinic Population
Services Needed as Seen by Clinician*
(N = 98)

1.	Counseling-psychotherapy-individual	77%
2.	Coordination	63%
3.	Psychotropic Drugs	61%
4.	Counseling-Family	60%
5.	Medical Treatment	46%
6.	Social Interaction	44%
7.	Relocation and Placement	27%
8.	Recreation and Leisure	27%
9.	Financial	23%
10.	Personal Care	19%
11.	Food Services	18%
12.	Transportation	15%
13.	Housing	14%
14.	Nursing Services	13%
15.	Checking Services	12%
16.	Assistance to find paid employment	11%
17.	Legal Services	10%
18.	Physical Therapy	9%
19.	Vocational Rehabilitation	7%
20.	Assistance to find unpaid employment	6%
21.	Day-Care Services	5%
22.	Respite Services	3%
23.	Surrogate Services	2%

* These services assessments were made before the current list had been defined (see Appendix B) and hence are not identical with them.

If one is to achieve the aim of defining "appropriate service packages" for individuals within a clinic, community, or institutional population, the functional status of these individuals must be assessed and a functional classification system developed. One possible functional classification system is represented by the Cumulative Impairment Score (CIS) mentioned previously. Another is represented by all the possible combinations of functioning on each of the five dimensions. This, however, results in 7,776 profiles, a number somewhat too large to use. A classification system which we have favored requires dichotomizing each dimension simply to represent an impaired or unimpaired state. All possible combinations of impaired/unimpaired across the five dimensions result in 32 functional equivalence classes (i.e., classes in which the members are functionally equivalent). As might be expected, clients were not distributed equally among these classes. As the extreme left-hand column, headed SEMPA, in Table 9 shows, 11 functional classes account for 80 percent of the clients in the clinic population.

Table 9

Average Number of Services Recommended
and CIS According to Functional Class for the Most
Common Functional Classes

SEMPA[a]	Functional Class	N	Average Number of Services	Average CIS
00000	0	11	3.7	10.9
00X00	2	5	3.6	12.8
00XX0	6	6	6.2	14.8
00X0X	12	10	6.4	16.8
X0XX0	16	5	5.0	18.6
00XXX	18	11	6.9	18.5
0XX0X	24	5	4.2	18.8
X0XXX	27	8	8.0	21.0
0XXXX	28	6	3.8	20.7
XXX0X	30	5	8.6	20.4
XXXXX	31	7	7.1	22.1
	Total	79	5.8	16.8

[a] SEMPA = Social resources, Economic resources, Mental health, Physical health, and ADL
X = Impaired functioning
0 = Unimpaired functioning

In Table 10, the mean number of services recommended by clinicians is listed for the most prevalent CISs. In this table it is obvious not only that the average number of services recommended gradually increases as CIS increases, but also that it does so at a rate lower than might be expected. This may indicate that individuals seeking help from a clinic such as the OARS Clinic may require a different "quality," rather than a greater variety, of services as their CISs increase. The lesser amount of services recommended for individuals with lower CISs may indicate their having taken greater preventive measures--measures to prevent institutionalization, for example. A reading of Appendix B of this manual shows that even when people are unimpaired they need certain services simply to remain unimpaired.

Table 10

Mean Number of Services Recommended by Clinicians
According to Cumulative Impairment Score (CIS) for the Most
Common Cumulative Impairment Scores

CIS	N	Average Number of Services
13-14	10	5.1
15-16	14	6.0
17-18	18	5.9
19-20	24	6.1
21-22	16	6.5
	82*	6.0

* Eighty-four percent (N = 82) of the clinic population of 98 had CIS scores in the range of 13-22. Those falling outside this range were not considered in this analysis.

In Table 9, the eleven most frequently occurring functional classes are listed with the average total number of services recommended for each class and its average Cumulative Impairment Score. Although the number of patients in some of these functional classes is quite small, some interesting patterns do emerge. As expected, the average CIS gradually increases as the number of dimensions which are impaired increases. However, the average total number of services recommended does not follow the same linear pattern. In particular, functional classes 24 and 28 have among the lowest number of average total services recommended, although the former includes three, and the latter four, impaired dimensions. In both of these functional classes economic resources is impaired. Thus, one may raise the question of whether or not the economic status of the subject being interviewed in the clinic relates to the recommendation of services.

As can be seen by the above preliminary analysis of clinic data, the methodology permits the analysis of particular patterns of impairment in an elderly clinic population, the services recommended by clinicians for them, and the

relationship between the two. The development of such "service packages" could
be of immense value for health planners. In addition, if resources permit, the
impact of the presence or absence of these services upon outcome and later functioning could be determined. This would be most valuable in determining the
cost effectiveness of the range of services available to an older population.
The Cleveland Survey (reported on in detail in Chapter 10) provides an opportunity
for such analyses.

Summary

Three populations of elderly individuals in Durham County were surveyed.
These surveys included 997 community-based elderly (with a mean age of 72.6, 66
percent of whom were white and 63 percent of whom were female), a clinic sample
of 98 individuals (with an average age of 70.4 years, of whom 67 percent were
white, 62 percent female), and an institutional population of 102 (with an average age of 79.3 years, 76 percent of whom were white and 71 percent female). Of
the community sample, 25 percent were impaired in physical health, 13 percent
were mentally impaired, and 14 percent were economically impaired. Nine percent
were socially impaired, and 21 percent were impaired in ADL. A majority (81
percent) of the clinic population was impaired in mental health, and roughly 50
percent was impaired on each of the other dimensions. Between 48 percent and 93
percent of the institutionalized population was impaired depending on dimensions.
Impairment in one dimension may frequently be correlated with impairment in one
or more additional dimensions, emphasizing the pattern of multiple impairments
encountered in working with the elderly.

Although functioning tends to decline over time in the community population,
there appears to have been a trend toward improvement in the clinic population.
The institutional population also shows decline in four dimensions with some
indication of improvement in mental health. Further outcome studies indicate
that males, whites, and individuals over the age of seventy-five are at greater
risk for institutionalization. Activities of daily living, physical health, and
mental health were all predictive of mortality in the outcome studies.

The Durham surveys indicate a significant level of impairment on each of the
five dimensions measured in all three populations studied. Although the majority
of elderly individuals are functioning quite well, there are a significant number
who show impairment in areas where the availability and utilization of various
services may in fact improve functional status or retard decline in functioning.
Such survey data can be most valuable in program planning and evaluation.

CHAPTER 10

THE CLEVELAND EXPERIENCE: FUNCTIONAL STATUS
AND SERVICES USE*

WILLIAM F. LAURIE

PROBLEM: To determine the impact of federal programs and other services on the well-being of older people, using basic research to provide a reliable methodology.

Systematic evaluation of complex programs in which many agencies and many different departments of government are involved has become a necessity. To assist the Congress and to demonstrate that meaningful multiprogram evaluations can be made, the U.S. General Accounting Office (GAO) in Cleveland, Ohio, decided to assess the impact of federal programs on older persons. Twenty-three federal programs administered by various agencies were selected. These agencies include the Departments of Agriculture; Health, Education and Welfare; Housing and Urban Development; and Labor and Transportation.

The proposed design for program evaluation required:

1. A reliable, valid measure of the multiple aspects of human functioning.

2. A specification and definition of services which could be used in quantifying data on services received.

3. A data set in which the impact of specified services on individuals with known levels of functioning could be assessed.

The Multidimensional Functional Assessment Questionnaire produced by the Older Americans Resources and Services (OARS) program of the Duke Center for the Study of Aging and Human Development provided the concepts and instruments to fit our needs.

The GAO selected programs serving older persons for study for many reasons: (1) there are over twenty million persons 65 years of age or older; (2) they

---

* Data in this chapter were published initially in "Report to Congress on the well-being of older people in Cleveland, Ohio," by the United States General Accounting Office (HRD-77-70), 19 April 1977. This chapter first appeared as "The Duke OARS methodology: Basic research and a practical application" in the Duke University Center for the Study of Aging and Human Development's *Center Reports on Advances in Research*, *1*, 2 (Summer 1977) and has been reprinted as "Population assessment for program evaluation" in G. L. Maddox (Ed.), *Assessment and evaluation strategies in aging: People, populations, and programs* (Durham, N.C.: Duke University Center for the Study of Aging and Human Development, 1978), pp. 100-110.

vary in age from 65 to over 125, with over 5,200 centenarians receiving social security payments; (3) they vary considerably in health, income, and housing; and (4) there are at least 134 federally sponsored or supported programs which provide assistance to older people.

Do large investments of public funds in programs for older people have the intended effect? Basic methodological research is essential to answering this question. The General Accounting Office was able to apply the basic research of Duke University in preparing an answer. Building on this knowledge, GAO-Cleveland used the additional data collected to determine important insights about the design of effective programs for the future. In essence, we now have an illustration of basic research useful to the program evaluator and a practical application of basic research.

Assessing Well-Being of Older Persons

The sample studied in Cleveland consisted of persons sixty-five years of age and older who were not institutionalized, that is, not in nursing homes or similar facilities. Sixteen hundred and nine older persons were seen by interviewers from Case Western Reserve University between June and November 1975. Each interview questionnaire, involving almost 100 questions and requiring about forty-five minutes to complete, was then reviewed for completeness and consistency of answers. This sample was reinterviewed one year later with the same questionnaire.

The questionnaire which was developed at Duke assessed the older person's status in five areas of functioning: (1) social, (2) economic, (3) mental health, (4) physical health, and (5) activities of daily living. The questions used to probe levels of functioning were drawn, insofar as possible, from existing literature. The distinctive aspect of the procedure was the format of questions in each area which permitted a convenient summary. Responses to questions during the interview summarized functional impairment of the respondents in each of the five areas, and a rating was assigned on a scale of 1 to 6: 1 = excellent, 2 = good, 3 = mildly impaired, 4 = moderately impaired, 5 = completely impaired. For example, after responses were received to twenty-two detailed questions on physical health, the respondent was placed in a category which described his or her health as follows:

1. *In excellent physical health.*
   Engages in vigorous physical activity, either regularly or at least from time to time.

2. *In good physical health.*
   No significant illnesses or disabilities found, and only routine medical care such as annual checkups required.

3. *Mildly physically impaired.*
   Has only minor illnesses and/or disabilities which might benefit from medical treatment or corrective measures.

4. *Moderately physically impaired.*

Has one or more diseases or disabilities which are either painful or which require substantial medical treatment.

5. *Severely physically impaired.*
    Has one or more illnesses or disabilities which are either severely painful or life threatening, or which require extensive medical treatment.

6. *Totally physically impaired.*
    Confined to bed and requiring full-time medical assistance or nursing care to maintain vital bodily functions.

A similar assessment procedure was applied to the categories of social resources, economic resources, mental health activities, and activities of daily living.

Summary Assessments Used in Cleveland

Although the questionnaire responses provide information on five discrete areas of human functioning, we wanted to consider the entire person, or what we defined as the *well-being* of the person. Therefore, the information in each of the five areas was combined into an assessment of the overall well-being of the individual as shown in the following groupings:

Description Based on Five Areas Included in Duke University Questionnaire

Well-Being

Unimpaired
  Excellent or good in all five areas of human functioning.
Slightly impaired
  Excellent or good in four areas.
Mildly impaired
  Mildly or moderately impaired in two areas, or mildly or moderately impaired in one area and severely or completely impaired in another.
Moderately impaired
  Mildly or moderately impaired in three areas, or mildly or moderately impaired in two and severely or completely impaired in one.
Generally impaired
  Mildly or moderately impaired in four areas.
Greatly impaired
  Mildly or moderately impaired in three areas, and severely and completely impaired in another.
Very greatly impaired
  Mildly or moderately impaired in all five areas.
Extremely impaired
  Mildly or moderately impaired in four areas and severely or completely impaired in the other, or severely or completely impaired in two or more areas.

Results of Cleveland Study: Distribution of Impairment

One of every five older persons in Cleveland whose well-being we assessed
was *unimpaired*; about 23 percent were *generally impaired* or worse, including 7
percent considered *extremely impaired*. Table 1 shows our projections of assessed
well-being.

Table 1

Projections of Assessed Well-Being in Cleveland

	1975 Estimate of People 65 and Over	
Category	Number	Percent
Unimpaired	13,400	21
Slightly impaired	13,200	21
Mildly impaired	11,500	18
Moderately impaired	10,300	17
Generally impaired	5,700	9
Greatly impaired	1,900	3
Very greatly impaired	2,300	4
Extremely impaired	4,300	7
TOTAL	62,000[a]	100

[a] Total includes noninstitutionalized older persons
in Cleveland only.

To identify differences in the status of older persons living in separate
geographic regions, we compared the results in Cleveland--a northern industrial
city of about 750,000 people--with a similar study in Durham, North Carolina--
a less industrialized city with a population of 105,000 and a more rural orientation. The Durham study was conducted in the spring of 1973 by the Duke Center
for the Study of Aging and Human Development. The Cleveland study was conducted
in the spring of 1975 using essentially the same questionnaire and methodology.
As can be seen from Table 2, the results from the two studies were very similar.

As is seen in Table 2, 57 percent of the older persons interviewed in
Cleveland had no worse than a mild impairment in any of five functional areas,
compared to 59 percent of the people in Durham. In Cleveland, 23 percent were
moderately impaired or worse in only one functional area, compared to 19 percent
in Durham; 20 percent of those in Cleveland were moderately impaired or worse
in two or more functional areas, compared to 22 percent in Durham.

Examining each functional area, we found the results of the two studies
were again similar. To illustrate, 70 percent of the older people interviewed
in Cleveland scored *excellent* or *good* in social functioning, compared to 73 percent in Durham. In the activities of daily living, 64 percent in both cities

were *excellent* or *good*. Table 3 reports on the distribution in each of the functional areas.

Table 2

Comparison of Cleveland and Durham
Findings on Impairment
(Percentages)

	Cleveland	Durham
No impairment/mild impairment	57	59
Moderate impairment or worse in one function	23	19
Moderate impairment or worse in two or more functions	20	22

Table 3

Comparison of Cleveland (Cl) and Durham (Du) Findings
on Functional Area Competency
(Percentages)

Rating	Social Cl	Du	Economic Cl	Du	Mental Health Cl	Du	Physical Health Cl	Du	Activities of Daily Living Cl	Du
Excellent or good	70	73	52	44	68	64	41	43	64	64
Mildly or moderately impaired	25	24	46	54	28	32	53	47	30	27
Severely or completely impaired	5	3	2	2	4	4	5	9	6	10

The similarity of functional status among older people in Durham and Cleveland reflects the similar demographic characteristics of the two populations. They only differences were (1) in race, with the Durham and Cleveland samples having more blacks represented than in the nationwide figures, and (2) in age distribution, with Cleveland having a larger percentage of very old persons. Table 4 shows the similar socioeconomic characteristics of the two populations.

Table 4

Socioeconomic Comparison of Cleveland and Durham
(Percentages)

	Cleveland Sample	Durham Sample	1974 Nationwide Sample
Sex			
Male	38	37	41
Female	62	63	59
Age			
65-74	59	68	63
75 and over	41	32	37
Race			
White	74	66	92
Black	26	34	8
Marital Status			
Single	7	5	8
Married	40	44	50
Widowed	46	46	37
Divorced or separated	7	5	5

Identifying Factors That Could Affect Well-Being

To identify those factors affecting the well-being of older people, we did several things:

1. Developed specific definitions of services provided older people and a technique for quantifying the services.

2. Identified the providers of the services--families and friends, Medicare and Medicaid, and over 118 social service agencies.

3. Obtained information during our interviews and from agencies and Medicare and Medicaid about the services provided to each person in our sample and the source and intensity of those services.

In defining and quantifying the services, we used a technique developed by the Duke Center on Aging which defines twenty-four basic service components according to five elements: purpose of the service, activity, relevant personnel, unit of measure, and example. As an instance, meal preparation was defined as follows:

Purpose: To prepare meals regularly for an individual.
Activity: Meal planning, food preparation, and cooking.
Relevant personnel: Cook, homemaker, family member.
Unit of measure: Meals.
Examples: Meals provided under 42 U.S.C. 3045 (supp. V, 1975), the Older Americans Act, Meals-on-Wheels programs.

We used the *unit of measure* to quantify the service along with the duration, or number of months, during which the service was received.

Based upon the procedure illustrated above, data were gathered on twenty-six generic service components provided to older people in Cleveland. However, to simplify the numbers, the variety of services being provided, and their many possible combinations, the individual services were grouped into types to enable meaningful analyses. The following groupings were formed based on the commonalities described below:

Home help--provided in the home by a minimally trained adult.
Medical help--provided by a medically trained adult.
Financial help--direct or in-kind financial assistance.
Assessment and referral--provided by an adult trained in evaluation and/or familiar with resources available to provide service.
Social/Recreational.
Transportation.

Table 5 shows the components of these generic services.

Table 5

Generic Service Components

Types of Service

Home Help

    Personal care
    Checking
    Homemaker
    Administrative and legal
    Meal preparation
    Continuous supervision

Medical Help

    Medical care
    Psychotropic drugs
    Supportive devices
    Nursing care
    Physical therapy
    Mental health

Financial Help

    Financial
    Housing
    Groceries and
        food stamps

Assessment and Referral

    Coordination, information,
        and referrals
    Overall evaluation
    Outreach

Social/Recreational

    Social/Recreational

Transportation

    Transportation

95

Services Affecting Well-Being

In the second phase of the Cleveland study, the impact of services on the well-being of older persons in our sample will be assessed. The first phase, reported here, has concentrated on descriptions of functioning, of generic services, and the distribution of impairment and services in Cleveland. Examples of the data we developed in the first phase and a discussion of what we plan to look for in the second phase are presented below.

Medical services. Our data indicate that some older persons who could probably benefit from medical services had not received them, although many others who were not impaired in physical health were receiving medical services, apparently as a preventive measure. Overall, about 5.7 percent of our sample were impaired in physical health but did not receive medical services; 25.8 percent of our sample were not impaired in physical health and were receiving medical services. Table 6 shows a breakdown of both health ratings and medical care received by the subjects in the Cleveland study.

Table 6

Health Rating of Subjects and Medical Care Received
(Percentages)

Physical Health Rating	Did Receive Medical Service	Did Not Receive Medical Service
Excellent or good	25.8	15.5
Mildly or moderately impaired	47.9	5.5
Severely or completely impaired	5.1	.2
TOTAL	78.8	21.2

In phase two we will assess whether or not the medical services had an effect on the physical health of the sampled older people. In the second phase we also expect to be able to determine whether changes in physical health over time can be attributed to the availability of medical services. If we find in the second phase, for instance, that older persons in good health receiving medical services maintain their good health and that those good-health individuals not receiving medical care become impaired, then we may want to recommend that outreach efforts be directed to older persons who are not yet impaired in physical health and who are not receiving medical services. As shown in Table 6, this latter group represents an estimated 15.5 percent of the population of older people in our sample.

If, however, we find that older persons impaired in physical health and receiving medical services fared better in general over the year than those not receiving medical services, we should consider recommending that outreach efforts be directed to those persons in the latter group, who make up about 5.7 percent of the population of older people.

Social/recreational services. Most older people receiving social/recreational services (82 percent) were assessed as being unimpaired socially, as demonstrated in Table 7, which shows those older persons who did and did not receive social/recreational services.

Table 7

Social/Recreational Services Received
(Percentages)

Assessed Level of Impairment in Social Functioning	Did Receive Services	Did Not Receive Services
Excellent or good	82	65
Mildly or moderately impaired	15	29
Severely or completely impaired	3	5
TOTAL	100	100

Data from the second phase will enable us to determine (1) whether most persons are impaired socially when social/recreational services are initially provided, or (2) whether the already socially impaired improve as a result of participating in social/recreational activities. If the first premise is supported, the question is: "Should services be provided to unimpaired older persons to prevent or slow down the decline in social functioning?" If the second premise is supported, the outreach efforts might be directed to provide services to the 34 percent who are already impaired socially.

Family and friends as a resource. For the most part, home help service and transportation were provided by the family or friends. Medical and social/recreational services were provided mostly by agencies; financial assistance and assessment and referral services came about evenly from family and friends and an agency. Table 8 shows the percent of sampled persons receiving each individual service by source. Overall, we estimate that about 80 percent of all services received by impaired older persons are provided informally by kinsmen and friends.

Each sampled older person was asked if he or she had a primary source of help if he or she became sick or disabled; 87 percent said they did. Most said they had someone who would take care of them as long as needed.

The most frequent primary source of available help was the older person's children: forty-two percent of those who said they had help available mentioned their children. The next most frequent source was the husband or wife: twenty-seven percent said the help would come from their spouse, followed by brother or

sister (10 percent), other relative (9 percent), and friend (8 percent). The
remaining percentage included all others.

Table 8

Individual Services Received
(Percentages)

Medical Services	Source			
	Family/Friends	Agency	Both	Total
Medical care	–	75	–	75
Psychotropic drugs	–	20	–	20
Supportive devices	–	15	–	15
Nursing care	3	3	1	7
Physical therapy	–	4	–	4
Mental health	–	3	–	3
Home Help Services				
Personal care	56	1	1	58
Checking	44	1	1	46
Homemaker	20	5	1	26
Administrative and legal	15	7	1	23
Meal preparation	13	8	1	22
Continuous supervision	6	1	1	8
Financial Assistance				
General financial	2	7	–	9
Housing	12	10	–	22
Groceries and food stamps	7	8	–	15
Assessment and Referral				
Coordination, information, and referral	8	3	1	12
Overall evaluation	–	8	–	8
Outreach	–	5	–	5
Social/Recreational (formal, organized activities outside the home)	–	30	–	30
Transportation	60	3	5	68

Since the family and friends are now providing home help and transporation services, it may well be that the family and friends of other older people could be encouraged and trained to provide similar services. Mechanisms to encourage family and friends to help older people could be identified, developed, and tested. These could include training for family and friends and financial incentives through the income tax system or direct payments. However, any such effort should be structured to encourage and support the many family members or friends who are currently serving older persons.

Location of services. There appears to be a mismatch between the location of official service agencies and the distribution of impairments among older persons. Services tend to be concentrated in the central city while impairments are more widely distributed. A substantial number of poor, impaired elderly were identified in suburban areas quite distant from service agencies.

Review

We were able to perform our study of the well-being of older people because basic research in this area had already been done. Through practical application, we were able to push the state of the art further by relating services to well-being status. Some other important observations:

1. By using the same functional assessment instrument (Duke OARS methodology) comparisons could be made between two different samples.

2. Needs assessment does not provide the same insights as functional assessment. Functional assessment provides a way to relate services to a well-being status. Needs assessment might provide insights into services related to activities of daily living, but not necessarily into all dimensions of older people, particularly the mental health dimension.

3. The GAO-Cleveland research illustrates the basic elements of a program evaluation design which has general applicability in communities with complex service systems. This program evaluation research logically leads from evidence about the impact of existing programs to a consideration of alternative allocation of resources in the future.

Chapter 11

Nursing Home Cost and Care: An Investigation of Alternatives*

Richard M. Burton, William W. Damon, David C. Dellinger,

Douglas J. Erickson, and David W. Peterson

Introduction

Nursing homes provide a high level of care for many of the elderly in the United States. Yet in recent years there has been a feeling that better alternatives exist for providing such care and that nursing homes are in some sense a default option, a service of dubious efficiency provided to sustain old folks abandoned by their families (*Gerontologist*, 1974). A theme which spontaneously draws adherents is "to free people from institutions," among which nursing homes are numbered.

In this chapter we examine the nursing home situation in Durham County, North Carolina, to assess the feasibility of returning people from nursing homes to community life through the provision in the community of selected gerontological care services. Finding this expensive, and finding that few people are likely to benefit from such a program, we then assess the demand for additional nursing home care, concluding that there are not great numbers of individuals in the community and in homes for the aged who should be moved to nursing homes. Consequently, at least for Durham County, it does not appear that many people would be made better off either by the movement of nursing home patients out into the community or by the movement of great numbers of community individuals into nursing homes. In part, these results are limited to Durham County, but a broader implication of the study is that one cannot achieve better care at lower cost for the elderly now in nursing homes by putting them back in the community. Thus, nursing homes are an economically reasonable alternative for a portion of the elderly population.

There are two major aspects to our investigation. The first is an assessment of the nature of nursing home care, of the patients in nursing homes, and of the feasibility and costs of permitting these patients to return to the community through the public provision of particular services. The second is an assessment of the demand for nursing home care by individuals not in nursing homes.

---

* The cost estimates used in this chapter are not current as of the publication date of this manual. This chapter, however, does illustrate a viable approach to the comparison of alternative forms of care which is possible only when functional status data and services production information are available in a standard form. This type of analysis does not require the technology matrix.

Data Source and Methodology

We have studied both data sources and methodology using a body of data and an analytical framework developed as part of the OARS project. Five groups of data are used in our analysis:

1. Institutional survey data
2. Community survey data
3. Cost survey data
4. North Carolina Blue Cross-Blue Shield data
5. Clinician evaluation data

The institutional survey was conducted in nursing homes, mental hospitals, and rest homes in Durham County. (See Chapters 7 and 9; and Pfeiffer, 1973a.) In all, 102 patients in such institutions were interviewed, and from each was obtained information concerning physical health, mental health, economic resources, social resources, and activities of daily living. Some of the details concerning this survey are included in Appendix 1 of this chapter.

The community survey was administered to a sample of 997 of about 10,000 elderly residents in the Durham County community. (See Chapters 7, 9; and Pfeiffer, 1973b.) The questionnaire used in the institutional survey was also used in the community survey. The cost survey involved the collection and verification of data on budgets and services rendered from all public and private agencies that are open to the community and that provide services to the elderly in Durham County. These sixteen agencies are listed in Appendix 2 of this chapter. The North Carolina Blue Cross-Blue Shield data consist of cost reports filed by nursing homes for Medicare and Medicaid reimbursement purposes. To obtain the clinical data, the psychiatrists and social workers who comprise the clinical staff of the Older Americans Resources and Services (OARS) team at the Duke University Center for the Study of Aging and Human Development evaluated the responses of each person interviewed in the institutional and community surveys, assigning each one an index, or rating, in each of five dimensions of functioning. In addition, the clinical staff advised us at regular intervals on the appropriateness of various types of care for specific patients.

Two analytical structures, previously developed by the OARS team, are used in our analysis. The first is the service package structure used for describing the basic elements of gerontological care. (See Chapter 4; Pfeiffer, 1973b.) In the service package structure, twenty-three elementary services are identi-fied,* of which the following set of services is characteristic of many nursing homes:

Hotel Services: living quarters, including room, bed, bath, etc.

---

* The service definitions which form the basis of the service package concept have been revised since the initial publication of the article which formed this chapter. Some of the services defined originally have been combined appropriately to form the current list of twenty-four service definitions found in Appendix B of this manual.

Food Services: meals for the patients.

Nursing Serivces: services which are normally performed by an R.N. or an L.P.N. (includes such services when provided by persons other than nurses).

Personal Care Services: services which aid clients in performing personal activities of daily living related to personal hygiene activities.

Medical Treatment: professional medical services, including drugs, medical supplies, tests, etc.

Physical Therapy: treatment by a physical therapist which is intended to rehabilitate a client's physical (nonmedical) problem.

In order to provide comparable services in alternative settings, additional services are necessary. These include:

Checking Services: daily contact with the client to assure well-being.

Transportation: rides to and/or from appointments, activities, etc.

Respite Care: temporary relief for a person who is taking care of a client. This service allows a family member, or whoever is responsible for the client, to "get away" for short periods; e.g., to shop or to go on a vacation.

The second structure of which we make use is the system of ratings which clinicians use to summarize the condition of each person interviewed in the institutional and community surveys. Each person interviewed is assigned a rating, an integer from one through six, in each of the following categories: (1) social resources, (2) economic resources, (3) mental health, (4) physical health, and (5) activities of daily living. A rating of one in any category indicates excellent functioning while a rating of six indicates severe impairment. The five single-interger ratings (one in each category) of each of these five categories characterize a particular class of patient.

Alternatives to Nursing Home Care for Individuals

Alternatives to nursing homes include public housing, homes for the aged, the individual's own home, and the home of a family. To assess these alternatives, we determined what services are actually provided by nursing homes, how these services would be provided in the alternative settings, and what the associated costs would be.

To establish a basis for our comparisons, we first estimated the cost of providing care in a nursing home. In Durham County, the average cost in 1972 for a publicly supported patient was $19.19, as determined from North Carolina

Blue Cross-Blue Shield data. Private patients in the same homes pay between $16.00 and $31.00 per day, an indication that different patients receive different services. Clearly, the costs are not the same for every patient in the nursing home, but, for simplicity, we shall use this average cost of $19.19 per day as a basis for comparing alternatives to the nursing home.

The nursing homes surveyed provide all patients with the services required for basic maintenance (hotel and food services) and a minimal level of nursing care, personal care, and medical and physical therapy services. The institutional survey (Whanger, 1973) revealed, in addition, that patients receive varying levels of nursing and personal care services, ranging from a few hours per day of supplementary care to continuous nursing surveillance. Thus, nursing homes provide not one, but a number of service packages which differ in the quantity of nursing and personal care provided.

Table 1 shows the estimated costs of providing services which are comparable to those received by all nursing home residents (basic maintenance and minimal nursing care, personal care, and medical and physical therapy services) in the four alternative settings. Comparable services in public housing and private homes include the checking services which are provided as a by-product in nursing homes, in homes for the aged, and for those living with a family. Comparable services in public housing, private homes, and family settings include the transportation necessary to obtain those services which are normally provided on site in nursing homes and homes for the aged. Respite care is included when the alternative is living with the family. The variation of costs for alternatives to this basic package is minimal, ranging from $13.72 to $20.31 per day, and these are not significantly different from the estimated $19.19 for delivery of the basic package in the nursing home.

As the level of nursing and personal care increase, the cost of comparable service packages in the alternative setting increases. Table 2 displays the estimated costs of five service packages which contain graduated levels of these two services. Costs increase dramatically as continuous nursing surveillance is added to the service package.

The institutional survey (Whanger, 1973) revealed that 87 percent (forty of forty-six) of the nursing home residents were receiving--and needed, in the judgment of the clinician making the assessment--nursing surveillance on a continuous basis. To provide equivalent services for these forty individuals is quite expensive, ranging from $74.00 per day in a family setting to $80.59 per day in public housing. (See Table 2, Alternative 6). The largest portion of these costs is an estimated $67.50 per day for the twenty-four-hour-per-day nursing surveillance. By most standards, the alternatives for these forty patients are not economically feasible.

The remaining 13 percent (six patients) did not, according to clinical judgment, need continuous nursing surveillance. One of these patients could receive comparable service (one hour of nursing, three hours of personal care, prepared food, etc.) in her own home at a comparable cost (see Alternative 2, Table 2), but she was a private patient in the home by choice. Two others were residing in the home temporarily to provide respite for their spouses. Three other patients could be relocated to an alternative setting, but there was no significant economic advantage in making such a relocation.

Table 1

Cost of Service Packages in Alternative Settings
Comparable to Minimal Nursing Home Services*

Alternative Settings

Service	Public Housing		Homes for the Aged		Own Home		With Family	
	Amount	Cost ($)	Amount	Cost ($)	Amount	Cost ($)	Amount	Cost ($)
Nursing (LPN)	1 hour	4.22	1 hour	4.22	1 hour	4.22	1 hour	4.22
Personal care	2 hours[a]	6.00	1 hour	3.00	2 hours[a]	6.00	1 hour	3.00
Living quarters	1 day	3.20	1 day	8.00				
Food, prepared	1 day	3.50	1 day		1 day	3.50		
Food, unprepared							1 day	1.50
Checking		.26				.26		
Transportation	.33 Trips	1.33			.33 Trips	1.33	.33 Trips	1.33
Respite care								1.87
Medical Rx		1.80		1.80		1.80		1.80
Total[b]		20.31		17.02		17.11		13.72

* Minimal Nursing Home Services include basic maintenance (food and living quarters services) and one hour of Nursing services, one hour of Personal care, occasional Physical therapy services daily, and limited Medical care (e.g., maintenance of medical records, pharmacy, drugs).

a Additional Personal care included for housecleaning chores.

b Does not include a nominal cost which would be incurred in arranging for those services normally provided in nursing homes.

104

Table 2

Cost of Service Packages in Alternative Settings
With Supplementary Nursing and Personal Care

Alternative	Total Amount		Alternative Settings			
	Nursing Services Hours/Day	Personal Care Services Hours/Day	Public Housing	Homes for the Aged	Own Home	Living With Family
2	0	1	23.31	20.02	20.11	16.72
3	1	0	24.53	21.24	21.33	17.94
4	1	1	27.53	24.24	24.33	20.94
5	8	0	35.59	32.30	32.39	29.00
6	24	0	80.59	77.30	77.39	74.00

The implication for the nursing home population surveyed is clear. For most of the patients in the nursing home, approximately 87 percent, the only suitable alternatives are economically unfeasible (easily about four times the cost of nursing homes). For the other patients, about 13 percent, alternatives outside the nursing home are available, but there would not be great reductions in costs if the alternatives were chosen. Moreover, in half of those cases where alternatives are feasible, the nursing home was selected by the individual. Thus, the nursing home appears to provide an economic and desirable alternative to many elderly people.

The cost estimates used in this analysis reflect the cost of the resources consumed in providing comparable services in alternative settings. Questions regarding who bears the cost and what the particular costs are to individuals are not addressed, even though these might be central issues in determining public policy. Most would agree that it is an appropriate goal in making public policy to seek alternatives which are efficient in the sense that they minimize the resources consumed for any given level of services. But public policy should go beyond this and address questions of fairness as well. For example, Table 1 shows that the estimated cost of providing comparable services is minimal if the services are provided in a family setting. The estimate of $15.72 includes those additional costs which would be incurred if the elderly persons were cared for in the home, including items such as additional food, nursing care, and personal care. What is not apparent is the fact that under current law, the $15.72 would probably be paid by the family while the $19.19 would be paid by the government if the elderly person remained in a nursing home. Under such an arrangement, it is questionable whether a family would choose to keep at home a person who is eligible for care in a nursing home at government expense. Moreover, if the presence of an elderly person in the house made it impossible for some family member to be gainfully employed, the cost to the family would be even greater.

It is clear that while the cost of alternatives in terms of resources consumed is essential for public policy analysis, it is not sufficient. The issue of who bears the costs must also be considered.

The Demand for Nursing Home Care

A question which naturally follows at this point is whether there are large numbers of people who are not in nursing homes, but who should be. The institutional survey and the community survey provided data related to this question.

In the institutional survey, fifty-six nonnursing home residents were evaluated and rated on the five dimensions of the OARS classification system. Of these fifty-six subjects, 29 percent (sixteen residents) had ratings which indicated that nursing home care might be an appropriate alternative. These sixteen potential candidates for nursing home care were individually evaluated to determine the appropriateness of a move to a nursing home. Two residents had been in nursing homes and had moved to rest homes, one had improved in health, and the other had sold his house and lived with his wife in the rest home. More typical were two bedridden stroke patients who had been long-term (six and eleven years) residents of a large rest home. Both were similar to many patients in nursing homes and were, in fact, receiving services comparable to those offered in nursing homes. (This rest home offered nursing home services to a very limited number of their patients but could not increase the number without changing its character as an institution.) Most of the sixteen residents were receiving appropriate care, and there were no apparent benefits to be derived from moving them to nursing homes.

The results of the community survey were more striking. Of the 997 people in the survey, only 3.7 percent (thirty-seven subjects) had ratings which indicated that nursing home care might be an appropriate alternative. Twenty-seven of these thirty-seven subjects were receiving appropriate care provided either by a spouse, by children, or by both. It is possible that some of these thirty-seven subjects could have been placed in nursing homes at government expense but were not, either because the families elected to keep them at home or because they were not aware of the alternative. Thus, the community survey indicates that there are very few, if any, elderly persons in the community who should be placed in nursing homes, a conclusion which reinforces our earlier one based on the institutional survey.

Results and Further Investigation

Our main conclusions are (1) that the hypothesis that many individuals who are being treated in nursing homes could be adequately treated elsewhere at lower cost is not substantiated, and (2) that there are few people in the community who should be receiving care in a nursing home but who are not. The first of these probably extends beyond Durham County since it seems reasonable that in many places the costs of nursing home care relative to alternative forms of care are at least qualitatively similar to those in Durham County. This assumed, we conclude that nursing homes are clearly a viable alternative for caring for the elderly.

The finding that there are not many potential nursing home clients may be particular to Durham County. In other localities, it is quite possible that there are many elderly persons who should be in nursing homes but are not, and it would be inappropriate to extend this part of our results beyond the boundaries of Durham County.

We conclude our analysis with an observation and a question concerning the nature of costs. We found that many nursing home patients could leave their institutions only if they had twenty-four-hour surveillance; a different alternative was not reasonable. Yet, we found the same type of individuals in the community who were not receiving the twenty-four-hour nursing surveillance and not incurring a $70 to $80 per day cost of care. These individuals had a spouse or other relative to provide the surveillance service and did not incur such a cost. Consequently, their out-of-pocket cost was less than that given in Tables 1 and 2 and was quite acceptable. Clearly, then, individuals other than nurses can provide this type of care. An while the manner of funding this service, and whether or not public programs should be instituted to generate more of this kind of care, is not clear, it is clear that nursing homes are efficient providers of care for many individuals.

REFERENCES

Gerontologist, 1974, *14*, No. 1. Whole number.

Pfeiffer, E. Community survey of 1,000 elderly persons. Paper presented at the 26th annual meeting of the Gerontological Society, Miami Beach, Florida, November, 1973a.

Pfeiffer, E. Designing systems of care: The clinical perspective. In E. Pfeiffer (Ed.), *Alternatives to institutional care for older Americans: Practice and planning*. Durham: Duke University Center for the Study of Aging and Human Development, 1973b.

Whanger, A. D. A study of the institutionalized elderly of Durham County. Paper presented at the 26th annual meeting of the Gerontological Society, Miami Beach, Florida, November, 1973.

Appendix 1

Composition of Sample
Institutional Survey of Durham County Elderly

	Type of Institution	Number of Such in County	Number of People in Sample	Percentage of Sample in each Type
1.	Retirement Home, infirmary section	1	0	0.0
2.	Retirement Home, domiciliary section	2	8	7.8
3.	Retirement Home, apartment section	1	0	0.0
4.	Small licensed home, family care (five or less residents)	45	21	20.6
5.	Licensed homes for aged	7	18	17.6
6.	Nursing Home or extended care facility	5	28	27.4
7.	Combination Home, rest home section	2	1	1.0
8.	Combination Home, nursing home section	2	12	11.8
9.	State Hospital, psychiatric wards	1	8	7.8
10.	State Hospital, nursing care wards	1	6	5.9
		67	102	99.9

Appendix 2

Durham County System
for the
Delivery of Services to the Elderly

Agencies in the System

Agricultural Extension Services

American Red Cross, Durham County Chapter

Community Mental Health Center

Coordinating Council for Senior Citizens

Department of Public Health

Department of Social Services (includes Medicaid)

Family Counseling Service, Inc.

Housing Authority of the City of Durham

Legal Aid Clinic

North Carolina State Division of Vocational Rehabilitation

Nursing Homes

Older Americans Resources and Services

Operation Breakthrough

Recreation Department

Social Security Administration (includes Medicare)

John Umstead Hospital (a state mental hospital)

CHAPTER 12

EMPLOYING THE DUKE OARS METHODOLOGY IN COST COMPARISONS: HOME SERVICES AND INSTITUTIONALIZATION*

WILLIAM F. LAURIE

In Chapter 10 we described how the Cleveland, Ohio, branch of the U.S. General Accounting Office (GAO) used basic research to provide a reliable methodology to assess the impact of federal programs and other services on the well-being of older persons. In particular, we described how GAO-Cleveland had employed the Multidimensional Functional Assessment Questionnaire to survey a sample population of 1,609 older persons living in Cleveland, Ohio. Having created rich data bases on both well-being and services, we can begin to answer a number of the important questions GAO-Cleveland was asked to consider. One of the most important of these questions was: "Taking the status of well-being of older persons into consideration, at what point does the cost of receiving services at home exceed the cost of institutionalization?" The following comments describe the results of our analysis in answering this question.

Overview

From our survey of 1,609 elderly persons in Cleveland, Ohio, several significant facts concerning the differences in the costs of services provided by family and friends, public agencies, and institutions emerged. Specifically, we found not only that the value of the home services provided by family and friends greatly exceeded the cost of home services provided by public agencies at public expense, but also that the total cost of all home services was greater than the cost of institutionalization, even for older persons who are greatly or extremely impaired (approximately 17 percent of those persons aged sixty-five and over). In addition, in examining the relationships which existed among (a) the Cleveland elderly at different levels of impairment, (b) the types of services they received, and (c) the providers of those services, we found that:

1. Although approximately 60 percent of persons who are extremely impaired

---

* Data in this chapter appeared originally in Comptroller General of the United States, "Report to Congress on home health--the need for a national policy to better provide for the elderly," U.S. General Accounting Office, HRD-78-19 (Washington, D.C.: U.S. General Accounting Office, 30 December 1977). This chapter first appeared under the same title, but in a slightly different form, in the Duke University Center for the Study of Aging and Human Development's *Center Reports on Advances in Research*, vol. 2, No. 2, Summer 1978.

live outside institutions, these persons require and receive many services at home (homemaker services, continuous supervision, transportation, housing, and social and recreational services, for example). We refer to these as *home services*, regardless of whether they are provided by family and friends or by public agencies.

2. As expected, older people who are more impaired receive more services, public and private, than do people who are less impaired.

3. Public agencies are currently spending less per person for home services than they spend for institutional care, regardless of the level of impairment of the person.

4. Fourteen percent of older people who are greatly or extremely impaired are at home, compared to 87 percent of those in institutions.

5. The services provided to the greatly or extremely impaired living at home are similar to the services they receive in institutions.

6. Family and friends provide over 50 percent of the services received by older persons at all impairment levels and over 70 percent of the services received by the greatly or extremely impaired elderly.

To aid in understanding our analysis in reporting these and other findings, brief descriptions of our methodology, our cost comparisons, and, finally, of the significant differences we found in impairment level and living arrangement between the institutionalized and noninstitutional elderly follow.

Methodology

Our analysis is based on an extensive data base developed in our survey of the well-being of older people in Cleveland, Ohio. This data base contains information on the characteristics of 1,609 people aged sixty-five years and over randomly sampled from the Cleveland population. Information on the services these people received has been collected in two phases over one and one-half years from one hundred and eighteen agencies and from the reports of older individuals themselves. (See Chapter 10 for a more detailed report on the initial information obtained from this sample.)

In studying the well-being status of older people, we used the Multidimensional Functional Assessment Questionnaire (MFAQ), which permits the assessment of functional status separately on each of five dimensions: (1) social resources, (2) economic resources, (3) mental health, (4) physical health, and (5) activities of daily living. We wanted to consider the entire person and, in particular, to concentrate on individual impairment level. There are a number of ways in which this can be done (see, e.g., Chapter 8), but the way we choose (see Chapter 10), a way which had not been employed previously, involved combining the separate status for each of the five dimensions to place individuals into the following eight groupings: (1) unimpaired, (2) slightly impaired, (3) mildly impaired, (4) moderately impaired, (5) generally impaired, (6) greatly impaired, (7) very greatly impaired, and (8) extremely impaired. In addition, for purposes of our analysis, we combined group 7 (very greatly impaired) and group 8 (extremely impaired), since the overall impairment of people in these two groups was similar.

Using the MFAQ and the service information gathered during the first phase of the survey, we determined (1) what home services each person received, (2) the source that provided each service, and (3) the average amount of service used by persons in each of the seven impairment levels. We then contacted twenty-seven federal, state, local, and private agencies to discuss home service costs and to gather cost data for the period October 1976 – March 1977. From this information, an average cost was estimated for each type of home service. These average costs appear reasonable in comparison to similar data compiled by the Mayor's Commission on Aging in Chicago, Illinois, and to data compiled by the Duke Center in Durham, North Carolina.

To develop home service costs for each impairment level we combined these four data elements:

1. The cost or value of each service.

2. The average monthly use of each service.

3. The percentage of persons at each impairment level receiving each service from an agency.

4. The percentage of persons at each impairment level receiving each service from family or friends.

The agency cost was calculated in terms of an average monthly cost per individual. This calculation included:

1. The percentage of persons receiving each service.

2. The monthly frequency of the use of each service.

3. The cost of each service.

The portion of services provided by agencies was funded primarily through federal sources and included services provided to older persons by government and private service providers.

This same process was repeated to determine the value of the home services provided by family and friends. In the absence of family and friends, any home services received would have to be from an agency. Therefore, *we assigned the same cost to family and friend services that we found for agencies.*

The two home service costs (agency or family and friends) were added to determine the total cost, or value, of home services provided for individuals at each impairment level, and the total service costs were plotted by impairment level. Finally, the resulting curve of cost by impairment level was compared to the cost of institutionalization based on January to February 1977 reimbursements to skilled nursing and intermediate care facilities in Ohio.

Cost Comparison: Noninstitutionalized and Institutionalized Older People
_____

In comparing the cost of maintaining older people in their homes to the
cost of maintaining them in institutions, we first analyzed each alternative
separately by impairment level and by noninstitutional and institutional status.
It should be remembered that about 5 percent of persons sixty-five and older
are in institutions at any point in time. We then compared the costs for both
groups to determine at what impairment level the total cost of keeping an older
person at home--including the value of the services provided by family and
friends--equaled the cost of institutionalizing a person at that level of
impairment.

While we do not believe that a decision to institutionalize an individual
who wants to remain at home should be based on cost comparisons alone, we do
believe that such comparisons provide some insight as to the economic, physical,
and social factors which have influenced such decisions.

Noninstitutionalized older people. Several factors contribute to an older
individual's ability to function outside an institution. One of these factors
is the services which compensate for impairment: people who are more impaired
receive more services than do people who are less impaired. As Table 1 shows,
transportation, checking (periodic monitoring by telephone or personal contact),
and social/recreational services are received by the less impaired, while, at
the more impaired levels, social/recreational services drop drastically and
nursing care, personal care, and continuous supervision increase significantly.
Eventually the most severely impaired people require almost constant and comprehensive care.

As level of impairment increases, so does the cost, or value, of home services. And, as can be seen in Table 2, at each level of impairment the value
of services provided by family and friends is substantially greater than the
cost of the services provided by agencies. Thus, the cost of maintaining the
most impaired persons at home is substantially greater than the cost of maintaining those who are less impaired, with family and friends shouldering a dominant
share of the costs.

An important aspect of institutional care is that a person receives a package of services with a variety of specific services as components. Home care
also requires a package of services, and the care needed by the greatly or
extremely impaired living at home is similar to that needed by comparably impaired persons in institutions. For example, an arthritic person may need
physical therapy twice a week but may also need help in getting out of bed or
in preparing his or her meals. As a person becomes more impaired, more services
must be added to the package, and the person's use of these services will increase.

Institutionalized older people. Five percent, or about 1.2 million, of the
23 million people sixty-five years and over reside in various types of institutions, from rest homes to skilled nursing facilities.

Cost data for Ohio's medical nursing homes, including intermediate care
and skilled nursing facilities, from January to February 1977 showed the average
total cost for long-term institutionalization reimbursed under Ohio's Medicaid

Table 1

The Primary Services Received
At Each Impairment Level

Impairment Level

Service	Unimpaired	Slightly	Mildly	Moderately	Generally	Greatly	Extremely
Transportation	X	X	X	X	X	X	X
Checking (periodic monitoring)	X	X	X	X	X	X	X
Social/recreational	X	X	X	X	X		
Homemaker			X	X	X	X	X
Housing			X	X	X	X	X
Administrative/legal				X	X	X	X
Meal preparation				X	X	X	X
Food, groceries				X	X	X	X
Personal care (aiding an individual with dressing, bathing, etc.)						X	X
Continuous supervision (full-time monitoring)							X
Nursing care (skilled care)							X

system was $597 per month per individual. However, offsets from Social Security, pensions, and other income from those individuals reduced the average cost to $458 per month per individual. Although these costs are based on Ohio data and will vary in other states, we compared them to national averages and found them to be representative.

Table 2

Average Monthly Cost or Value of Home Services Per Individual

Impairment level	Service Provider		
	Family and friends	Agency	Total
Unimpaired	$ 37	$ 26	$ 63
Slightly	63	47	110
Mildly	111	65	176
Moderately	181	78	259
Generally	204	100	304
Greatly	287	120	407
Extremely	673	172	845

Institutional costs include room and board, laundry, medical equipment, medical supplies (over-the-counter drugs and supportive devices, for example), personal care, nursing care, supportive rehabilitative services, and social/recreational activities. Doctor fees, prescription drugs, and other medical costs are not included in either the costs of institutionalization or home services because medical expenditures are generally related to physical conditions and should be similar for people in institutions and for people living at home.

Break-even point. The graph in Figure 1 compares the cost of home services with the cost of institutionalization with level of impairment taken into account. As shown, there is a point in the impairment scale, falling within the greatly impaired level, where home service costs, including the value of services provided by family and friends, equal institutional costs. Thereafter, the cost of home services increases significantly over the cost of institutionalization.

About 10 percent of the noninstitutionalized older people fall in the area above the break-even point. However, on the average, a majority of the cost at all impairment levels is borne by family and friends, not by agencies. In fact, family and friends provide over 50 percent of the services received at all impairment levels by those living at home, and, at the greatly impaired level--

115

Figure 1

Comparison of Estimated Monthly Cost
of Home Services and Institutionalization at Each Impairment Level per Individual

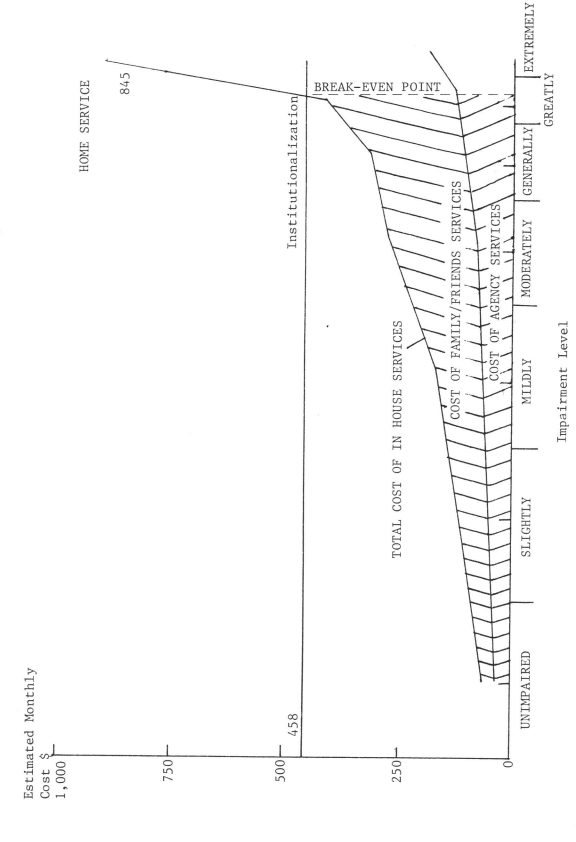

SOURCE: Comptroller General of the United States. Report to Congress on home health--the need for a national policy to better provide for the elderly. U.S. General Accounting Office, HRD-78-19. Washington, D.C.: U.S. General Accounting Office, December 1977.

116

where the break-even point falls--family and friends are providing over $287 per month for services for every $120 being spent by agencies. As shown in Table 3, the family and friends' portion of home services reaches 80 percent at the extremely impaired level.

Table 3

Service Cost Allocation (Percentages)

	Service Provider	
Impairment level	Family and friends	Agency
Unimpaired	59	41
Slightly	57	43
Mildly	63	37
Moderately	70	30
Generally	67	33
Greatly	71	29
Extremely	80	20

Other Differences: Impairment Level and Living Arrangement

In addition to differences in costs, two other significant differences emerged when institutionalized and noninstitutionalized elderly were commpared: level of impairment and living arrangement.

Impairment level. Table 4 indicates a substantial difference in level of impairment between the institutionalized and noninstitutionalized populations. Specifically, 87 percent of the elderly persons living in institutions are estimated to be greatly or extremely impaired, while 14 percent of those living in the community are estimated to be at this level of impairment. To determine, for each impairment level, what percentage of the elderly was institutionalized, we combined our data on community resident Cleveland elderly with data obtained in the Duke OARS institutional survey. (The OARS institutional survey is described in Chapter 7.) This combination was possible since the Durham and Cleveland populations had similar demographic characteristics. As Table 5 shows, a clear relationship exists between impairment level and institutionalization, with the greatest probability of institutionalization existing at the extremely impaired level, where 37 percent are in institutions.

Table 4

Impairment Levels of Institutionalized
and Noninstitutionalized People (Percentages)

Impairment level	Noninstitutionalized people		Institutionalized people[a]	
Unimpaired	21		1	
Slightly	21		1	
Mildly	18	86	2	13
Moderately	17		5	
Generally	9		4	
Greatly	7		11	
Extremely	7	14	76	87
	100		100	

[a] Based on a survey of institutionalized elderly reported in
E. Pfeiffer (Ed.), *Multidimensional functional assessment: The
OARS methodology--a manual*. Durham, N.C.: Duke University
Center for the Study of Aging and Human Development, 1975.

Table 5

Impairment Levels of the Total Population
and the Institutionalized (Percentages)

Impairment Level	Total Older Population		In Institutions
Unimpaired	20		00.2
Slightly	20		00.2
Mildly	18		00.6
Moderately	16		01.6
Generally	9		02.2
Greatly	7	17	07.8
Extremely	10		37.0
	100		

Living arrangement. Few institutionalized older people had a spouse or lived with their children at the time they were institutionalized. Seventeen people in our Cleveland sample, or about 1 percent, were institutionalized within one year after our data were gathered. Table 6 compares the seventeen institutionalized people with the twenty-one people who were greatly or extremely impaired and illustrates the importance of living arrangements in preventing institutionalization. None of those institutionalized had a spouse or lived with their children; over three-fourths had lived alone. In comparison, 29 percent of the greatly or extremely impaired people living in the community were married and an additional 25 percent lived with their children.

Table 6

Living Arrangement of Greatly or Extremely Impaired
Elderly Entering Institutions (Percentages)

With Whom Living	Greatly or Extremely Impaired		Entered Institutions	
Spouse	29 }		–	
Offspring	25 }	54	–	
Relative	10 }		18 }	
Friend	5 }	15	6 }	24
No one		31		76
		100		100

Other studies have shown similar results. Data gathered on institutionalized people in Durham, North Carolina, for example, showed that approximately 90 percent were married (Pfeiffer), and a twenty-year Duke University study has shown that those who have no spouse or children are more likely to be institutionalized (Palmore).

Having recognized the importance of living arrangements, we can examine the status of the noninstitutionalized population and identify those older people that have a high probability of being institutionalized. Specifically, the 31 percent of the greater or extremely impaired who live alone are at high risk for institutionalization.

The final phase of the GAO-Cleveland study will analyze changes in well-being over time and identify factors contributing to these changes. The data developed during this phase of the Cleveland study will also make it possible to examine further the people identified as having a high risk of being institutionalized and to determine which services, if available, may enable these people to function in the community. By relating changes in well-being to services received, we may also identify when it would be less costly to maintain high risk individuals at home.

Conclusions

The true costs of maintaining the impaired elderly in their own homes have been largely hidden because the greatest portion of such costs represents the services provided by family and friends rather than those provided at public expense. The importance of family and friends is evidenced by the fact that the greatly or extremely impaired elderly who live with their spouses or children generally are not institutionalized whereas those who live alone usually are. Thus, the potential for home health benefits as an alternative to institutionalization depends to a large degree on a person's living arrangements and the support of family and friends.

REFERENCES

Palmore, E. (Ed.), *Normal aging I*. Durham, N.C.: Duke University Press, 1970.

Pfeiffer, E. (Ed.), *Multidimensional functional assessment: The OARS methodology--a manual*. Durham, N.C.: Duke University Center for the Study of Aging and Human Development, 1975.

CHAPTER 13

THE USE OF THE OARS MULTIDIMENSIONAL FUNCTIONAL ASSESSMENT PROCEDURE IN CLINICAL TRAINING

DAN BLAZER

The OARS Geriatric Evaluation and Treatment Clinic at the Duke University Center for the Study of Aging and Human Development has served as a training site for clinicians for over five years. Central to the training curriculum in the OARS Clinic has been the OARS multidimensional functional assessment methodology. In this chapter, the use of the OARS Multidimensional Functional Assessment Questionnaire as a method for training clinicians will be discussed.

The OARS Clinic was initially developed as a part of the OARS program of policy research on alternatives to institutionalization and has as its goals evaluative research, training, and service delivery. In general, the OARS Clinic serves as a model evaluation and treatment facility for the elderly, and its evaluation procedures include (in addition to the OARS Multidimensional Functional Assessment Questionnaire) a clinicial assessment of psychosocial status and a medical evaluation. In particular, however, the clinic also provides a variety of basic services to the elderly. These include mental health services (individual psychotherapy, group psychotherapy, and family therapy), psychotropic drug services, medical services (medical review), nursing services, relocation and placement services, administrative, legal, and protective services, and coordination of services. (All of these are described in detail in Appendix B.) Additional services available in Durham County include financial assistance (e.g., through the Department of Social Services), continuing supervision (day-care), and homemaker services. Thus, systematic multidimensional evaluation and coordination of service delivery are basic to the philosophy of the OARS Clinic.

The staff of the OARS Clinic reflects a multidimensional and interdisciplinary concept of service delivery. The core staff of this clinic includes a half-time director (a psychiatrist), a part-time medical director (an internist), a full-time clinical supervisor and training coordinator, a half-time clinical geropsychiatrist, a half-time social worker, a part-time nurse, a full-time assessment worker, a full-time record librarian, and a full-time secretary.

Trainees from a variety of disciplines rotate through the clinic, providing its clients with the services described above, and all trainees learn the OARS assessment procedure as an essential part of their clinical experience in the OARS Clinic. These trainees include: (1) social work students from the University of North Carolina School of Social Work, (2) nursing students (both graduate and undergraduate) from the Duke University School of Nursing, (3) family medicine residents from the Department of Community and Family Medicine at the Duke University Medical Center, (4) geropsychiatry fellows from the Geropsychiatry Training Program of the Duke University and John Umstead Hospitals, (5) medical students from the Duke University School of Medicine, (6) law students from the Duke University School of Law, and (7) pastoral counsellors from the Clinical Pastoral Education Program at the Duke University Medical Center. In addition, plans are underway to develop a training program for psychology interns in the Division of Medical Psychology of the Department of Psychiatry at the Duke University Medical Center and psychiatric residents from the Duke University Department of Psychiatry.

Following a screening procedure for the appropriateness of a referral, each referred client is administered the OARS Multidimensional Functional Assessment Questionnaire and undergoes an in-depth clinical assessment by an intake clinician. This clinician may be a physician, a social worker, a psychologist, a nurse, or a pastoral counsellor. Impairments in five dimensions of functioning--social resources, economic resources, mental health, physical health, and activities of daily living--and the need for particular services are all assessed to provide information for the assignment of the client to one or more clinicians for additional evaluation and/or treatment and service delivery coordination. Table 1 illustrates the intake form used by clinicians to outline both major problems and an appropriate service plan.

The OARS assessment procedure has been found to be beneficial in training clinicians in at least four areas: (1) health care planning, (2) working as a member of an interdisciplinary team, (3) the evaluation of the "whole" person, and (4) the systematic evaluation of service delivery and follow-up. The following paragraphs outline briefly, but specifically, the value of the OARS assessment procedure as an effective tool for learning in each of these four areas of training.

Training and Health Care Planning

In the best of all possible worlds, informed program planners identify and implement a program designed specifically to ameliorate a particular problem and mobilize appropriate resources. In the everyday world, planners who lack the information necessary for precise problem definition, evaluation, and coordination of service delivery *do* make attempts to consider community needs and resources available in health care planning. Clinicians, however, are rarely trained to think in terms of overall health care needs and rarely have available to them the data that directly relate to the service needs of the community in which they work. The OARS Clinic is an exception to this rule.

The OARS policy research project included an epidemiologic survey of functional impairments among persons sixty-five years of age and older in the county served by the OARS Clinic. (The results of this survey are reported in Chapter 9.) Since impairment does not automatically translate into demand for service, data were also made available on perceived need of individual services and needs as predicted by clinicians evaluating ninety-eight consecutive referrals to the clinic. The OARS Clinic, therefore, serves as an example of a clinic facility established to meet a specific need within a community; that is, the clinic was specifically patterned to meet the need for systematic screening and management planning for older persons residing in a county where those services were not available.

In training clinicians in the OARS Clinic we frequently refer to the OARS

Table 1

January, 1977   OARS - SERVICE SUMMARY   (check one)

OARS # _____   Phone # _____   Clinician: _____   Service Provision:
                                                                          Client can go
Name: _____ Age: _____ Rating: S ____   _____ to services.
                                                       E ____   Services brought
Address: _____ Marital Status _____ M ____   _____ to client.
                                                       P ____
Living Arrangements - (current) _____ A ____   Setting
                                                                Recmnd: Home _____
Past Psychiatric Hospitalization _____   Rest H _____
                                                                        Nursing H _____
                                                                        Gen. Hosp. _____
                                                                        Mental Hosp. ____

	Rec'd 6 mos	Still Rec'd	Clin Recc	PROVIDER (Comment/Quantity)	PROBLEMS
1. Transportation					1 = MAJOR (only 1 prbm)
2. Social Recreation					2 = OTHER (multiple OK)
3. Employment					___ Housing ___ Financial-general
4. Sheltered Emp.					___ $-medical care ___ $-budget
5. Ed. Emp					___ $-institution support
6. Remedial Training					___ Family ___ Marital
7. Mental Out Patient: ___ In Patient: ___					___ Loneliness ___ Loss of loved one ___ Emotional ___ Behavioral
8. Psychotropic Drugs					___ Memory loss/ intellect impairment
9. Personal Care					___ Legal
10. Nursing Care					___ Med. equip/prosths devices
11. Medical Services					___ Visiting health nurse
12. Supp. & Prostheses					___ Physical therapy
13. Physical Therapy					___ Admission general hospital
14. Continuous Supvsn.					___ Admission nursing home
15. Checking					___ Admission rest home, retire- ment home
16. Relocation & Plcemnt					___ Admission psych
17. Homemaker Household					___ Assessment of need for institutional & appro. inst. place
18. Meal Preparation					___ Employment
19. Admin, Legal & Prot.					___ Homemaker service ___ Food prep/delivery
20. Sys Multdimen Eval					___ Transportation ___ Gen. info on aging
21. Financial Assistance					___ Recreation/social
22. Food					___ Adjustment retire- ment
23. Living Quarters					___ Other: _____
24. Coord, Info & Ref.					_____

I.   Initial Goals

II. Initial Service Plan

III. Date of Staffing: _____   Assigned Clinician:
     Provisional Assessment (including diagnosis):
     Disposition:
     Estimated Length of Service: Attending Physician Signature:

                                              _____

Community Survey, for an awareness of the magnitude of the impairments within a community (as well as the knowledge of the well-being of most older people) provides clinicians with a social context for the problems they are likely to encounter in individual clients. The awareness of being one part of the whole system of service delivery facilitates the translation of abstract concepts of health care needs into concrete activities.

Training and Evaluating the "Whole" Person

A multitude of professionals and nonprofessionals from a variety of disciplines presently work with the elderly. Unfortunately, however, many disciplines are becoming increasingly specialized, and fragmentation of service delivery and of the conceptualization of impairment in the elderly has become a real problem. Thus, the need for integration of our evaluation procedures as well as coordination of service delivery has become paramount.

The use of the OARS Multidimensional Functional Assessment Questionnaire provides striking evidence for the clinical trainee that the elderly have multiple impairments which cut across professional boundaries. The elderly person who is impaired in one area is likely to be impaired in another. In addition, the exercise of asking specific questions about each of the five areas of impairment provides at least one situation in which the trainee must survey the "whole person" in a systematic manner. With the availability of the initial assessment data and consultation with other disciplines within the clinic, each trainee is encouraged to serve as the "primary clinician" for a certain number of clients. Based on the philosophy of multidimensional functional assessment, the responsibilities of this primary clinician include: (1) continued assessment of the total needs of the client, (2) obtaining consultation from other disciplines when necessary, (3) consultation about the referral process, and (4) coordination of service delivery.

Training and Working as a Team

The OARS Multidimensional Functional Assessment Questionnaire provides a common language for clinicians from a variety of disciplines to discuss the impairments and needs of elderly clients. The profiles of impairment indicate the need of professionals from a number of disciplines in caring for the impaired elderly. The distribution of assessed needs for generic services (i.e., the "service package" described below) provides some indication of the relative needs of special expertise from various staff members.

Few would dispute that teamwork is an essential part of delivering services to older people; but the implementation of a multidimensional and interdisciplinary team is another matter. The OARS Clinic has made great strides in providing a training model for teamwork, however, and the success of this clinic is related significantly to the use of the OARS assessment procedure.

Training for Service Delivery and Follow-up

The OARS assessment procedure provides a framework in which systematic planning for service delivery can be carried a step beyond "clinical judgment." Table 1 provides an example of the OARS "Service Summary" used in the systematic development of "service packages"--a set of services assigned to a particular individual. Significantly, while there continue to be variations among individuals, patterns for developing services do emerge, and certain profiles of impairment necessarily imply the delivery of certain services.

In addition, to alleviate the problems which plague service providers in their follow-up evaluations, the OARS questionnaire may also be used as a follow-up procedure when it is paired with systematic questioning concerned with the actual receipt of specific services. Not only does this model provide trainees with an overview of the discrepancy between service planning, actual service delivery, and outcome, but it also provides them with a model for evaluating interventions and outcomes as well.

Training Procedures

Each clinical trainee participates in a one-and-one-half-day training program in the use of the OARS methodology. This training program includes: (1) a videotaped introduction to functional assessment and needs assessment, (2) a videotaped administration of the questionnaire, (3) an in-depth discussion of interviewer skills using a questionnaire format, (4) a discussion of particular problems in using the OARS questionnaire and how these are managed, (5) practice in administering and rating the questionnaire, and (6) a general discussion of the uses of the questionnaire. This training session is encouraged for *all* OARS users to insure the reliability of data collection and has proven to be equally valuable for researchers and clinicians.

In addition, all clinical trainees are given the opportunity to administer the OARS questionnaire to one or two actual clients with whom they work as intake clinicians. Ratings of the trainees are compared to those of experienced raters. After this experience, the clinical trainee uses the questionnaire data--as do all OARS clinicians--in evaluation and service planning.

Summary

The experience in the OARS Clinic and other training settings indicates that the OARS Multidimensional Functional Assessment Questionnaire can be a valuable adjunct to clinical training. The specific areas where such an instrument can be of value are indicated above. Naturally, the OARS instrument does not replace basic clinical evaluation, but it is a useful prelude to such evaluation. At the same time, if the use of the questionnaire occurs in a setting not conducive to comprehensive evaluation and service delivery, it may prove quite frustrating to the clinician. However, the overview provided by the use of this instrument both in evaluating the individual and in evaluating groups of individuals provides a picture of the function and needs of the individual and the community that is not ordinarily perceived by the clinical trainee.

Chapter 14

Experience Using the OARS Methodology in a
Family Medicine Residency Program

James T. Moore

The Duke-Watts Family Medicine Program has a dual mission of providing services and educating resident physicians receiving advanced training. There are presently a total of thirty-nine residents in the three-year training program, and all of them are exposed to many aspects of geriatric medicine. Approximately 300 elderly patients are seen each month in the ambulatory Family Medicine Center. About 100 of these patients are admitted each year to the local acute hospital, and about 40 patients from the program are in nursing homes at any given time. Residents are responsible for patient care in each of these sites.

We have used the OARS methodology in a variety of ways in meeting our goals of service and resident education. Specifically, we have surveyed patient functional impairment to assure that we offer appropriate services to our patients; we have audited medical records in order to determine whether or not resident physicians recognize patient problems; we have used the OARS methodology as the central feature of a research demonstration project that evaluated the impact of information about patient problems on physician behavior; and, finally, we have used the OARS assessment procedure as a guide to develop a curriculum in geriatric medicine for family medicine residents. Following are brief reviews of our experience in each of these areas.

Patient Functional Status Survey

In order to determine the functional impairment of our patients, we surveyed 130 of the 226 patients over age sixty who were seen for the first time at the Family Medicine Center during a twelve-month period. All patients who could be interviewed within two weeks after their first visit were included. Patients were interviewed by an intake worker who visited them in their homes and who completed the OARS Multidimensional Functional Assessment Questionnaire.

Table 1 summarizes the functional impairments of the Family Medicine patients interviewed. Thirty-two percent of the patients suffered social impairment, 33 percent economic impairment, 13 percent mental impairment, 56 percent physical impairment, and 28 percent were impaired in their ability to perform activities of daily living.

Table 2 shows the number of dimensions on which Family Medicine patients were impaired. Twenty-five percent of these patients were not impaired on any of the five dimensions; 26 percent were impaired on one dimension, 25 percent on two, 11 percent on three, 8 percent on four, and 5 percent were impaired on all five dimensions assessed.

Table 1

Percentage of Family Medicine Patients Age Sixty
and Over Impaired, by Dimension
(N = 130)

Dimensions	Percentage of Patients Impaired
Social	32
Economic	33
Mental	13
Physical	56
ADL	28

Impairment = Functional rating of 4, 5, or 6

Table 2

Number of Dimensions Impaired Among Family
Medicine Patients Age Sixty and Over
(N = 130)

Number of Dimensions Impaired	Percentage of Patients Impaired
None	25
One	26
Two	25
Three	11
Four	8
Five	5

Impairment = Functional rating of 4, 5, or 6

Table 3 summarizes the need for services reported by older Family Medicine patients. For example, 47 percent of the patients reported that they needed medication for their nerves, and 45 percent reported a need for information about the types of services available to them, etc. In general, patients report many needs for services that are not being met, and many of these needs directly affect an individual's health status.

Table 3

Percentage of Family Medicine Patients Age Sixty and Over
Reporting Need for Selected Services
(N = 130)

Psychotropic Drugs	47	Transportation	28
Information	45	Legal Aid	23
Checking Services	45	Continuous Sup'n.	17
Household Help	37	Personal Care	16
Social-Rec. Activities	33	Counseling	16
Meal Prep. Aid	30	Nursing Care	15
Systematic Eval.	30	Relocation	10

This survey provided a compelling argument that the Family Medicine Program reassess its service delivery component to assure that patients obtain assistance in these areas which affect their health status. As a result of this survey, the Family Medicine Program is presently designing a program of patient education which will help elderly patients obtain these services.

This survey of ambulatory patients also has encouraged us to perform a similar survey of those patients who are institutionalized either in the acute hospital or in local long-term care facilities. This study is presently underway and will provide two additional ways of using the OARS methodology: We will use it to evaluate the impact of team conferences on patient care, and we will use it to compare patient populations across training sites. That is, we will be able to compare patient characteristics in the ambulatory setting, acute hospital, and nursing homes. This information will help in planning both service and educational programs.

Medical Record Audit

We have also applied the OARS methodology to help audit medical records. We developed a form for auditing the medical records of Family Medicine patients which was designed to determine whether or not physicians recorded in the patient record a functional assessment for each of the dimensions evaluated by the OARS methodology. The use of this audit in the Family Medicine Program confirmed our impression that physicians do not routinely demonstrate an understanding of the multidimensional functional approach to patient assessment. The medical records reflected a diagnosis-orientation rather than the functional approach so important in working with the elderly. Our impression that physicians seldom list problems except those in the area of physical problems was also confirmed.

Impact of OARS-based Patient Data on Medical Resident Practice

The OARS methodology was also used in an educational research demonstration project in the Family Medicine Program. The purpose of this project was to determine the effect of exposing residents to information about a patient's functional status. During the survey of the 130 patients mentioned previously, residents were randomly assigned to two groups. One group received verbal feedback from the intake interview; the other group did not. Midway through the study period, the groups crossed over so that all residents ultimately were exposed to feedback. The chart audit form described above was used to determine the effect of this feedback on resident behavior. At the beginning of the research demonstration, residents were exposed to the concept of multidimensional functional assessment and the OARS methodology in a series of conferences, but no special effort was made to force residents to adopt this model. In other words, we taught this concept in the same way that much medical education is taught normally. This research demonstration project showed that the residents' exposure to information about their patients in this manner had no effect on the medical record.

Relevance to Geriatric Medicine Curriculum

The research demonstration project was extremely important in the development of a geriatric medicine curriculum in the Family Medicine Program. The demonstration that more than information is required to alter behavior dramatized the need for such training and has encouraged the residency program to emphasize measurement of physician behavior as part of the evaluation of this curriculum.

The OARS methodology has helped define our curriculum in geriatric medicine for Family Medicine residents. It has been useful both in defining content and in selecting instructional and evaluation methods. The survey of patient needs helped define part of the content of the curriculum. For example, residents will learn how to help patients receive needed services which were identified in the survey. The assessment skills on which the OARS methodology is based are a central part of the present curriculum. Residents are now required to demonstrate proficiency in performing a multidimensional functional assessment of their elderly patients. Experience with the OARS methodology also helped define our instructional method. Because the research demonstration showed that residents do not routinely document input from other health professionals when it is needed, team conferences were instituted as a routine part of the residency training. These team conferences include social workers, nursing personnel, dietitians, and physical therapists. To insure that the plans formulated in these conferences are implemented, the resident is responsible for completing a team conference summary that not only details the problems to be addressed and the plans for each problem, but also identifies the person or persons responsible for implementing each plan.

The research demonstration also helped determine evaluation methods to be used in both our educational and our service programs. We have chosen to include resident behavior in evaluating our curriculum. While knowledge and attitudes are clearly important in working with the elderly, it is difficult to define a program as successful unless the desired behavior is observed.

In summary, the OARS methodology has had an effect on all components of the Family Medicine Program. The service delivery component has changed better to address the needs of the population served; the style of practice has changed as team conferences have become routine; the physician education component of the residency has changed as a result of information obtained by the patient survey and the medical record audit; and the OARS methodology has also stimulated research by the residency. In addition, research projects planned or underway include an evaluation of a patient education program designed to improve patient use of community services and an evaluation of service delivery to patients in hospitals and long-term care facilities.

PART IV

TRAINING IN ADMINISTRATION
OF THE OARS QUESTIONNAIRE

CHAPTER 15

ADMINISTRATION OF THE OARS MULTIDIMENSIONAL
FUNCTIONAL ASSESSMENT QUESTIONNAIRE

CONNIE SERVICE AND BECKY HERON

The OARS Multidimensional Functional Assessment Questionnaire (MFAQ), reproduced in full in Appendix A of this manual, consists of two parts: Part A and Part B. Part A is designed to assess the functioning of individuals, particularly in the areas of mental and physical health, economic and social resources, and activities of daily living, and it forms the basis for making quantitative judgments of individuals on each of these five dimensions on a six-point scale. Part B of the questionnaire explores what services individuals are receiving, with what intensity they are being received, who is providing them, and subjects' perceived need for services.

The entire questionnaire takes about forty-five minutes to administer. However, while most people choose to administer the entire questionnaire--both Part A and Part B--some people may be interested in only one part, and they should note that the two parts can be administered separately, in which case the guide appearing at the end of this chapter, and again in Appendix A, should be followed. If information is desired from both Parts A and B, *both* should be administered on the *same* occasion.

While it is designed to produce similar results in the hands of both professionals and laymen, the MFAQ is a structured instrument which requires rigid, but easily mastered, techniques of administration. In addition, reliability requires that the meaning of the MFAQ's assessment strategy be understood by all users. Hence, for these reasons, and because only a thorough understanding of the instrument--its limitations as well as its uses--can provide users with a reliable and effective method for gathering information about individuals and/or populations, the OARS staff makes training available in the administration and in the uses of the MFAQ once each month and functions continually as a source of assistance to aid in any problems and to answer any questions concerning the instrument.

Definitions

Subject, or S: The person about whom the questionnaire is seeking information.

Informant: A person who knows the subject well--a relative, a household member, or someone taking care of the subject--and who answers some questions about and/or for the subject.

Respondent: Anyone answering a question, either subject or informant.

Ratings

After completing the questionnaire, the interviewer is to make a quantitative judgment of the subject on each of the five scales: social resources, economic resources, mental health, physical health, and activities of daily living. The scales are found on pages 38 through 42 of the questionnaire, and the interviewer is to circle the *one specific* number from one to six on each scale which best describes the subject of that particular interview.

Although the rater should use the description of levels for each scale to arrive at the appropriate level, the basic meanings of the six levels, which are the same for all five scales, should be kept in mind:

> 1 = Excellent
> 2 = Good
> 3 = Mildly impaired
> 4 = Moderately impaired
> 5 = Severely impaired
> 6 = Totally impaired

A trained person who has not seen the subject may later rate him or her based on the recorded information.

Administration of the Questionnaire

The OARS MFAQ is not intended to be an open-ended instrument. It asks specific questions and limits answers to specific categories. *Questions should be asked exactly as they are written* so that results from subject to subject are comparable. The interviewer should maintain an unhurried, objective manner but should try to control any excessive talking on the part of the respondent, who should be gently urged on to the next question.

Most of the questions require the respondent to choose among specific answer options. If the respondent does not answer with an option, or qualifies one, the options should be repeated and the subject asked to make a choice. For example, if the subject, in answer to "How would you rate your health. . . ?" says "Good--most of the time," ask if, in general, it was excellent, good, fair, or poor. The interviewer is to circle the number which precedes the correct answer option. These numbers, with the exception of "1 Yes," "0 No," and the ADL section have no consistent meaning.

If the subject will not or cannot answer a question, the "Not answered" option should be circled and an explanation provided, such as "IDK" for "I don't know" or "Subject refused." If a question is left blank it must be assumed that it was not asked. In probing for scorable answers the interviewer should take care not to influence the answer or overly irritate the subject. It is helpful to mark all repeated questions and probes with a "Q" (question) to indicate that the answer was difficult to elicit.

Some questions--such as question 44, for example, "Do you have any of the following illnesses at the present time?"--have many sections to be checked.

The interviewer *must ask each subquestion separately* and check the "YES" or "NO" for each. A blank does not mean "NO."

Since the questionnaire responses may later be coded and computerized, only codable responses are acceptable. For example, in answer to "How many times did you see a doctor last year?" neither "3 to 4 times" nor "regularly" can be coded, so interviewers are asked to probe and so indicate. However, interviewer notations explaining inconsistencies, or anything unusual, are very helpful to coders. In addition, an accurate answer occasionally may just not fit one of the answer options. In that case, please write in the answer so that a coding decision may be made later.

Statements to the interviewer which are not to be read to the subject have been printed in capital letters throughout the questionnaire. Explicit instructions to the interviewer have also been bracketed. *These instructions are very important.*

Guiding Principle

The general principle which should guide the interviewer throughout the whole questionnaire is to get the best, most complete information in every case. It is better to get too much information than not enough.

Questionnaire Outline

The entire MFAQ asks questions about the "Subject" we wish to assess and is set up in sections which deal with different aspects of his or her functioning and use of services. The Preliminary Questionnaire is a mental status examination designed to help interviewers decide if subjects are capable of answering the rest of the "factual" questions for themselves (this process will be described below) and also provides evidence of intellectual functioning. Questions 1 through 5 are *demographic questions*. The five major dimensions of functioning cover questions 6 through 70. Questions 6 through 14 inquire about the *social resources* of subjects; 15 through 30 their *economic resources*; 31 through 36 (and the Preliminary Questionnaire) their *mental health*; 37 through 55 their *physical health*; and 56 through 70 their *ability to perform the activities of daily living*. Each of these sections has been labeled. Question 71 inquires about services: the kinds and amounts of services subjects are receiving, from whom they receive them, and subjects' perceived need for services.

Questions 73 through 82 are to be asked of a reliable informant, if one is available. If an informant is not available at the time of the interview, a callback need not be made to find one, unless, of course, the subject is unreliable (defined below). It is assumed that an informant will always be available in an institution.

The remaining questions are to be answered by the interviewer immediately after leaving the interview site. Questions 83 through 86 seek information about the interview and the quality of the data obtained. In questions 87 through 96 interviewers are asked not only for their impressions of the subject based upon the total interviewer experience with the subject and/or the informant, but also for any other impressions gathered from the environment. In questions 97 through 101 the interviewer is asked to rate the subject's current level of function on each of the five dimensions--social resources, economic resources, mental health, physical health, and activities of daily living (ADL).

Reliable Subject

Most subjects will be able to answer the questions reliably, but occasionally a decision will be required as to the subject's ability to answer. The Preliminary Questionnaire (Pfeiffer, 1975a) on page two of the MFAQ gives an indication of the subject's reliability. A total error score of 4 or more is an indication that the subject may be unable to give correct factual answers. Other factors, however, should be weighed. If the subject's educational level (question 5) is very low (3rd grade or less), it may account for some of the errors. If there is an indication that the subject may not be reliable, *nevertheless ask questions 5 through 14.* If the subject gives good answers, continue the questionnaire; if not, ask the subject only the subjective questions (those in boxes) described below. Special care should be taken when interviewing mentally retarded subjects since their answers may appear valid but may be distorted, particularly when reporting amounts of anything within periods of time.

Acceptable Informant

An acceptable informant must be eighteen years of age or older, or have been married (if younger than eighteen), and well enough mentally and physically to answer reliably for the subject. Acceptable informants, in order of preference, are:

1. A member of the household related to the subject by blood, marriage, or adoption.

2. Someone responsible for the care of the subject.

3. A member of the household unrelated to the subject.

4. A member of the subject's immediate family but not living in the household.

The word *respondent* applies to either subject or informant, whoever is answering the question.

Subjective/"Factual" Questions

Throughout the questionnaire are subjective and what we call *factual* questions. The subjective questions deal with the subjects' feeling about things and so must be answered by subjects only. In the case of factual questions, however, accuracy is important; so if subjects are unreliable an acceptable informant should answer these questions for them.

The subjective questions have been outlined by boxes on the questionnaire so that the interviewer can easily identify them. The factual questions, which are not boxed, are to be asked of subjects if they are reliable. Otherwise, factual questions should be asked of the informant. One set of questions is to be asked of an informant if one is available in all circumstances.

In summary:

If the subject is reliable:

1. Ask all questions through page 32, and make a brief concluding statement.

2. If an informant is available, ask questions 73 through 82.

If the subject is unreliable:

1. Ask the subject all the boxed questions.

2. Ask the informant all other questions (except those questions clearly marked to be answered by the interviewer).

Get the best, most complete data available; that is, if the informant cannot answer a question for the subject and the subject seems to know the answer, use the subject's answer. Occasionally a subject will be completely unable to answer even subjective questions. In this case, get an "informant only" interview—one in which only the factual, or unboxed, questions are answered.

Privacy

Each respondent, subject or informant, should be seen alone. The interviewer should state that the interview needs to be conducted with the subject alone and, if an informant is present, that there are also questions for him or her, also to be asked alone. If it is *impossible* to see the subject alone, whoever is present must be asked not to speak. If the subject insists on remaining while the informant is interviewed, the interviewer may find some of the questions, 73 through 82, too embarrassing to administer and should so indicate on the questionnaire.

Introductory Statement

Just prior to beginning the interview, interviewers should again reassure subjects of the confidentiality of their answers and of the importance of their contribution to the project. Subjects should then be told: "I am going to be asking you lots of questions. Some of them may not seem to apply to you, but please bear with me and answer them as best you can. These questions were designed to apply to many different kinds of people, but it is important that each person answer them all."

Questions Requiring Special Consideration

A few of the items on the questionnaire require special consideration from the interviewer. The remainder of this chapter will be concerned with their description, beginning with a discussion of the Preliminary Questionnaire (PQ) and progressing, in order of occurrence, through question 101. In addition, a guide to the administration of the institutional form of the MFAQ and a guide to the separate administrations of Part A and Part B of the MFAQ appear at the end of this chapter.

Question
Number

PQ   The Preliminary Questionnaire should be approached in a very matter-of-fact manner. Despite the apprehension of many new interviewers, subjects answer these questions readily. However, if subjects seem disconcerted by the questions, a statement such as "I know they seem silly, but please bear with me; I have to ask them," or something similar, should put them at ease. An answer is correct only if all parts of it are correct. For example, if a subject gives the correct month and year for "What is the date today?" but fails to give the correct day, the whole answer is wrong. Every part of each question should be asked and the answers recorded. For example, all of the following information should be recorded, in the space provided, for the first question on the Preliminary Questionnaire:

MONTH   DAY   YEAR

All ten questions of the Preliminary Questionnaire should be asked of all subjects (unless there are problems in their understanding them because of language difficulties or deafness). A score of 10 errors is a meaningful score, but unless *every* question is asked we cannot assume that the total number of errors is 10.

4.   When date of birth and age conflict, we assume that the date of birth is correct if it is reasonable and compute age from it.

7.   Please include parents-in-law under "Parents"; brothers and sisters-in-law under "Brothers and sisters"; etc. Foster parents, however, should be included under "Others" and "Foster parents" indicated.

10.   Question 10 applies to social relationships at work as well as outside of work.

14.   Question 14 asks if there is "anyone who would give you any help at all if you were sick or disabled. . . ?" This question is in the social resources section and therefore applies to social, not economic, support. It does not apply to paid workers.

16.   Please note that this question asks for the work done throughout *most*
        of the subject's life. Only one occupation can be coded. It is very
        important that the occupation be specifically described since this ques-
        tion is a major indicator of socioeconomic status. If the subject was
        a farmer, for instance, being a tenant farmer would be quite different
        from being a farm owner. The size of the farm is also very important.
        Occupations like "engineer" are not specific enough. Is the subject
        a train engineer or a civil engineer, or does the subject perhaps own
        a company? If the subject was a factory worker, find out what the sub-
        ject's particular job was in the factory.

17.   This question is to be answered if the subject was ever married, even
        if the former spouse is no longer living.

17a.   Here again, elicit the work done the longest, and specify the job in
        detail.

18-22. Income, reserves, debts, etc. are generally shared by a married couple.
        Therefore, questions about finances, ownership, and obligations refer
        to the couple if the subject is married and to the individual if he
        or she is not.

18.   Regular assistance from family members applies only to regular contri-
        butions of money. Family aid in the form of providing a place to live,
        having the subject for meals, etc. should not be included in question
        18, but is covered elsewhere. Since it is important to know the total
        income figure for the subject, if *any* amounts are not included in ques-
        tion 18, then question 18a must be asked.

18a.   Since some people are very sensitive about revealing their income, an
        income card should be shown to subjects when question 18a is asked and
        subjects requested to reply with the letter which represents their in-
        come category. Be sure to establish the correct letter, especially
        if the subject replies with an amount which would be quite different
        if it were a monthly rather than a yearly figure.

19.   Question 19 asks how many people altogether live on the reported in-
        come. This should include the subject and any others, such as the
        spouse, who receive more than half of their support from this income.

21.   Question 21 asks about assets and financial resources. This should in-
        clude savings, stocks and bonds, real estate holdings, etc. that could
        aid in an emergency.

34.   Question 34 is, in fact, a psychiatric evaluation (Pfeiffer, 1975b).
        Although some of the questions may seem ridiculous to subjects, it is
        important that they answer them as they best apply to them. In answer-
        ing any queries subjects may have, you should be careful to tell them
        only that you are interested in the problems and needs of people in

general and ask them to try and answer as best they can. Since some less intelligent people may have trouble with word meanings in this section, the interviewer may define difficult words as necessary, being *extremely careful* not to interpret the meaning of the sentence or change it in any way. We do not want this to be an intelligence test, but the schedule is set up so that the subject's interpretation of each question is important.

The answers to these questions which are in the pathological direction are in capital letters. If the sum of responses in capital letters is 5 or more there are probably psychiatric problems. The higher the number over 5, the stronger the evidence.

42-44.   It is very important that both interviewer and subject remain aware of the particular time span on certain questions. Question 42 asks for information on the *past month*; 44, at the *present time*. In asking these questions the interviewer should repeat the introductory question often, stressing the time span. In asking question 42, for example, the interviewer might say: "Have you had any arthritis medication in the past month? How about prescription pain killers? Have you taken any high blood pressure medicine in the past month?"

56-69.   Questions 56 through 69 are the OARS scale for determining the subject's capacity to carry out the activities of daily living, that is, capacity for self-care. The questions ask "Can you. . . ?" rather than "Do you. . . ?" since, for example, subjects may not cook or do housework because husbands or wives do these things for them, yet be perfectly capable of doing them themselves.

The interviewer is cautioned to be aware that not only physical disabilities cause a subject to require help with ADL activities. Some subjects who are physically capable of ADL activities may nevertheless be unable to perform them regularly because of dementia, depression, intellectual deficit, etc., in which case the answer is "1 with some help" or "0 Unable. . . ." Subjects unable to do something regularly are considered to need help or to be unable even though they may be able to perform the activity occasionally.

Since there is a specific transportation question within the activities of daily living questions, transportation should not influence the answers for such things as shopping and doing laundry. We want to know the subject's capacity (ability) to go shopping or do laundry. Subjects may not do their own shopping because they have no transportation, but if they are capable of doing it regularly they should get a 2 answer.

69.   If, in answer to Question 69, subjects wet or soil themselves less than once a week, they are considered not to wet or soil themselves and the "Never" option should be circled.

70.   Be sure to get full information on helpers. In follow-up studies these persons may be crucial in locating the subject.

71.   Utilization of Services. Question 71 (subquestions 1 through 24) asks about services that the subject may or may not be receiving. Each subquestion asks about a specific service, which has been labeled. The numbers correspond with those of the service list in Appendix B. Although subquestions about each service are not identical, they do follow a general pattern. For most questions we wish to know if the subject has gotten the service at all within the past six months and, if so, who provided it and in what quantity. We then ask if the subject is still receiving the service and if he or she perceives a need for it. The need question applies whether or not the subject is receiving the service. For example, in subquestion 2, some subjects may be receiving social/recreational services and yet say they really do not need it, while others who are getting it may feel they do need it.

Since it is often difficult for subjects to think in terms of "the past six months," the interviewer is asked to calculate in advance what period the past six months has covered and to remind the subject that it means, for example, since last June. This procedure has been indicated in subquestions 2, 3, and 7, but the interviewer is urged to repeat it when necessary to insure that the subject is answering in terms of the past six months.

In the services section an additional burden is placed on the interviewer to get "the best possible information." In most cases the questions are clear and straightforward, but some will require further explanation. It is important that the interviewer understand what is meant by each service and make sure that the respondent, either subject or informant, also understands.

Services with Special Problems

(2) SOCIAL/RECREATIONAL SERVICES are any *planned* and *organized* activities designed to increase a person's social interaction or foster creative use of leisure time. Social clubs, church clubs and groups (excluding church services), hobby, recreation, and special interest groups as well as volunteer projects and all classes taken for pleasure or self-enrichment are examples. Planned and organized crafts and hobbies, etc. should also be included.

(4) SHELTERED EMPLOYMENT applies to employment in special industries, offices, or shops designed to employ the impaired or handicapped. Goodwill Industries and industries for the blind are examples.

(5) EDUCATIONAL SERVICES, EMPLOYMENT RELATED includes any training to prepare a person for a job. Secretarial courses, professional schools

(dental or law), retraining for older workers, and on-the-job training such as apprenticeships are all examples.

(6) REMEDIAL TRAINING is any training--except physical therapy, which is covered separately (see subquestion 13)--designed to improve the capabilities of a person whose abilities are limited. Included are speech therapy, remedial reading or literacy courses, reality orientation, training in self-care for the mentally or physically impaired, training for the blind, etc.

(7) MENTAL HEALTH SERVICES includes family or marital counseling along with all forms of individual or group mental health counseling or psychotherapy. Evaluation for psychiatric hospitalization is also included.

(9) PERSONAL CARE SERVICES refers to daily help in bathing, dressing, grooming, feeding, and toilet care. A weekly trip to the hairdresser would not be included.

(10) NURSING CARE, as defined here, can be provided by a nurse or by someone else. In this set of questions we wish to know about treatments or medications provided by or monitored by a nurse, attendant, family member, or someone else. Administration of medicine--either orally or in injections--catheter care, changing dressings, and taking of blood pressure and temperature are all examples. But nursing care here *does not* include other services--personal care services, continuous supervision, etc.--even when they are performed by a nurse.

(13) PHYSICAL THERAPY must be a *planned* set of physical exercises, massages, or treatments, but may be supervised by an attendant, a nurse, a family member, or by a physical therapist.

(14) CONTINUOUS SUPERVISION applies to continuous, twenty-four-hour-a-day monitoring of an individual. Someone need not always be in the room with the person but must be nearby--within calling distance. Individuals who have to have someone with them twenty-four hours a day--and need a sitter if, for example, a daughter goes to the drug store--are receiving continuous supervision. In a nursing home continuous supervision is available for all if needed, since there is always a nurse available; but we ask whether or not someone "had to be with you all the time to look after you?" In other words, continuous supervision exists only if supervision is provided as a necessity and not when it occurs just because of the presence of others.

(15) CHECKING SERVICES. Usually, subjects who have received continuous supervision in the past six months are asked only subquestion 15c, but an occasional exception occurs. If the subject is no longer receiving continuous supervision he or she may now be receiving checking. In that case, do *not* skip the checking questions since it is necessary to know if the subject received checking after the continuous supervision stopped.

(17)   HOMEMAKER-HOUSEHOLD SERVICES asks, "Did someone *have to* help you
with routine household chores. . . ?" not, "Did someone help you. . . ?"
We do not want to know, for example, about the wife who cleans, does
laundry, etc. for her husband, *unless* it is required because he couldn't
do it for himself.

(18)   MEAL PREPARATION also asks, "Did someone *have to* prepare meals
for you," not "Did someone prepare meals for you?"

(19)   ADMINISTRATIVE, LEGAL, AND PROTECTIVE SERVICES apply to any help
subjects have had in managing business and administrative affairs--
legal help, someone paying bills for the subject (with the subject's
money), and help with business dealings, such as that with landlords,
for example.   An extreme case is that of guardianship.

(20)   SYSTEMATIC MULTIDIMENSIONAL EVALUATION must be of the individual's
overall functioning, including social and economic resources and mental
and physical health.   The gathering of information in these areas is
not sufficient; it must be evaluated.   Examples are case conferences
on a patient by a doctor, a social worker, and others; staff conferences
on patients in nursing homes; or a case review of a client in a multidisciplinary clinic.

(24)   COORDINATION, INFORMATION, AND REFERRAL SERVICES asks "Did someone see to it that you got the kinds of help that you needed?"   It
goes on to say, ". . . did someone give you information about the kind
of help that is available or put you in touch with those who could help
you?"   We are not interested here in a casual referral, for example,
of a friend saying, "You really should check with the Senior Center.
They could help you."   We want to know here about people who take
responsibility for seeing to it that the subject gets the kinds of
help he or she needs.

73-82.   Questions 73-82 follow the concluding statement to the subject and
should be asked of an informant if one is available.   This should not
be done in the subject's presence.   (See Privacy, above.)

74.   Question 74, like the identical Question 14, which is asked only of
the subject, does not apply to paid help for the subject if sick or
disabled but, rather, to family, friends, and neighbors.   It is a social
rather than an economic support question and has been included under
that title within the informant questions.

83.   Length of interview should include only the time with the subject or
informant(s) in filling out pages 2 through 35.

86a.   Additional information about the physical and/or mental state of the
subject may be obtained in 86a.   We want to know if the subject refused or if the informant refused for him or her and why.   It is also

very important to know if the subject is too sick or too mentally disturbed to talk to the interviewer or if perhaps the subject is deaf or in a coma.

87-96.   In questions 87-96 interviewers are asked to give their impressions of subjects based on experience with the subject, information from the informant, the subject's environment, etc. In some cases the interviewer will feel there has been insufficient information to answer some of these questions and should so indicate. But even in an informant-only interview generally enough information is obtained from the informant to answer these questions. The interviewer is urged to answer all of the questions or as many as possible based upon whatever information and evidence were gathered.

97-101.   Ratings. Please also read the information on ratings provided in the introduction to this chapter. The five rating scales are designed to help the interviewer make a summary assessment of the subject. These judgments are to be based on the interviewer's overall impression of the subject from information contained in the survey questionnaire and from all other sources. The interviewer will rate the subject's current level of function on socal resources (questions 6-14, 73, 74, 87, and 88), economic resources (15-30, 75, 89-91), mental health (the Preliminary Questionnaire and questions 31-36, 76-80, and 92-95), physical health (37-55, 81, 82, and 96), and activities of daily living (56-69). Although the interviewer should use the descriptions of levels for each scale to arrive at the appropriate level of functioning, the basic meaning of the six levels should be kept in mind (see Ratings, above):

> 1 = Excellent
> 2 = Good
> 3 = Mildly impaired
> 4 = Moderately impaired
> 5 = Severely impaired
> 6 = Totally impaired

Ratings should be based on the subject's functional level *at the time of the interview* even if the condition is viewed as temporary. The interviewer must circle a specific level number, even when finding it difficult to choose between two levels. Ratings between numbers--such as a rating between 2 and 3--are not permissible.

97.   THE SOCIAL RESOURCES RATING SCALE incorporates two concepts: how satisfying the subjects' social network is to them, and the adequacy of social support in case of disability. The most common combinations are listed as examples in the scales, but the interviewer is reminded to return to the basic meaning of the scales for guidance when the subject does not fit a description.

98.   THE ECONOMIC RATING SCALE incorporates two concepts in various combinations: the adequacy of the subjects' income and the presence or

absence of reserves that could help in times of trouble. It is often impossible to rate economic status based on monetary income and reserves alone, since many subjects are receiving supplements to their income in the form of such things as meals and housing provided by their families, or are living in subsidized public housing or receiving food stamps or regular meals from a federal program. The adequacy of income, for purposes of rating, therefore, should incorporate these supplements.

The interviewer is reminded that if the subject does not fit one of the categories described, the overall meaning of the numbered ratings should be used.

99.   The term *psychiatric symptoms* refers not only to psychotic symptoms, but also to depression, hypochondriasis, etc.

100.   The term *disability* refers here to any deficit such as a missing limb, paralysis, a nonfunctioning internal organ, etc. In some cases these disabilities have been compensated for so well that they no longer present a physical problem or require treatment. In other cases the disability either alone or in combination with illness is disabling or requires treatment. The scale attempts to describe varying degrees of physical impairment. Again, when in doubt revert to the overall descriptions.

Institutional Form of the
OARS Multidimensional Functional Assessment Questionnaire

For interviewing anyone residing in an institution, the Institutional form of the Multidimensional Functional Assessment Questionnaire should be used. Although basically the same as the noninstitutional form, the institutional form has been modified somewhat. Questions that have been radically modified or changed have been flagged with "(Inst.)." Additional questions have been designated by the number of the preceding question plus a capital letter. For example, on the Institutional form, three new questions follow Question 74. They have been numbered 74A, 74B, and 74C. In the questionnaire reproduced in this manual, items asked solely in institutions have been italicized.

Areas Requiring Particular Attention

Question
Number

(Page 1)   If the place of interview is an institution, or if the subject resides in one, it is extremely important that both the name of that institution and the kind of institution it is be carefully recorded. We need to know if the institution serves any particular disability group and what its official level of care is.

PQ   In the Preliminary Questionnaire, number 4 applies only if subjects have a phone of their own since we cannot expect them to know the phone number of their institutions. In 4a, any reasonable address is acceptable.

8.   Question 8 asks how many people subjects know well enough to visit with. We wish to know how many people they know well enough to spend some time with, chatting, etc.

10.   In question 10 we wish to know if, when in the institution, the subject interacts—chats or visits—with other people. This question includes any social contact with others in the institution, or with visitors from outside.

18, 18a.   In obtaining income amounts from institutionalized subjects, the interviewer is cautioned that Social Security payments may be going, all or in part, directly to the institution. The interviewer should ascertain the total amount of Social Security the subject gets, including what goes to the home, and enter it. Other types of government payments and insurance which go to the institution and which the subject otherwise would not receive should not be entered in 18 and 18a but, rather, recorded in 24, "Who pays for your stay here?"

98.   As stated on the ECONOMIC RATING SCALE, subjects' incomes are considered adequate if all their needs are being met. Housing and food needs are generally well met in an institution and medical needs are attended to.

The subject may or may not, however, have adequate clothing and small luxuries provided. The rating should describe the economic situation of the subject alone at this point in time and should not reflect the economic conditions of his or her spouse or family.

Separate Assessments of Functional Status and Services Utilization

The OARS functional assessment procedure incorporates two major areas of interest, one dealing with functional assessment, the other with services utilization and perceived need for services.

Since many users want to get information in both areas, most choose to administer the entire instrument. However, some persons may be interested only in one part, or may be particularly concerned with time. They should note that this instrument can be divided into a Part A, Assessment of Individual Functioning, and a Part B, Assessment of Services Utilization, by using the following procedure:

Part A. Assessment of Individual Functioning.

Cover Sheet; Preliminary Questionnaire; questions 1-23, 26-40, 42-70, 73-101.

Part B. Assessment of Services Utilization.

Cover Sheet; Preliminary Questionnaire; questions 1-4, 71, 83-85, Services Supplement.

Note: To facilitate interviewing, services items should be asked in numerical order, and items on the Services Supplement (printed immediately following the questionnaire, at the end of Appendix A) must therefore be interleaved with items in question 71. It should be noted that no coding columns have been provided for the Services Supplement.

REFERENCES

Pfeiffer, E. A short, portable mental status questionnaire for the assessment of organic brain deficit in elderly patients. *Journal of the American Geriatrics Society*, 1975a, *23*, 10, 433-441.

Pfeiffer, E. A short psychiatric evaluation schedule. Paper presented at the 28th Annual Meeting, Gerontological Society, Louisville, Kentucky, October 26-30, 1975b.

APPENDICES

APPENDIX A

The OARS Multidimensional Functional
Assessment Questionnaire and Services Supplement*

Forms for Community and Institutional Use

The OARS Multidimensional Functional Assessment Questionnaire has been designed for use with adults living in the community, and when it is administered to adults residing in institutions minor changes are necessary to make it appropriate to that situation. The questionnaire reproduced here is a composite of the community and institutional forms. Items used only in an institutional setting as well as specific directions for the use of the questionnaire in institutions have been printed in italics. We recommend that the two versions be kept separate when they are actually used.

Separate Assessment of Individual Functional Status and Services Utilization

The OARS functional assessment procedure incorporates two major areas of interest, one dealing with functional assessment, the other with services utilization and perceived need for services.

Since many users want to get information in both areas, most choose to administer the entire instrument. However, some persons may be interested only in one part, or may be particularly concerned with time. They should note that this instrument can be divided into a Part A, Assessment of Individual Functioning, and a Part B, Assessment of Services Utilization, by using the following procedure.

Part A.   Assessment of Individual Functioning.
Cover Sheet; Preliminary Questionnaire; questions 1-23, 26-40, 42-70, 73-101.

Part B.   Assessment of Services Utilization.
Cover Sheet; Preliminary Questionnaire; questions 1-4, 71, 83-85, Services Supplement.

Note: To facilitate interviewing, services items should be asked in numerical order; items on the attached *Services Supplement* must therefore be interleaved with items in question 71. It should be noted that no coding column has been provided for the Services Supplement. The Services Supplement constitutes the last item in Appendix A.

---

* A detailed guide to the administration of the OARS Multidimensional Functional Assessment Questionnaire is provided in Chapter 15.

OARS MULTIDIMENSIONAL FUNCTIONAL ASSESSMENT QUESTIONNAIRE   CARD 1

Subject # _____
                                                                    1-4

Subject Number _____   Card # _____ 01
                                                                    5-6
Subject's Address _____
                  Street & Number   City   State   Mo   Day   Yr

Date of Interview _____
                                                        7-8 9-10 11-12
Time Interview Began _____

Interviewer's Name _____
                                                            13-14
Relationship of Informant to Subject _____
                                                             15
Place of Interview (SPECIFY HOME OR PROPER NAME AND OFFICIAL
TYPE OF INSTITUTION.)

_____
                                                             16
Subject's Residence if Not the Place of Interview (SPECIFY
HOME OR PROPER NAME AND OFFICIAL TYPE OF INSTITUTION.)

_____
                                                            17-18

OLDER AMERICANS RESOURCES AND SERVICES PROGRAM
OF THE
DUKE UNIVERSITY CENTER FOR THE STUDY OF AGING AND HUMAN DEVELOPMENT
DURHAM, NORTH CAROLIAN 27710

April, 1975

(152)

NOTE: *MATERIAL IN ITALICS*

1. *WHEN THIS QUESTIONNAIRE IS USED FOR PERSONS IN INSTITUTIONS ADDITIONS IN ITALICS SHOULD BE INCLUDED AND ITALICIZED DIRECTIONS FOLLOWED.*
2. *DO NOT USE MATERIAL IN ITALICS FOR PERSONS NOT LIVING IN INSTITUTIONS.*
3. *CODING COLUMNS HAVE NOT BEEN PROVIDED FOR ITEMS ASKED SOLELY OF INSTITUTIONAL RESIDENTS. USERS MAY ADD CODING COLUMNS FOR THESE ITEMS.*

PRELIMINARY QUESTIONNAIRE
[ASK QUESTIONS 1-10 AND RECORD ALL ANSWERS. (ASK QUESTION 4a. ONLY IF SUBJECT HAS NO TELEPHONE.) CHECK CORRECT (+) OR INCORRECT (−) FOR EACH AND RECORD TOTAL NUMBER OF ERRORS BASED ON TEN QUESTIONS.]

1 +	0 −	
		1. What is the date today? _____ Month Day Year
		2. What day of the week is it? _____
		3. What is the name of this place? _____

		4. What is your telephone number? _____
		
		   a. [ASK ONLY IF SUBJECT DOES NOT HAVE A PHONE.]
		      What is your street address?
		
		      _____

		5. How old are you? _____
		6. When were you born? _____ Month Day Year
		7. Who is the president of the U.S. now? _____
		8. Who was the president just before him? ____
		9. What was your mother's maiden name? _____

		10. Subtract 3 from 20 and keep subtracting 3 from each new number you get, all the way down.
		
		   _____
		   [CORRECT ANSWER IS: 17, 14, 11, 8, 5, 2.]

_____ Total number of errors.

1. Telephone number [IF SUBJECT IS RELIABLE TRANSFER FROM
   PRELIMINARY QUESTIONNAIRE; OTHERWISE, OBTAIN FROM INFORMANT
   OR LOOK ON TELEPHONE.] _____

CARD 1

2. Sex of Subject
   1 Male
   2 Female

_____
32

3. Race of Subject
   1 White (Caucasian)
   2 Black (Negro)
   3 Oriental
   4 Spanish American (Spanish surname)
   5 American Indian
   6 Other
   - Not answered

_____
33

4. [GET FROM PRELIMINARY QUESTIONNAIRE IF SUBJECT IS RELIABLE;
   FROM INFORMANT IF NOT.]
   a. When were you born? _____
                            (Month)   (Day)   (Year)

Mo   Day   Y
34-35 36-37 3

   b. How old are you? _____

_____
40-42

5. How far did you go (have you gone) in school?
   1 0-4 years
   2 5-8 years
   3 High school incomplete
   4 High school completed
   5 Post high school, business or trade school
   6 1-3 years college
   7 4 years college completed
   8 Post graduate college
   - Not answered

_____
43

SOCIAL RESOURCES

Now I'd like to ask you some questions about your family and friends.

6. Are you single, married, widowed, divorced or separated?
   1 Single
   2 Married
   3 Widowed
   4 Divorced
   5 Separated
   - Not answered

   (Inst.)
   [IF "2" ASK a.]

   a. Does your spouse live here also?
   1 Yes
   2 No
   - Not Answered

Inst.: Do not ask 7. Ask 7. (Inst.) instead.

7. Who lives with you?

CARD 1

[CHECK "YES" OR "NO" FOR EACH OF THE FOLLOWING.]

	1	0	
	YES	NO	
45			No one
46			Husband or wife
47			Children
48			Grandchildren
49			Parents
50			Grandparents
51			Brothers and sisters
52			Other relatives [Does not include in-laws covered in the above categories.]
53			Friends
54			Non-related paid* helper [*Includes free room]
55			Others [SPECIFY.] _____

_____

7. *(Inst.) In the past year about how often did you leave here to visit your family and/or friends for weekends, or holidays, or to go on shopping trips or outings?*
   1 Once a week or more
   2 1-3 times a month
   3 Less than once a month or only on holidays
   4 Never
   - Not answered

8. How many people do you know well enough to visit with in their homes?
   3 Five or more
   2 Three to four
   1 One to two
   0 None
   - Not answered

56

9. About how many times did you talk to someone--friends, relatives, or others on the telephone in the past week (either you called them or they called you)? [IF SUBJECT HAS NO PHONE, QUESTION STILL APPLIES.]
   3 Once a day or more
   2 2-6 times
   1 Once
   0 Not at all
   - Not answered

57

10. *(Inst.) Substitute italized paragraph.*

10. How many times during the past week did you spend some time with someone who does not live with you, that is you went to see them or they came to visit you, or you went out to do things together?

    How many times in the past week did you visit with someone, either with people who live here or people who visited you here?
    3 Once a day or more
    2 2-6 times
    1 Once
    0 Not at all
    - Not answered

58

11. Do you have someone you can trust and confide in?
    2 Yes
    0 No
    - Not answered

59

12. Do you find yourself feeling lonely quite often, sometimes, or almost never?
    0 Quite often
    1 Sometimes
    2 Almost never
    - Not answered

60

13. Do you see your relatives and friends as often as you want to or are you somewhat unhappy about how little you see them?
    1 As often as wants to
    2 Somewhat unhappy about how little
    - Not answered

61

14. Is there someone *(Inst.: outside this place)* who would give you any help at all if you were sick or disabled, for example your husband/wife, a member of your family, or a friend?
    1 Yes
    0 No one willing and able to help
    - Not answered

62

  IF "YES" ASK a. AND b.

  a. Is there someone *(Inst.: outside this place)* who would take of you as long as needed, or only for a short time, or only someone who would help you now and then (for example, taking you to the doctor, or fixing lunch occasionally, etc.)?
      1 Someone who would take care of Subject indefinitely (as long as needed)
      2 Someone who would take care of Subject for a short time (a few weeks to six months)
      3 Someone who would help the Subject now and then (taking him to the doctor or fixing lunch, etc.)
      - Not answered

63

  b. Who is this person?

    Name _____

    Relationship _____

64

ECONOMIC RESOURCES

Now I'd like to ask you some questions about your work situation.

ARD 1

15. Are you presently:

[CHECK "YES" OR "NO" FOR EACH OF THE FOLLOWING.]

	1	0	
	YES	NO	
65			Employed full-time
66			Employed part-time
67			Retired
68			Retired on disability
69			Not employed and seeking work
70			Not employed and not seeking work
71			Full-time student
72			Part-time student

16. What kind of work have you done most of your life?

[CIRCLE THE MOST APPROPRIATE.]

    1 Never employed
    2 Housewife
    3 Other [STATE THE SPECIFIC OCCUPATION IN DETAIL.] _____

73

74 (occupation) _____
    - Not answered

17. Does your husband/wife work or did he/she ever work? [QUESTION
     APPLIES ONLY TO SPOUSE TO WHOM MARRIED THE LONGEST.]
     1 Yes
     2 No
     3 Never married
     - Not answered

75

[IF "YES" ASK a.]

a. What kind of work did or does he/she do?

    [STATE THE SPECIFIC OCCUPATION IN DETAIL.] _____

76

    _____

    _____

CARD 2

18. Where does your income (money) come from (yours and your husband's/ wife's)?

[CHECK "YES" OR "NO" FOR EACH OF THE FOLLOWING AND IF "YES" ENTER THE AMOUNT AND CIRCLE "Weekly", "Monthly", OR "Yearly".]

S# ____ 1-4

Card# __02__ 5-6

CODE 1 Yes
         0 No

1 YES	0 NO	IF YES HOW MUCH			
			Weekly Monthly Yearly	Earnings from employment (wages, salaries or income from your business)	7
			Weekly Monthly Yearly	Income from rental, interest from investments, etc. [Include trusts, annuities, & payments from insurance policies & savings.)	8
			Weekly Monthly Yearly	Social Security (Include Social Security disability payments but not SSI.)	9
			Weekly Monthly Yearly	V.A. benefits such as G.I. Bill, and disability payments	10
			Weekly Monthly Yearly	Disability payments not covered by Social Security, SSI, or VA. Both government & private, & including Workmen's Compensation	11
			Weekly Monthly Yearly	Unemployment Compensation	12
			Weekly Monthly Yearly	Retirement pension from job	13
			Weekly Monthly Yearly	Alimony or child support	14
			Weekly Monthly Yearly	Scholarships, stipends (Include only the amount beyond tuition.)	15
			Weekly Monthly Yearly	Regular assistance from family members (including regular contributions from employed children)	16
			Weekly Monthly Yearly	SSI payments (yellow government check)	17
			Weekly Monthly Yearly	Regular financial aid from private organizations and churches	18
			Weekly Monthly Yearly	Welfare payments or Aid for Dependent Children	19
			Weekly Monthly Yearly	Other	20

[IF COMPLETE INCOME AMOUNTS ARE OBTAINED IN QUESTION 18 SKIP TO QUESTION 19, BUT IF ANY AMOUNTS ARE MISSING ASK a.]

CARD 2

IF ALL AMOUNTS
OBTAINED ON 18,
TOTAL AND CODE
IN 18a.

a. How much income do you (and your husband/wife) have a year?

[SHOW ANNUAL INCOME LADDER AND CIRCLE THE LETTER WHICH
IDENTIFIES EITHER YEARLY OR MONTHLY INCOME CATEGORY.]

CODE		YEARLY	MONTHLY
01	A.	0 − $499	(0 − $41)
02	B.	$500 − $999	($42 − $83)
03	C.	$1,000 − $1,999	($84 − $166)
04	D.	$2,000 − $2,999	($167 − $249)
05	E.	$3,000 − $3,999	($250 − $333)
06	F.	$4,000 − $4,999	($334 − $416)
07	G.	$5,000 − $6,999	($417 − $583)
08	H.	$7,000 − $9,999	($584 − $833)
09	I.	$10,000 − $14,999	($834 − $1249)
10	J.	$15,000 − $19,999	($1250 − $1666)
11	K.	$20,000 − $29,999	($1667 − $2499)
12	L.	$30,000 − $39,999	($2500 − $3333)
13	M.	$40,000 or more	($3334 or more)

21-22

23-24

19. How many people altogether live on this income (that is it provides at least half of their income)? _____

(Inst.) [PREFACE 20. WITH]
Do you own, rent, or maintain a home outside of this place?
    1 Yes
    2 No
    - Not answered
[IF "YES" ASK 20; IF "NO" SKIP TO 21.]

20. Do you own your own home?
    1 Yes
    0 No ─────────────────────→ [IF "NO" ASK c. AND d.]
    - Not answered

25

[IF "YES" ASK a. AND b.]

a.
26

a. How much is it worth?
    1 Up to $10,000
    2 $10,000 − $24,000
    3 $25,000 − $50,000
    4 More than $50,000
    - Not answered

b.
27

b(1)
28

b. Do you own it outright
    or are you still pay-
    ing a mortgage?
    1 Own outright
    2 Still paying
    - Not answered

c.
29

[IF 2 ASK (1).]

c(1)
30

(1) How much is the
     monthly payment?
    1 0 − $59
    2 $60 − $99
    3 $100 − $149
    4 $150 − $199
    5 $200 − $249
    6 $250 − $349
    7 $350 up
    8 Not answered

d.
31

c. Do you (and your husband/
    wife) pay the total rent for
    your house (apartment) or do
    you contribute to the cost,
    or does someone else own it
    or pay the rent?
    1 Subject pays total rent
    2 Subject contributes to
       the cost
    3 Someone else owns it or
       pays the rent (Subject
       doesn't contribute)
    - Not answered
[IF 1 OR 2 ASK (1.).]
(1.) How much rent do you pay?
    1 0 − $59 per month
    2 $60 − $99 per month
    3 $100 − $149
    4 $150 − $199
    5 $200 − $249
    6 $250 − $349
    7 $350 up
    - Not answered

d. Do you live in public housing
    or receive a rent subsidy?
    1 No, neither
    2 Yes, live in public housing
    3 Yes, receives a rent subsidy
    - Not answered

21. Are your assets and financial resources sufficient to meet emergencies?
    1 Yes
    0 No
    - Not answered

_____
32

22. Are your expenses so heavy that you cannot meet the payments, or can you barely meet the payments, or are your payments no problem to you?
    1 Subject cannot meet payments
    2 Subject can barely meet payments
    3 Payments are no problem
    - Not answered

_____
33

23. Is your financial situation such that you feel you need financial assistance or help beyond what you are already getting?
    1 Yes
    0 No
    - Not answered

_____
34

Inst.: Do not ask 24. Ask 24.(Inst.) instead.

24. Do you pay for your own food or do you get any regular help at all with costs of food or meals?
    1 Subject pays for food himself
    2 Subject gets help
    - Not answered

_____
35

[IF 2 ASK a.]

a. From where?
   [CHECK "YES" OR "NO" FOR EACH OF THE FOLLOWING.]

1	0		
YES	NO		
		Family or friends	36
		Food stamps	37
		Prepared food (meals) from an agency or organization program [SPECIFY NUMBER OF MEALS PER WEEK.] _____	38

_____
39-40

24. *(Inst.) Who pays for your stay here?*
    Check "YES" or "NO" FOR EACH OF THE FOLLOWING.

YES	NO	
		Yourself (or your husband/wife)
		Other relatives
		Insurance, such as Medicare or Blue Cross/Blue Shield
		Public or private agency or any government source such as Medicaid or V.A.
		Other [*SPECIFY.*] _____

RD 2　　　*Inst.: Do not ask 25.*

25. Do you feel that you need food stamps?
　　　1　Yes
　　　0　No
　　　-　Not answered

41 ———

26. Are you covered by any kinds of health or medical insurance?
　　　1　Yes
　　　0　No
　　　-　Not answered

42 ———

[IF "YES" ASK a.]

a.　What kind?

[CHECK "YES" OR "NO" FOR EACH OF THE FOLLOWING.]

1 YES	0 NO	
		Medicaid
		Medicare Plan A only (hospitalization only)
		Medicare Plan A and B (hospitalization and doctor's bills)
		Other insurance: hospitalization only (Blue Cross or other)
		Other insurance: hospitalization and doctor's bills (Blue Cross and Blue Shield, major medical or other)

43 ———

44 ———

45 ———

46 ———

47 ———

27. Please tell me how well you think you (and your family) are
　　　now doing financially as compared to other people your age--
　　　better, about the same, or worse?
　　　[PROBE AS NECESSARY.]
　　　2　Better
　　　1　About the same
　　　0　Worse
　　　-　Not answered

48 ———

28. How well does the amount of money you have take care of your
　　　needs--very well, fairly well, or poorly?
　　　2　Very well
　　　1　Fairly well
　　　0　Poorly
　　　-　Not answered

49 ———

29. Do you usually have enough to buy those little "extras";
　　　that is, those small luxuries?
　　　2　Yes
　　　0　No
　　　-　Not answered

50 ———

CARD 2

30. Do you feel that you will have enough for your needs in the future?
    2   Yes
    0   No
    -   Not answered

51

MENTAL HEALTH

Next, I'd like to ask you some questions about how you feel about life.

31. How often would you say you worry about things--very often, fairly often, or hardly ever?
    0   Very often
    1   Fairly often
    2   Hardly ever
    -   Not answered

52

32. In general, do you find life exciting, pretty routine, or dull?
    2   Exciting
    1   Pretty routine
    0   Dull
    -   Not answered

53

33. Taking everything into consideration how would you describe your satisfaction with life in general at the present time-- good, fair, or poor?
    2   Good
    1   Fair
    0   Poor
    -   Not answered

54

ARD 2

DE

Yes

No

34. Please answer the following questions "Yes" or "No" as they apply to you now. There are no right or wrong answers, only what best applies to you. Occasionally a question may not seem to apply to you, but please answer either "Yes" or "No", whichever is more nearly correct for you.

[CIRCLE "YES" OR "NO" FOR EACH.]

(1) Do you wake up fresh and rested most mornings?...............yes NO

(2) Is your daily life full of things that keep you interested?..yes NO

(3) Have you, at times, very much wanted to leave home?..........YES no

(4) Does it seem that no one understands you?....................YES no

(5) Have you had periods of days, weeks, or months when you couldn't take care of things because you couldn't "get going"?..YES no

(6) Is your sleep fitful and disturbed?..........................YES no

(7) Are you happy most of the time?..............................yes NO

(8) Are you being plotted against?...............................YES no

(9) Do you certainly feel useless at times?.....................YES no

(10) During the past few years, have you been well most of the time?..yes NO

(11) Do you feel weak all over much of the time?.................YES no

(12) Are you troubled by headaches?..............................YES no

(13) Have you had difficulty in keeping your balance in walking?..YES no

(14) Are you troubled by your heart pounding and by a shortness of breath?..YES no

(15) Even when you are with people, do you feel lonely much of the time?..YES no

Sum of Responses in Capital letters _____

Sum of Responses in Capital Letters

70-71

(163)

35. How would you rate your mental or emotional health at the present time—excellent, good, fair, or poor?
    3 Excellent
    2 Good
    1 Fair
    0 Poor
    - Not answered

72

36. Is your mental or emotional health now better, about the same, or worse than it was five years ago?
    3 Better
    2 About the same
    0 Worse
    - Not answered

73

PHYSICAL HEALTH

CARD 3

Let's talk about your health now.

S# ____
1-4

37. About how many times have you seen a doctor during the past six months other than as an inpatient in a hospital? [EXCLUDE PSYCHIATRISTS.]

Card# 03
5-6

_____ Times

7-9

38. During the past six months how many days were you so sick that you were unable to carry on your usual activities—such as going to work or working around the house?
    0 None
    1 A week or less
    2 More than a week but less than one month
    3 1-3 months
    4 4-6 months
    - Not answered

10

39. How many days in the past six months were you in a hospital for physical health problems?

_____ Days

11-13

40. How many days in the past six months were you in a nursing home, or rehabilitation center for physical health problems?

_____ Days

14-16

41. Do you feel that you need medical care or treatment beyond what you are receiving at this time?
    1 Yes
    0 No
    - Not answered

17

ARD 3

L.

42. I have a list of common medicines that people take. Would you please tell me if you've taken any of the following in the past month.

[CHECK "YES" OR "NO" FOR EACH MEDICINE.]

1 YES	0 NO	
		Arthritis medication
		Prescription pain killer (other than above)
		High blood pressure medicine
		Pills to make you lose water or salt (water pills)
		Digitalis pills for the heart
		Nitroglycerin tablets for chest pain
		Blood thinner medicine (anticoagulants)
		Drugs to improve circulation
		Insulin injections for diabetes
		Pills for diabetes
		Prescription ulcer medicine
		Seizure medications (like Dilantin)
		Thyroid pills
		Cortisone pills or injections
		Antibiotics
		Tranquilizers or nerve medicine
		Prescription sleeping pills (once a week or more)
		Hormones, male or female (including birth control pills)

DE # OF
thers"
AT CANNOT
ENTERED
ABOVE
TEGORIES.

43. What other prescription drugs have you taken in the past month?

[RECORD THE "others". THEN ENTER THEM IN APPROPRIATE CATEGORIES ABOVE IF POSSIBLE.]

[SPECIFY.] _____

36-37

_____

_____

44. Do you have any of the following illnesses at the present time?

[CHECK "YES" OR "NO" FOR EACH OF THE FOLLOWING. IF "YES", ASK:
 "How much does it interfere with your activities, not at all,
 a little (some), or a great deal?" AND CHECK THE APPROPRIATE BOX.]

CODE
0,1,2,3
OR 4 FOR
YES BUT
NOT HOW
MUCH.

[IF "YES", ASK:] How much does it interfere with your activities?

		0	1	2	3		
YES	NO	NOT AT ALL	A LITTLE	A GREAT DEAL			
					Arthritis or rheumatism	3
					Glaucoma	3
					Asthma	4
					Emphysema or chronic bronchitis	4
					Tuberculosis	4
					High blood pressure	4
					Heart trouble	4
					Circulation trouble in arms or legs	4
					Diabetes	4
					Ulcers (of the digestive system)	4
					Other stomach or intestinal disorders or gall bladder problems	4
					Liver disease	4
					Kidney disease	50
					Other urinary tract disorders (including prostate trouble)	5
					Cancer or Leukemia	5
					Anemia	5
					Effects of stroke	5
					Parkinson's Disease	5
					Epilepsy	56
					Cerebral Palsy	5
					Multiple Sclerosis	58
					Muscular Dystrophy	59
					Effects of Polio	60
					Thyroid or other glandular disorders	61
					Skin disorders such as pressure sores, leg ulcers or severe burns	62
					Speech impediment or impairment	63

ARD 3

45. Do you have any physical disabilities such as total or partial paralysis, missing or non-functional limbs, or broken bones?
    0 No
    1 Total paralysis
    2 Partial paralysis
    3 Missing or non-functional limbs
    4 Broken bones
    - Not answered

_____
64

46. How is your eyesight (with glasses or contacts), excellent, good, fair, poor, or are you totally blind?
    1 Excellent
    2 Good
    3 Fair
    4 Poor
    5 Totally blind
    - Not answered

_____
65

47. How is your hearing, excellent, good, fair, poor, or are you totally deaf?
    1 Excellent
    2 Good
    3 Fair
    4 Poor
    5 Totally deaf
    - Not answered

_____
66

48. Do you have any other physical problems or illnesses at the present time that seriously affect your health?
    1 Yes
    0 No
    - Not answered

_____
67

    [IF "YES" SPECIFY.] _____

                         _____

SUPPORTIVE DEVICES AND PROSTHESES

49. Do you use any of the following aids all or most of the time?

[CHECK "YES" OR "NO" FOR EACH AID.]

CARD 3

1 YES	0 NO		
		Cane (including tripod-tip cane)	68
		Walker	69
		Wheelchair	70
		Leg brace	71
		Back brace	72
		Artificial limb	73
		Hearing aid	74
		Colostomy equipment	75
		Catheter	76
		Kidney dialysis machine	77
		Other [SPECIFY.] _____	78

CARD 4

S# _____
        1-4

Card# ___04___
        5-6

50. Do you need any aids (supportive or prosthetic devices, in-
    including false teeth) that you currently do not have?
    1 Yes
    0 No
    - Not answered

        7

[IF "YES", ASK a.]

a. What aids do you need? [SPECIFY.]

_____

_____

_____

        8-9

51. Do you have a problem with your health because of drinking
    or has your physician advised you to cut down on drinking?
    1 Yes
    0 No
    - Not answered

        10

52. Do you regularly participate in any vigorous sports activity such as hiking, jogging, tennis, biking, or swimming?
    - 1 Yes
    - 0 No
    - \- Not answered

11

53. How would you rate your overall health at the present time-- excellent, good, fair, or poor?
    - 3 Excellent
    - 2 Good
    - 1 Fair
    - 0 Poor
    - \- Not answered

12

54. Is your health now better, about the same, or worse than it was five years ago?
    - 3 Better
    - 2 About the same
    - 0 Worse
    - \- Not answered

13

55. How much do your health troubles stand in the way of your doing the things you want to do--not at all, a little (some) or a great deal?
    - 3 Not at all
    - 2 A little (some)
    - 0 A great deal
    - \- Not answered

14

ACTIVITIES OF DAILY LIVING

Now I'd like to ask you about some of the activities of daily living, things that we all need to do as a part of our daily lives. I would like to know if you can do these activities without any help at all, or if you need some help to do them, or if you can't do them at all.

[BE SURE TO READ ALL ANSWER CHOICES IF APPLICABLE IN QUESTIONS 56. THROUGH 69. TO RESPONDENT.]

Instrumental ADL

56. Can you use the telephone...
    - 2 without help, including looking up numbers and dialing
    - 1 with some help (can answer phone or dial operator in an emergency, but need a special phone or help in getting the number or dialing),
    - 0 or are you completely unable to use the telephone?
    - \- Not answered

15

57. Can you get to places out of walking distance...
    2 without help (can travel alone on buses, taxis, or drive your own car),
    1 with some help (need someone to help you or go with you when traveling) or
    0 are you unable to travel unless emergency arrangements are made for a specialized vehicle like an ambulance?
    - Not answered

_____
16

58. Can you go shopping for groceries or clothes [ASSUMING S HAS TRANSPORTATION]...
    2 without help (taking care of all shopping needs yourself, assuming you had transportation),
    1 with some help (need someone to go with you on all shopping trips),
    0 or are you completely unable to do any shopping?
    - Not answered

_____
17

59. Can you prepare your own meals...
    2 without help (plan and cook full meals yourself),
    1 with some help (can prepare some things but unable to cook full meals yourself),
    0 or are you completely unable to prepare any meals?
    - Not answered

_____
18

60. Can you do your housework...
    2 without help (can scrub floors, etc.),
    1 with some help (can do light housework but need help with heavy work),
    0 or are you completely unable to do any housework?
    - Not answered

_____
19

61. Can you take your own medicine...
    2 without help (in the right doses at the right time),
    1 with some help (able to take medicine if someone prepares it for you and/or reminds you to take it),
    0 or are you completely unable to take your medicines?
    - Not answered

_____
20

62. Can you handle your own money...
    2 without help (write checks, pay bills, etc.),
    1 with some help (manage day-to-day buying but need help with managing your checkbook and paying your bills),
    0 or are you completely unable to handle money?
    - Not answered

_____
21

Physical ADL

63. Can you eat...
    2 without help (able to feed yourself completely),
    1 with some help (need help with cutting, etc.),
    0 or are you completely unable to feed yourself?
    - Not answered

22 _____

64. Can you dress and undress yourself...
    2 without help (able to pick out clothes, dress and
       undress yourself),
    1 with some help,
    0 or are you completely unable to dress and undress
       yourself?
    - Not answered

23 _____

65. Can you take care of your own appearance, for example
    combing your hair and (for men) shaving...
    2 without help,
    1 with some help,
    0 or are you completely unable to maintain your
       appearance yourself?
    - Not answered

24 _____

66. Can you walk...
    2 without help (except from a cane),
    1 with some help from a person or with the use of a
       walker, or crutches, etc.,
    0 or are you completely unable to walk?
    - Not answered

25 _____

67. Can you get in and out of bed...
    2 without any help or aids,
    1 with some help (either from a person or with the
       aid of some device),
    0 or are you totally dependent on someone else to
       lift you?
    - Not answered

26 _____

68. Can you take a bath or shower...
    2 without help,
    1 with some help (need help getting in and out of
       the tub, or need special attachments on the tub),
    0 or are you completely unable to bathe yourself?
    - Not answered

27 _____

69. Do you ever have trouble getting to the bathroom on time?
    2 No
    0 Yes
    1 Have a catheter or colostomy
    - Not answered

28 _____

    [IF "YES" ASK a.]

    a. How often do you wet or soil yourself (either day or night)?
        1 Once or twice a week
        0 Three times a week or more
        - Not answered

29

70. Is there someone who helps you with such things as shopping, housework, bathing, dressing, and getting around?
      1 Yes
      0 No
      - Not answered

30

[IF "YES" ASK a. AND b.]

    a. Who is your major helper?

        Name _____   Relationship _____

31

    b. Who else helps you?

        Name _____   Relationship _____

32

UTILIZATION OF SERVICES

71. Now I want to ask you some questions about the kinds of help you are or have been getting or the kinds of help that you feel you need. We want to know not only about the help you have been getting from agencies or organizations but also what help you have been getting from your family and friends.

        TRANSPORTATION
    (1) Who provides your transportation when you go shopping, visit friends, go to the doctor, etc.?

        [CHECK "YES" OR "NO" FOR EACH.]

1	0		
YES	NO		
		Yourself	33
		Your family or friends	34
		Use public transportation (bus, taxi, subway, etc.)	35
		Public agency [SPECIFY.] _____	36
		Other [SPECIFY.] _____	37

(172)

RD 4

a. On the average how many round trips do you make a week?
    0 None
    1 Less than one a week
    2 One to three a week
    3 4 or more
    - Not answered

b. Do you feel you need transportation more often than it is available to you now for appointments, visiting, social events, etc.?
    1 Yes
    0 No
    - Not answered

SOCIAL/RECREATIONAL SERVICES

(2) In the past six months (since _____ [SPECIFY MONTH.]) have you participated in any planned and organized social or recreational programs or in any group activities or classes such as arts and crafts classes? [EXCLUDE EMPLOYMENT-RELATED CLASSES.]
    1 Yes
    0 No
    - Not answered

[IF "NO" SKIP TO c.; IF "YES" ASK a., b., AND c.]

a. About how many times a week did you participate in these activities?
    1 Once a week or less
    2 2-3 times a week
    3 4 times a week or more
    - Not answered

b. Do you still participate in such activities or groups?
    1 Yes
    0 No
    - Not answered

c. Do you feel you need to participate in any planned and organized social or recreational programs or in any group activities or classes?
    1 Yes
    0 No
    - Not answered

EMPLOYMENT SERVICES

(3) Has anyone helped you look for or find a job or counseled you in regard to getting employment in the past six months (since _____ [MONTH])?
    1 Yes
    0 No
    - Not answered

[IF "NO" SKIP TO b.; IF "YES" ASK a. AND b.]

a. Who helped you?
    1 Family members or friends
    2 Someone from an agency
    3 Both
    - Not answered

_____
45

b. Do you feel you need someone to help you find a job?
    1 Yes
    0 No
    - Not answered

_____
46

SHELTERED EMPLOYMENT
(4) During the past six months have you worked in a place like a sheltered workshop which employs people with disabilities or special problems?
    1 Yes
    0 No
    - Not answered

_____
47

[IF "NO" SKIP TO b.; IF "YES" ASK a. AND b.]

a. Do you still work there?
    1 Yes
    0 No
    - Not answered

_____
48

b. Do you feel you need to work in a sheltered workshop?
    1 Yes
    0 No
    - Not answered

_____
49

EDUCATIONAL SERVICES, EMPLOYMENT RELATED
(5) In the past six months have you had any occupational training or on the job training to further prepare you for a job or career?
    1 Yes
    0 No
    - Not answered

_____
50

[IF "NO" SKIP TO c.; IF "YES" ASK a., b., AND c.]

a. Was this full or part-time training?
    1 Full-time
    2 Part-time
    - Not answered

_____
51

b. Are you still in classes or training?
    1 Yes
    0 No
    - Not answered

_____
52

RD 4

c. Do you feel you need education or on the job training
to prepare you for a job?
1 Yes
0 No
- Not answered

53

REMEDIAL TRAINING
(6) In the past six months have you had any remedial training
or instruction in learning basic personal skills, for
example speech therapy, reality orientation, or training
for the blind or physically or mentally handicapped?
[EXCLUDE PHYSICAL THERAPY.]
1 Yes
0 No
- Not answered

54

[IF "NO" SKIP TO c.; IF "YES" ASK a., b., AND c.]

a. On the average about how many training sessions a week
did you have over the past six months?
1 Less than one a week
2 One a week
3 Two or more a week
- Not answered

55

b. Are you currently receiving this type of training or
instruction?
1 Yes
0 No
- Not answered

56

c. Do you think you need remedial training or instruction
in basic personal skills?
1 Yes
0 No
- Not answered

57

MENTAL HEALTH SERVICES
(7) Have you had any treatment or counseling for personal or
family problems or for nervous, or emotional problems in
the past six months, that is, since _____ [SPECIFY MONTH.]?
1 Yes
0 No
- Not answered

58

[IF "NO" SKIP TO d.; IF "YES" ASK a., b., c., AND d.]

a. Were you hospitalized for nervous, or emotional problems
at any time during this period? (Last six months)
1 Yes
0 No
- Not answered

59

b. During the past six months how many sessions have you had with a doctor, psychiatrist or counselor for these problems (other than those when you were an inpatient in the hospital)? CARD 4

    0 None, had treatment only as an inpatient
    1 Less than 4 sessions (only occasionally or for evaluation)
    2 4-12 sessions
    3 13 or more sessions
    - Not answered

         60

c. Are you still receiving this help?
    1 Yes
    0 No
    - Not answered

         61

d. Do you feel that you need treatment or counseling for personal or family problems or for nervous or emotional problems?
    1 Yes
    0 No
    - Not answered

         62

PSYCHOTROPIC DRUGS

(8) Have you taken any prescription medicine for your nerves in the past six months, like medicine to calm you down or to help depression?
    1 Yes
    0 No
    - Not answered

         63

[IF "NO" SKIP TO b.; IF "YES" ASK a. AND b.]

a. Are you still taking it?
    1 Yes
    0 No
    - Not answered

         64

b. Do you feel you need this kind of medicine?
    1 Yes
    0 No
    - Not answered

         65

PERSONAL CARE SERVICES

(9) In the past six months has someone helped you with your personal care, for example helping you to bathe or dress, feeding you, or helping you with toilet care?
    1 Yes
    0 No
    - Not answered

         66

[IF "NO" SKIP TO d.; IF "YES" ASK a., b., c., AND d.]

a. Who helped you in this way?
     1 Unpaid family members or friends
     2 Someone hired to help you in this way
        or someone from an agency
     3 Both
     - Not answered

_____
67

b. On the average, how much time per day has this
   person helped you to bathe, dress, eat, go to the
   toilet, etc.?
     1 Less than ½ hour per day
     2 ½ to 1½ hours per day
     3 More than 1½ hours per day
     - Not answered

_____
68

c. Are you still being helped in this way?
     1 Yes
     0 No
     - Not answered

_____
69

d. Do you feel you need help with bathing, dressing,
   eating, or going to the toilet, etc.?
     1 Yes
     0 No
     - Not answered

_____
70

NURSING CARE
(10) During the past six months have you had any nursing care,
     in other words did a nurse or someone else give you treat-
     ments or medications prescribed by a doctor? [EXCLUDE
     NURSING CARE WHILE IN THE HOSPITAL.]
     1 Yes
     0 No
     - Not answered

_____
71

[IF "NO" SKIP TO e.; IF "YES" ASK a., b., c., d., AND e.]

a. Who helped you in this way?
     1 Unpaid family members or friends
     2 Someone hired to help you in this way
        or someone from an agency
     3 Both
     - Not answered

_____
72

b. On the average, how many hours a day did you receive
   this help?
     0 Only occasionally, not every day
     1 Gave oral medicine only
     2 Less than ½ hour per day
     3 ½ to 1 hour per day
     4 More than 1 hour per day
     - Not answered

_____
73

S#
1-4

c. For how long did you have this help within the past six months?
    1 Less than one month
    2 1-3 months
    3 More than 3 months
    - Not answered

Card#   05
5-6

_____
7

d. Are you still receiving nursing care?
    1 Yes
    0 No
    - Not answered

_____
8

e. Do you feel you need nursing care?
    1 Yes
    0 No
    - Not answered

_____
9

PHYSICAL THERAPY
(13) During the past six months have you received physical therapy?
    1 Yes
    0 No
    - Not answered

_____
10

[IF "NO" SKIP TO d.; IF "YES" ASK a., b., c., AND d.]

a. Who gave you physical therapy or helped you with it?
    1 Unpaid family members or friends
    2 Someone hired to provide this or someone from an agency
    3 Both
    - Not answered

_____
11

b. On the average how many times a week did someone help you with your physical therapy activities?
    1 Less than once a week
    2 Once a week
    3 2 or more times a week
    - Not answered

_____
12

c. Are you still receiving physical therapy?
    1 Yes
    0 No
    - Not answered

_____
13

d. Do you think you need physical therapy?
    1 Yes
    0 No
    - Not answered

_____
14

CONTINUOUS SUPERVISION

CARD 5

(14) During the past six months was there any period when someone had to be with you all the time to look after you?
   1 Yes
   0 No
   - Not answered

_____
15

[IF "NO" SKIP TO c.; IF "YES" ASK a., b., AND c.]

   a. Who looked after you?
      1 Unpaid family members or friends
      2 Someone hired to look after you or someone from an agency
      3 Both
      - Not answered

_____
16

   b. Do you still have to have someone with you all the time to look after you?
      1 Yes
      0 No
      - Not answered

_____
17

   c. Do you feel you need to have someone with you all the time to look after you?
      1 Yes
      0 No
      - Not answered

_____
18

CHECKING SERVICES

Inst.: Ask only (15)c.

(15) [IF S IS STILL RECEIVING CONTINUOUS SUPERVISIONS, ASK ONLY c.]

[PERSONS WHO NEED CHECKING WHO ARE LIVING IN INSTITUTIONS OR WITH FAMILY MEMBERS MAY BE PRESUMED TO BE RECEIVING IT.]

During the past six months have you had someone regularly (at least five times a week) check on you by phone or in person to make sure you were all right?
   1 Yes
   0 No
   - Not answered

_____
19

[IF "NO" SKIP TO c.; IF "YES" ASK a., b., AND c.]

   a. Who checked on you?
      1 Unpaid family members or friends
      2 Someone from an agency, a volunteer, or someone hired to help you
      3 Both
      - Not answered

_____
20

b. Is someone still checking on you at least five times a week?
1 Yes
0 No
- Not answered

21

c. Do you feel you need to have someone check on you regularly (at least five times a week) by phone or in person to make sure you are all right? [CIRCLE "NO", IF S FELT HE NEEDED CONTINUOUS SUPERVISION, (14c.)].
1 Yes
0 No
- Not answered

22

RELOCATION AND PLACEMENT SERVICES
(16) In the past six months have you had any help in finding a new place to live, or in making arrangements to move in? [THIS INCLUDES PLACEMENT IN INSTITUTIONS.]
1 Yes
0 No
- Not answered

23

[IF "NO" SKIP TO b.; IF "YES" ASK a. AND b.]

a. Who helped you with this?
1 Unpaid family members or friends
2 Other, such as someone from an agency
3 Both
- Not answered

24

b. Do you feel you need help in finding a (another) place to live?
1 Yes
0 No
- Not answered

25

HOMEMAKER-HOUSEHOLD SERVICES

Inst.: Ask only (17)d.

(17) During the past six months did someone have to help you regularly with routine household chores such as cleaning, washing clothes, etc.? That is did your wife/husband or someone else have to do them because you were unable to?
1 Yes
0 No
- Not answered

26

[IF "NO" SKIP TO d.; IF "YES" ASK a., b., c., AND d.]

RD 5

a. Who helped with household chores?
    1 Unpaid family members or friends
    2 Other, such as a paid helper or agency person
    3 Both
    - Not answered

27 _____

b. For about how many hours a week did you have to
    have help with household chores?
    1 Less than 4 hours a week
    2 4-8 hours a week (a half-day to a day)
    3 9 or more hours a week (more than one day a week)
    - Not answered

28 _____

c. Are you still getting this kind of help?
    1 Yes
    0 No
    - Not answered

29 _____

d. Do you feel you need help with routine housework?
    1 Yes
    0 No
    - Not answered

30 _____

MEAL PREPARATION

Inst.: Ask only (18)c.

(18) During the past six months did someone regularly have to
      prepare meals for you? That is did your wife/husband or
      someone else regularly cook because you were unable to,
      or did you have to go out for meals?
      1 Yes
      0 No
      - Not answered

31 _____

[IF "NO" SKIP TO c.; IF "YES" ASK a., b., AND c.]

a. Who prepared meals for you?
    1 Unpaid family members or friends
    2 Other, such as a paid helper or agency person
    3 Both
    - Not answered

32 _____

b. Is someone still having to prepare meals for you?
    1 Yes
    0 No
    - Not answered

33 _____

c. Do you feel that you need to have someone regularly
    prepare meals for you because you can't do it yourself?
    1 Yes
    0 No
    - Not answered

34 _____

ADMINISTRATIVE, LEGAL, AND PROTECTIVE SERVICES

(19) During the past six months has anyone helped you with any legal matters or with managing your personal business affairs or handling your money, for example paying your bills for you?

    1 Yes
    0 No
    - Not answered

_____
35

[IF "NO" SKIP TO c.; IF "YES" ASK a., b., AND c.]

    a. Who helped you?
        1 Family members or friends
        2 A lawyer, the Legal Aid Society, other agency personnel, or someone hired to help you?
        3 Both
        - Not answered

_____
36

    b. Are you still getting help with legal matters or with managing your personal business affairs?
        1 Yes
        0 No
        - Not answered

_____
37

    c. Do you think you need help with these matters?
        1 Yes
        0 No
        - Not answered

_____
38

SYSTEMATIC MULTIDIMENSIONAL EVALUATION

(20) In the past six months has anyone like a doctor or social worker thoroughly reviewed and evaluated your overall condition including your health, your mental health, and your social and financial situation?

    1 Yes
    0 No
    - Not answered

_____
39

    a. Do you think you need to have someone review and evaluate your overall condition in this way?
        1 Yes
        0 No
        - Not answered

_____
40

COORDINATION, INFORMATION AND REFERRAL SERVICES

(24) During the past six months did someone see to it that you got the kinds of help you needed? In other words did someone give you information about the kind of help that is available or put you in touch with those who could help you?

    1 Yes
    0 No
    - Not answered

_____
41

CARD 5

[IF "NO" SKIP TO c.; IF "YES" ASK a., b., AND c.]

a. Who was this person?
   1 A family member or a friend
   2 Someone from an agency
   3 Both
   - Not answered

42

b. Is there still someone who sees to it that you get the kinds of help you need? In other words is there someone who gives you information about the kind of help that is available or puts you in touch with those who can help you?
   1 Yes
   0 No
   - Not answered

43

c. Do you feel you need to have someone organize or coordinate the kinds of help you need and make arrangements for you to get them?
   1 Yes
   0 No
   - Not answered

44

72. QUESTION 71 WAS ASKED OF:
     1 Subject
     2 Informant
     3 Both

45

CONCLUDING STATEMENT TO THE SUBJECT

[MAKE A BRIEF CONCLUDING STATEMENT TO THE SUBJECT INDICATING THE CONCLUSION OF THE INTERVIEW AND EXPRESSING YOUR APPRECIATION FOR HIS COOPERATION.]

QUESTIONS TO BE ASKED OF AN INFORMANT
BASED ON HIS KNOWLEDGE OF THE SUBJECT

[IF THE SUBJECT IS UNRELIABLE THESE QUESTIONS <u>MUST</u> BE ASKED OF AN
INFORMANT.]
[IF THE SUBJECT IS RELIABLE, THE QUESTIONS MUST BE ASKED IF AN
INFORMANT IS AVAILABLE.]

CARD 5

SOCIAL RESOURCES

73. How well does _____ (Subject) get along with his/her family
and friends--very well, fairly well, or poorly (has considerable
trouble or conflict with them)?
   1 Very well
   2 Fairly well (has some conflict or trouble with them)
   3 Poorly (has considerable trouble or conflict with them)
   - Not answered

46

74. Is there someone *(Inst.: outside of this place)* who would help
          (Subject) at all if he/she were sick or disabled,
for example his/her husband or wife, a member of the family or
a friend?
   1 Yes
   0 No
   - Not answered

47

[IF "YES" ASK a. AND b.]

a. [CIRCLE THE MOST APPROPRIATE.]

Is there someone *(Inst.: outside of this place)* who would
take care of him/her as long as needed, or only for a short
time, or only someone who would help now and then (for
example, taking him/her to the doctor, fixing lunch, etc.)?
   1 Someone who would take care of Subject indefinitely
      (as long as needed)
   2 Someone who would take care of Subject a short time
      (a few weeks to six months)
   3 Someone who would help him now and then (taking him
      to the doctor or fixing lunch, etc.)
   - Not answered

48

b. Who is this person?

Name _____

Relationship _____

49

Ask only of institutionalized.

74A. How much does _____ (Subject) socialize with others in this institution--A lot, some, very little, or not at all?
    1 A lot
    2 Some
    3 Very little
    4 Not at all
    - Not answered

74B. About how many times a month does _____ (Subject) visit with someone from outside of this place, either they come for a visit, or he/she goes to visit them?
    0 Very little (less than once a month)
    1 Once or twice a month
    2 3 or 4 times a month
    3 Once or twice a week
    4 3 or more times a week
    - Not answered

74C. Is _____ (Subject) in a self-contained apartment, on a ward, or in a one, two, three, or four bed room?
    1 Self-contained apartment
    2 Ward
    3 One bed room
    4 Two bed room
    5 Three bed room
    6 Four bed room
    7 Other [SPECIFY.] _____
    - Not answered

ECONOMIC RESOURCES

75. In your opinion are _____'s (Subject's) needs for the following basic necessities being well met, barely met, or are they not being met?

[CHECK THE APPROPRIATE BOX FOR EACH NEED.]

2 WELL MET	1 BARELY MET	0 NOT MET	
			Food
			Housing
			Clothing
			Medical care
			Small luxuries

50 ___

51 ___

52 ___

53 ___

54 ___

MENTAL HEALTH

76. Does _____ (Subject) show good, common sense in making judgments and decisions?
   1 Yes
   0 No
   - Not answered

55 ___

77. Is _____ (Subject) able to handle (cope with) major problems which occur in his/her life?
   1 Yes
   0 No
   - Not answered

56 ___

78. Do you feel that _____(Subject) finds life exciting and enjoyable?
   1 Yes
   0 No
   - Not answered

57 ___

79. How would you rate _____'s (Subject's) mental or emotional health or ability to think at the present time compared to the average person living independently--excellent, good, fair, or poor?
   3 Excellent
   2 Good
   1 Fair
   0 Poor
   - Not answered

58 ___

80. Is _____ (Subject's) mental or emotional health or ability to think-- better, about the same, or worse than it was five years ago?
   3 Better
   2 About the same
   0 Worse
   - Not answered

59 ___

PHYSICAL HEALTH

81. How would you rate _____(Subject's) health at the present time--excellent, good, fair, or poor?
    3 Excellent
    2 Good
    1 Fair
    0 Poor
    - Not answered

_____
60

82. How much do _____ (Subject's) health troubles stand in the way of his/her doing the things he/she wants to do--not at all, a little (some), or a great deal?
    3 Not at all
    2 A little (some)
    0 A great deal
    - Not answered

_____
61

[THE REMAINING QUESTIONS ARE TO BE ANSWERED BY THE INTERVIEWER IMMEDIATELY AFTER LEAVING THE INTERVIEW SITE.]

83. Length of interview _____
                                        Minutes

_____
62-64

84. Factual information obtained from:
    1 Subject
    2 Relative
    3 Other [SPECIFY.] _____

_____
65

85. Factual questions (obtained from Subject and/or informant) are:
    1 Completely reliable
    2 Reliable on most items
    3 Reliable on only a few items
    4 Completely unreliable

_____
66

86. Subjective questions (those in boxes, obtained from Subject only) are:
    1 Completely reliable
    2 Reliable on most items
    3 Reliable on only a few items
    4 Completely unreliable
    5 Not obtained

_____
67

    [IF 5 ANSWER a.]

    a. Why didn't the Subject answer the Subjective questions? [BE SPECIFIC.]

    _____

_____
68-69

    _____

    _____

SOCIAL RESOURCES

CARD 5

87. Which of the following best describes the availability of help for the Subject if he(she) were sick or disabled?

[CIRCLE THE MOST APPROPRIATE.]

1 At least one person could and would take care of the Subject indefinitely (as long as needed).
2 At least one person could and would take care of the Subject for a short time (a few weeks to 6 months).
3 Help would only be available now and then for such things as taking him(her) to the doctor, fixing lunch, etc.
4 No help at all (except possible emergency help) would be available.

70

88. Which of the following best describes the Subject's social relationships?

[CIRCLE THE MOST APPROPRIATE.]

1 Very satisfactory, extensive
2 Fairly satisfactory, adequate
3 Unsatisfactory, of poor quality, few

71

ECONOMIC RESOURCES

89. In your opinion which of the following best describes the Subject's income?
1 Ample
2 Satisfactory
3 Somewhat inadequate
4 Totally inadequate
5 No income at all

72

90. In your opinion does the Subject have any financial reserves?
1 Yes, has reserves
0 No, has (little or) no reserves

73

91. In your opinion which of the following statements best describes the extent to which the Subject's needs are being met?
1 Food, housing, clothing, and medical needs are met; Subject can afford small luxuries.
2 Food, housing, clothing, and medical needs are met; Subject cannot afford small luxuries.
3 Either food, or housing, or clothing, or medical needs are unmet; Subject cannot afford small luxuries.
4 Two or more basic needs (housing, food, clothing, medical care) are unmet; Subject cannot afford small luxuries.

74

MENTAL HEALTH   CARD 5

92. Is it your impression that the Subject shows good, common
    sense in making judgments and decisions?
    1 Yes
    0 No
    - Not answered
                                                                    _____
                                                                       75

93. Is it your impression that the Subject is able to handle
    (cope with) major problems which occur in his/her life?
    1 Yes
    0 No
    - Not answered
                                                                    _____
                                                                       76

94. Is it your impression that the Subject finds life exciting
    and enjoyable?
    1 Yes
    0 No
    - Not answered
                                                                    _____
                                                                       77

                                                                    CARD 6

                                                              S# _____
                                                                     1-4

95. During the interview did the Subject's behavior strike you   Card# __06__
    as: 5-6

    [CHECK "YES" OR "NO" FOR EACH OF THE FOLLOWING.]

1	0		
YES	NO		
		Mentally alert and stimulating	_____ 7
		Pleasant and cooperative	_____ 8
		Depressed and/or tearful	_____ 9
		Withdrawn or lethargic	_____ 10
		Fearful, anxious, or extremely tense	_____ 11
		Full of unrealistic physical complaints	_____ 12
		Suspicious (more than reasonable)	_____ 13
		Bizarre or inappropriate in thought or action	_____ 14
		Excessively talkative or overly jovial, or elated	_____ 15

PHYSICAL HEALTH

96. Is the Subject either extremely overweight, or malnourished
    and emaciated?
    0 No, neither
    1 Yes, extremely overweight
    2 Yes, malnourished or emaciated
    - Not answered
                                                                    _____
                                                                       16

SOCIAL RESOURCES RATING SCALE

_____
17

97. [RATE THE CURRENT SOCIAL RESOURCES OF THE PERSON BEING
     EVALUATED ALONG THE SIX-POINT SCALE PRESENTED BELOW.
     CIRCLE THE <u>ONE</u> NUMBER WHICH BEST DESCRIBES THE PERSON'S
     PRESENT CIRCUMSTANCES. SOCIAL RESOURCES QUESTIONS ARE
     NUMBERS 6-14, 73, 74, *74A*, *74B*, *74C*, 87 AND 88.

   1. <u>Excellent social resources</u>.
       Social relationships are very satisfying and extensive;
       at least one person would take care of him(her)
       indefinitely.

   2. <u>Good social resources</u>.
       Social relationships are fairly satisfying and
       adequate and at least one person would take care
       of him(her) indefinitely.
       OR
       Social relationships are very satisfying and extensive;
       and only short term help is available.

   3. <u>Mildly socially impaired</u>.
       Social relationships are unsatisfactory, of poor quality,
       few; but at least one person would take care of him(her)
       indefinitely.
       OR
       Social relationships are fairly satisfactory, adequate;
       and only short term help is available.

   4. <u>Moderately socially impaired</u>.
       Social relationships are unsatisfactory, of poor quality,
       few; and only short term care is available.
       OR
       Social relationships are at least adequate or satisfactory;
       but help would only be available now and then.

   5. <u>Severely socially impaired</u>.
       Social relationships are unsatisfactory, of poor quality,
       few; and help would only be available now and then.
       OR
       Social relationships are at least satisfactory or adequate;
       but help is not even available now and then.

   6. <u>Totally socially impaired</u>.
       Social relationships are unsatisfactory, of poor quality,
       few; and help is not even available now and then.

ECONOMIC RESOURCES RATING SCALE   CARD 6

98. [RATE THE CURRENT ECONOMIC RESOURCES OF THE PERSON BEING EVALUATED
     ALONG THE SIX-POINT SCALE PRESENTED BELOW. CIRCLE THE ONE NUMBER
     WHICH BEST DESCRIBES THE PERSON'S PRESENT CIRCUMSTANCES. ECONOMIC
     QUESTIONS ARE NUMBERS 15-30, 75, AND 89-91.]

     1. Economic Resources are excellent.   18
         Income is ample; Subject has reserves.

     2. Economic Resources are satisfactory.
         Income is ample; Subject has no reserves
         or
         Income is adequate; Subject has reserves.

     3. Economic Resources are mildly impaired.
         Income is adequate; Subject has no reserves
         or
         Income is somewhat inadequate; Subject has reserves.

     4. Economic Resources are moderately impaired.
         Income is somewhat inadequate; Subject has no reserves.

     5. Economic Resources are severely impaired.
         Income is totally inadequate; Subject may or may not
         have reserves.

     6. Economic Resources are completely impaired.
         Subject is destitute, completely without income or reserves.

     [INCOME IS CONSIDERED TO BE ADEQUATE IF ALL THE SUBJECT'S
     NEEDS ARE BEING MET.]

MENTAL HEALTH RATING SCALE

99. [RATE THE CURRENT MENTAL FUNCTIONING OF THE PERSON BEING EVALUATED ALONG THE SIX-POINT SCALE PRESENTED BELOW. CIRCLE THE ONE NUMBER WHICH BEST DESCRIBES THE PERSON'S PRESENT FUNCTIONING. MENTAL HEALTH QUESTIONS ARE THE PRELIMINARY QUESTIONNAIRE, AND NUMBERS 31-36, 76-80, AND 92-95.]

1. Outstanding mental health.
   Intellectually alert and clearly enjoying life. Manages routine and major problems in his life with ease and is free from any psychiatric symptoms.

2. Good mental health.
   Handles both routine and major problems in his life satisfactorily and is intellectually intact and free of psychiatric symptoms.

3. Mildly mentally impaired.
   Has mild psychiatric symptoms and/or mild intellectual impairment. Continues to handle routine, though not major, problems in his life satisfactorily.

4. Moderately mentally impaired.
   Has definite psychiatric symptoms, and/or moderate intellectual impairment. Able to make routine, common-sense decisions, but unable to handle major problems in his life.

5. Severely mentally impaired.
   Has severe psychiatric symptoms and/or severe intellectual impairment, which interfere with routine judgments and decision making in every day life.

6. Completely mentally impaired.
   Grossly psychotic or completely impaired intellectually. Requires either intermittent or constant supervision because of clearly abnormal or potentially harmful behavior.

PHYSICAL HEALTH RATING SCALE

100. [RATE THE CURRENT PHYSICAL FUNCTIONING OF THE PERSON BEING
EVALUATED ALONG THE SIX-POINT SCALE PRESENTED BELOW. CIRCLE
THE ONE NUMBER WHICH BEST DESCRIBES THE PERSON'S PRESENT
FUNCTIONING. PHYSICAL HEALTH QUESTIONS ARE NUMBERS 37-55,
81, 82 AND 96.]

20

1. In excellent physical health.
   Engages in vigorous physical activity, either regularly or
   at least from time to time.

2. In good physical health.
   No significant illnesses or disabilities. Only routine
   medical care such as annual check ups required.

3. Mildly physically impaired.
   Has only minor illnesses and/or disabilities which might
   benefit from medical treatment or corrective measures.

4. Moderately physically impaired.
   Has one or more diseases or disabilities which are either
   painful or which require substantial medical treatment.

5. Severely physically impaired.
   Has one or more illnesses or disabilities which are either
   severely painful or life threatening, or which require
   extensive medical treatment.

6. Totally physically impaired.
   Confined to bed and requiring full time medical assistance
   or nursing care to maintain vital bodily functions.

PERFORMANCE RATING SCALE FOR
ACTIVITIES OF DAILY LIVING

CARD 6   101.   [RATE THE CURRENT PERFORMANCE OF THE PERSON BEING EVALUATED
ON THE SIX-POINT SCALE PRESENTED BELOW. CIRCLE THE ONE NUMBER
WHICH BEST DESCRIBES THE PERSON'S PRESENT PERFORMANCE. ACTIVI-
TIES OF DAILY LIVING QUESTIONS ARE NUMBERS 56-69.]

21

1. Excellent ADL capacity.
Can perform all of the Activities of Daily Living without
assistance and with ease.

2. Good ADL capacity.
Can perform all of the Activities of Daily Living without
assistance.

3. Mildly impaired ADL capacity.
Can perform all but one to three of the Activities of Daily
Living. Some help is required with one to three, but not
necessarily every day. Can get through any single day
without help. Is able to prepare his/her own meals.

4. Moderately impaired ADL capacity.
Regularly requires assistance with at least four Activities
of Daily Living but is able to get through any single day
without help. Or regularly requires help with meal
preparation.

5. Severely impaired ADL capacity.
Needs help each day but not necessarily throughout the day
or night with many of the Activities of Daily Living.

6. Completely impaired ADL capacity.
Needs help throughout the day and/or night to carry out
the Activities of Daily Living.

* *

Summary of Ratings

Social Resources   _____

Economic Resources   _____

Mental Health   _____

Physical Health   _____

Activities of Daily Living   _____

Cumulative Impairment Score   _____
22-23   (Sum of the five ratings)

OARS MULTIDIMENSIONAL FUNCTIONAL ASSESSMENT QUESTIONNAIRE

SERVICES SUPPLEMENT

MEDICAL SERVICES

(11) Have you received a medical examination or medical treatment for physical health problems from a physician, physician's assistant, or nurse in the past six months, that is since _____ (specify month)?
  1 Yes
  0 No
  − Not answered

  a. How often in the past six months did you receive this care?

      _____ Times

  b. Are you still receiving medical care?
      1 Yes
      0 No
      − Not answered

  c. Do you feel that you need medical care or treatment beyond what you are presently receiving?
      1 Yes
      0 No
      − Not answered

SUPPORTIVE DEVICES AND PROSTHESES

(12) Do you use any of the following aids all or most of the time? (CHECK "YES" OR "NO" FOR EACH AID).

YES	NO	
		Cane (including tripod-tip cane)
		Walker
		Wheelchair
		Leg brace
		Back brace
		Artificial limb
		Hearing Aid
		Colostomy equipment
		Catheter
		Kidney dialysis machine
		Other (SPECIFY.) _____

a. Do you need any aids (supportive or prosthetic devices) that you currently do not have?

    1 Yes
    0 No
    – Not answered

(IF "YES", ASK b.)

b. What aids do you need? (SPECIFY)

_____

_____

_____

FINANCIAL ASSISTANCE

(21) What is your total monthly income from all sources (e.g., work, rents, interest, social security, SSI, pensions, VA, disability, support payments, etc.)

(SHOW INCOME LADDER AND CIRCLE THE LETTER WHICH
IDENTIFIES EITHER YEARLY OR MONTHLY INCOME CATEGORY.)

	YEARLY	MONTHLY
A.	0 – $499	(0 – $41)
B.	$500 – $999	($42 – $83)
C.	$1,000 – $1,999	($84 – $166)
D.	$2,000 – $2,999	($167 – $249)
E.	$3,000 – $3,999	($250 – $333)
F.	$4,000 – $4,999	($334 – $416)
G.	$5,000 – $6,999	($417 – $583)
H.	$7,000 – $9,999	($584 – $833)
I.	$10,000 – $14,999	($834 – $1249)
J.	$15,000 – $19,000	($1250 – $1666)
K.	$20,000 – $29,000	($1667 – $2499)
L.	$30,000 – $39,000	($2500 – $3333)
M.	$40,000 or more	($3334 or more)

How many people altogether live on this income (that is it provides at least half of their income)? _____

b. Are you presently getting:

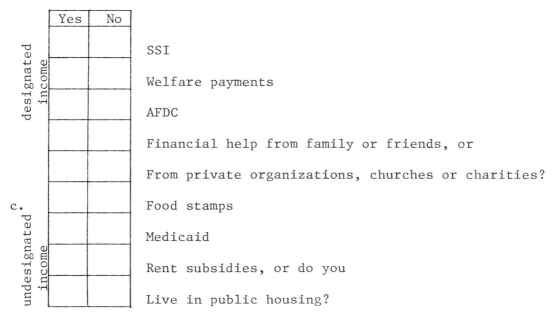

	Yes	No	
designated income			SSI
			Welfare payments
			AFDC
			Financial help from family or friends, or
			From private organizations, churches or charities?
c. undesignated income			Food stamps
			Medicaid
			Rent subsidies, or do you
			Live in public housing?

d. Is your financial situation such that you feel you need financial assistance or help beyond what you are already getting?
    1 Yes
    0 No
    - Not answered

FOOD, GROCERIES

(22) Do you pay for your own food or do you get any regular help at all with costs of food or meals?
    1 Subject pays for food himself
    2 Subject gets help
    - Not answered

    (IF 2 ASK a.)

    a. From where?
        (CHECK "YES" OR "NO" FOR EACH OF THE FOLLOWING.)

YES	NO	
		Family or friends
		Food stamps
		Prepared food (meals) from an agency or organization program (SPECIFY NUMBER OF MEALS PER WEEK) _____

LIVING QUARTERS

(23) Do you have a decent place in which to live?
    1 Yes
    0 No
    - Not answered

APPENDIX B

LIST OF GENERIC SERVICES: DESCRIPTIONS AND DEFINITIONS*

APRIL, 1975

LIST OF SERVICES

1. Transportation
2. Social/Recreational Services
3. Employment Services
4. Sheltered Employment
5. Educational Services, Employment Related
6. Remedial Training
7. Mental Health Services
8. Psychotropic Drugs
9. Personal Care Services
10. Nursing Care
11. Medical Services
12. Supportive Devices and Prostheses
13. Physical Therapy
14. Continuous Supervision
15. Checking Services
16. Relocation and Placement Services
17. Homemaker-Household Services
18. Meal Preparation
19. Administrative, Legal, and Protective Services
20. Systematic Multidimensional Evaluation
21. Financial Assistance
22. Food, Groceries
23. Living Quarters (Housing)
24. Coordination, Information, and Referral Services

* Developed by the Staff of the OARS Program, Duke University
Center for the Study of Aging and Human Development.

EXPLANATORY NOTES REGARDING SERVICE CATEGORIZATION

A. *Basic Maintenance Services* are those services required by all persons, healthy or impaired. They include the need for food stuffs (i.e., groceries), living quarters, and transportation. It is never a question of whether these services are to be provided but, rather, a question of who is to provide them. Healthy individuals residing in their own homes provide these services for themselves. However, individuals who have multiple impairments and who have become institutionalized must have these basic maintenance services become part of the total service packages which must be provided for them.

B. *Supportive Services* are those services which are provided to impaired individuals which in themselves do not improve the basic functional capacity of the individual but which serve to maintain functioning. In this category are personal care services, homemaker-household services, checking or continuous supervision, meal preparation, and administrative, legal, and protective services.

C. *Remedial or Rehabilitative Services* are those services which can, or are designed to, improve the basic functional capacity of an impaired individual. This category includes all the remaining services. The criterion which has been used for labelling a service as *remedial* requires that the service have a probability of improving the functional rating of an individual on one of the five dimensions.

CATEGORIES OF SERVICES

A. Basic Maintenance Services

1. Transportation
22. Food, Groceries
23. Living Quarters (Housing)

B. Supportive Services

9. Personal Care Services
14. Continuous Supervision
15. Checking Services
18. Meal Preparation
17. Homemaker-Household Services
19. Administrative, Legal, and Protective Services

C. Remedial Services

2. Social/Recreational Services
3. Employment Services
4. Sheltered Employment
5. Educational Services, Employment Related
6. Remedial Training
7. Mental Health Services
8. Psychotropic Drugs
10. Nursing Care
11. Medical Services
12. Supportive Devices and Prostheses
13. Physical Therapy
16. Relocation and Placement Services
20. Systematic Multidimensional Evaluation
21. Financial Assistance
24. Coordination, Information, and Referral Services

DEFINITIONS OF GENERIC SERVICES

1. TRANSPORTATION

Purpose: To provide access (outside of walking distance) to the community, e.g., to service providers, businesses, friends, leisure activities, and special events.

Activity: Transporting an individual from one place to another.

Unit of Measure: Passenger round trips.

2. SOCIAL/RECREATIONAL SERVICES

Purpose: To increase the quality and quantity of an individual's social interactions; to foster skills in making creative use of nonwork time, including artistic and intellectual development.

Activity: Social interaction and planned and organized activities (for either individuals or groups) to provide creative expression; physical, mental, and intellectual development; or community involvement.

Relevant Personnel: Social worker, activity therapist, volunteer coordinator, social club personnel, recreation worker, occupational therapist, educational personnel, crafts teacher.

Unit of Measure: Sessions.

Examples: Social clubs, recreation groups, church groups, hobby groups, special interest groups, volunteer projects, friendly visitors, adult education classes, craft courses, speed reading, painting, crafts, hobbies.

3. EMPLOYMENT SERVICES

Purpose: To provide assistance in finding employment.

Activity: Aiding an individual in finding employment by counseling and/or by referring the job applicant to businesses and agencies seeking employees.

Relevant Personnel: Employment counselor, social worker, guidance counselor, family member.

Unit of Measure: Number of times such assistance was provided.

4. SHELTERED EMPLOYMENT

Purpose: To provide employment for people who, because of physical or mental impairment, cannot find a job in the competitive labor market.

Activity: Providing the setting, supervision, materials and/or equipment necessary to allow handicapped or impaired people to work.

Relevant Personnel: Workshop supervisor, rehabilitation counselor, special education personnel.

Unit of Measure: Hours of employment.

Examples: Goodwill Industries, Industries for the Blind.

5. EDUCATIONAL SERVICES, EMPLOYMENT RELATED

Purpose: To develop or improve occupational skills in order to make the individual more readily employable.

Activity: Formal courses or instruction planned to develop occupational skills in either a preparatory or a remedial manner.

Relevant Personnel: Teacher, instructor, or training supervisors in educational, business, or industrial settings.

Unit of Measure: Training session hours.

Examples: Shorthand and typing courses in preparation for a secretarial career, professional schools (e.g., dental and law), beautician's college, training courses for older services workers, on the job training, apprenticeship programs.

6. REMEDIAL TRAINING
(This does *not* include physical therapy.)

Purpose: To improve the capabilities of an individual who is unable to perform some basic personal or instrumental functions because of trauma, illness, deprivation, or other impairment.

Activity: An organized course of instruction or training, including the development of personal skills necessary for self-maintenance or for further learning.

Relevant Personnel: Speech therapist, specialized educational personnel, attendant, family member.

Unit of Measure: Sessions.

Examples: Speech therapy, remedial reading or literacy course, reality orientation, training in self-care for the mentally or physically impaired, training for the blind.

7. MENTAL HEALTH SERVICES

Purpose: To identify and evaluate mental impairments which relate to both intra and interpersonal relationships, including individual, marital, familial, and environmentally related problems; to provide counseling and/or therapy in order to aid the individual to resolve these problems or to cope with them.

Activity: Mental health evaluation, diagnosis, and treatment.

Relevant Personnel: Psychiatrist, social worker, psychologist, nurse; educational, rehabilitation, and pastoral counselors.

Unit of Measure: Sessions.

Examples: Psychotherapy (individual or group), counseling, crisis intervention, evaluation of need for psychiatric hospitalization.

8. PSYCHOTROPIC DRUGS

Purpose: To improve the mood and/or psychological function of an individual who is symptomatic, manifesting either anxiety, depression, and thought disturbances or physical symptoms with psychological overlay.

Activity: Evaluation of need for psychotropic drugs; prescribing and/or dispensing of psychotropic drugs.

Relevant Personnel: Any physician.

Examples: Valium, Librium, Thorazine, Mellaril, Stelazine, Elavil, Triavil, Tofranil, Miltown, Equanil, Haldol.

9. PERSONAL CARE SERVICES

Purpose: To aid an individual in performing the personal physical activities of daily living.

Activity: Aiding an individual with bathing, dressing, grooming, feeding, and toilet care.

Relevant Personnel: L.P.N., attendant, volunteer, family member.

Unit of Measure: Contact hours.

10. NURSING CARE

Purpose: To coordinate, implement, and monitor the plan of care prescribed by a health care professional.

Activity: Administration and/or monitoring of prescribed medication or treatment regimens; health counseling; communication with primary clinician and other health team personnel.

Relevant Personnel: R.N., L.P.N., attendant, family member.

Unit of Measure: Contact hours.

Examples: Administration of oral medications, intramuscular or intravenous therapy, catheter care, dressings, taking blood pressure.

11. MEDICAL SERVICES

Purpose: To maintain and/or improve an individual's physical therapy.

Activity: Medical history taking and performance of physical examinations; evaluation, treatment, and monitoring of acute and chronic illnesses.

Relevant Personnel: Physician, physician's assistant, nurse practitioner.

Unit of Measure: Number of visits
                   Drugs: Dollars
                   Procedures: Dollars

Examples: Annual physical health checkups, prescribing medical treatment or regimen, surgical procedures, radiation therapy, special diagnostic procedures--e.g., gastrointestinal series, lumbar puncture.

12. SUPPORTIVE DEVICES AND PROSTHESES

Purpose: To compensate for physical disability that interferes with an individual's independent functioning, or to correct physical deformity cosmetically.

Activity: To supply and/or fit the appropriate device.

Relevant Personnel: Orthopedist, prosthetist, brace fitter, corsetiere (breast prostheses), othe. personnel involved in the creating and fitting of devices.

Unit of Measure: Dollars.

Examples: Walker, wheelchair, leg brace, artificial limb, hearing aid, kidney dialysis machine, facial prostheses.

13. PHYSICAL THERAPY

Purpose: To assist an individual in achieving partial or total use of some portion of the body which is not functioning normally.

Activity: A planned set of physical exercises and/or massages and treatments.

Relevant Personnel: Physical therapist, individual (either professional or nonprofessional) who has been trained to administer and follow a set of prescribed exercises--e.g., attendant, nurse, family member.

Unit of Measure: Sessions.

14. CONTINUOUS SUPERVISION

Purpose: To supervise an individual who cannot be left alone.

Activity: Monitoring an individual's activities to assure safety and well-being and to be available to respond readily to immediate needs and emergency situations.

Relevant Personnel: Family member, institutional personnel, paid companion, attendant.

Examples: Constantly supervising a person with severe memory loss and confusion either in that person's own home or in an institution.

15. CHECKING SERVICES

Purpose: To monitor an individual periodically to make sure he or she has not become ill and unable to get help.

Activity: Establishing regular telephone or personal contact (at least five times per week) with an individual.

Relevant Personnel: Agency worker, institutional personnel, family member.

Examples: Agency or volunteer program which maintains lists of subscribers who are contacted regularly; family or friends either who live with the individual or who regularly check on him or her; service provider who sees the individual at least five times/week.

16. RELOCATION AND PLACEMENT SERVICES

Purpose: To help an individual locate and secure a new place to live.

Activity: Locating available and suitable places to live and assisting in contracting for a new place to live, including institutional placements.

Relevant Personnel: Social worker, case worker, housing authority personnel, family member.

Unit of Measure: Moves.

17. HOMEMAKER-HOUSEHOLD SERVICES

Purpose: To aid regularly in the performance of necessary homemaker and household activities.

Activity: General household work, including cleaning, laundry, shopping for food and clothing, and basic home maintenance.
(NOTE: This does *not* include such things for which one would ordinarily hire a specialist--e.g., a plumber, house painter, or gardener.)

Relevant Personnel: Homemaker, housekeeper, attendant, family member.

Unit of Measure: Hours.

18. MEAL PREPARATION

Purpose: To prepare meals regularly for an individual.

Activity: Meal planning, food preparation, and cooking.

Relevant Personnel: Cook, homemaker, family member.

Unit of Measure: Meals.

19. ADMINISTRATIVE, LEGAL, AND PROTECTIVE SERVICES

Purpose: To aid and assist an individual in dealing with administrative affairs.

Activity: Acting as an intermediary, advisor, or guardian for the individual in dealings with agencies, businesses, landlords, etc.; aiding with business affairs--e.g., paying bills.

Relevant Personnel: Lawyer, social worker, guardian, institutional personnel, consumer advocate, family member.

Unit of Measure: Hours.

20. SYSTEMATIC MULTIDIMENSIONAL EVALUATION

Purpose: To evaluate systematically an individual's overall condition.

Activity: The systematic evaluation of an individual's overall functional state, including physical and mental health, social and economic resources, and capacity for self-care.

Relevant Personnel: A multidisciplinary team or group; individuals specially trained in multidimensional assessment, such as a specially trained social worker, nurse, psychiatrist, or family practitioner.

Unit of Measure: Number of hours spent in evaluation.

Examples: Evaluation of a person by a multiservice center; complete medical, psychiatric, and social workup of a new patient in a group medical practice.

21. FINANCIAL ASSISTANCE

Purpose: To insure an individual has sufficient income to maintain an adequate standard of living.

Classes of Financial Assistance:

   a) UNDESIGNATED: Money provided to be used entirely at the discretion of the individual.

       Unit of Measure: Dollars.

       Examples: SSI (Supplemental Security Income), Welfare payments, Aid for Dependent Children, financial assistance from family members, financial aid from private organizations or churches, charity.

b) DESIGNATED: Money or subsidies provided for specific uses.

  Unit of Measure: Dollars or dollar equivalent of designated aid.

  Examples: Food stamps, Medicaid, public housing, rent subsidies.

22. FOOD, GROCERIES

Purpose: To provide the raw materials for meal preparation.

Materials: Groceries, such as canned goods, produce, meat, and dairy products.

Unit of Measure: Dollars.

Examples: Groceries purchased by an individual for personal use; food provided for an individual by family--e.g., weekly groceries given to an aged person by his or her adult children; food provided by an institution for one of it's residents--e.g., the food a patient eats while in a hospital.

23. LIVING QUARTERS (HOUSING)

Purpose: To provide a habitable place to live.

Materials: Room, bed, other furnishings, toilet.

Unit of Measure: Dollars.

Examples: Room, appartment, or other living quarters provided by an individual for personal use; room, etc. provided for an individual by family-- e.g., an aged person living with married daughter and her family in their home; room, etc. provided by an institution for a resident-- e.g., room in a rehabilitation center, nursing home, hospital, etc.

24. COORDINATION, INFORMATION, AND REFERRAL SERVICES

Purpose: To insure that an individual receives an integrated set of services appropriate to his or her situation.

Activity: Designing an appropriate service program, providing information about available sources of help, making referrals to other agencies or professionals, including aiding with appointments, coordinating, implementing, and monitoring the entire treatment program.

Relevant Personnel: Social worker, health professional, allied health personnel, family member.

Unit of Measure: Hours.

APPENDIX C

Preliminary Listing of OARS Users and the Purposes for Which They Have Used the Instrument

Name, Address, and Telephone Number | Purpose

S. Ray Beckler
Community Life Program
P.O. Box 189
Elizabeth City, North Carolina
(919) 338-3935

We used the OARS questionnaire as an assessment of needs of the elderly. We attempted, as needs were found, to try to resolve them. The assessment became a route to service for the elderly by the Community Life Program.

* *

Lowell A. Borgen, Ph.D.
Warner Lambert/Parke Davis
   Pharmaceutical Laboratories
2800 Plymouth Road
Ann Arbor, Michigan   48105
(313) 994-3500 x277

We may use the OARS questionnaire as a screening instrument in geriatric trials of investigational antisenility drugs.

* *

William C. Byrd
P.O. Box 2931
University Station
Greenville, North Carolina   27834
(919) 757-6961 x237

To illustrate need for multidimensional assessment and interdisciplinary development of a service package.

* *

Scott Cassady
Office of Evaluation
Department of Health and Rehabilitative
   Services
1323 Winewood Boulevard
Tallahassee, Florida   32301
(904) 488-8722

I am conducting an evaluation research project on different approaches to supporting frail aging persons in the community. The MFAQ has been administered to a sample of clients in seven different programs across the state and will be readministered to these respondents after one year. The MFAQ has two basic functions in this study: (1) to enable us to control for level of client impairment when comparing performance data of the various programs; (2) to show comparative rates of change (if any) between the two administrations.

Name, Address, and Telephone Number	Purpose
Janet B. Chermak P.O. Box 31128 Crabtree Valley Station Raleigh, North Carolina 27604 (919) 782-8736	Informational. I was interested in different assessment systems and the MFAQ was looked at together with other systems.

* *

Michael A. Cilley Adult Day Health Center 220 Kennedy Memorial Drive Waterville, Maine 04901 (207) 873-0146	Our use of the MFAQ will be three-fold: (1) it will be a primary assessment tool for determining eliqibility for admission, (2) it will be used by the multidisciplinary team in formulating treatment regime, (3) it will be used for gauging progression or regression in the different dimensions on a six-month basis.

* *

Elizabeth Clagett Director of Social Services Central Montana Hospital Lewistown, Montana 59457	Used among nursing home patients to examine the effect of a program intended to encourage greater participation among nursing home residents.

* *

Sarah N. Cohen, CSW GAPS Project Director Social Work Department Lenox Hill Hospital 100 East 77th Street New York, New York 10021	The OARS questionnaire will be used to help the hospital social worker complete discharge plans for elderly, disabled, and socially isolated patients, facilitating the transition from hospital to home or other setting.

* *

Dr. Benjamin Danis Benjamin Rose Institute Cleveland, Ohio (216) 621-7201	Three hundred community resident clients are being examined, and these data will be compared with data obtained by the GAO from a random sample of Cleveland elderly. The findings will be used in a number of ways: (1) comparison with GAO data to determine what sample of elderly is being served; (2) assessment of whether needs are being met; (3) development of

Name, Address, and Telephone Number	Purpose
Dr. Benjamin Danis (continued)	innovative services; (4) internal reserarch purposes, in combination with other information on these clients. A survey of institutionalized residents is also being planned.

* *

Therese Diaz, ACSW, Project Manager Geriatric Clinical Evaluator Project Institute for the Study of Aging 1217A Dickinson Drive (Building 49A) P.O. Box 248106, University of Miami Coral Gables, Florida 33124 (305) 284-4011	"A New Specialist, the Geriatric Clinical Evaluator" is a two-year pilot training and demonstration program funded through an AoA grant to the Institute for the Study of Aging of the University of Miami in collaboration with the Miami Jewish Home and Hospital for the Aged. The Geriatric Clinical Evaluator is a person who can function maximally in a multiservice delivery system. Through didactic and field experiences, the Geriatric Clinical Evaluator will gain expertise in physical, psychological, social, and economic evaluation and become familiar with community resources, thus becoming the entry point of a multiservice geriatric team. Currently enrolled in the seven-module, one-hundred-hour program are thirty agency-based social workers and nurses who have committed themselves to a weekly block of time. Upon completion, a certificate in Geriatric Clinical Evaluation will be offered by the Project.

* *

G. J. Endres, M.A. Consultant, Metro Services 10333 Seminole Boulevard (Apartment #5) Largo, Florida 33540 (813) 391-4712	Interested in using OARS assessment in developing congregate housing and nonsheltered services to prevent unnecessary institutionalization.

Name, Address, and Telephone Number	Purpose
Michael Errecart Macro Systems 1110 Fidler Lane Silver Spring, Maryland 20910 (301) 652-5121 or 588-5484	A modified version was used in a test of its suitability as a tool for HEW policy making.

* *

Michele J. Foley Adult Foster Care Program Catholic Social Services 50 South Detroit Street Xenia, Ohio 45385	The OARS questionnaire is used in client assessment.

* *

Janice Friedman, BSW Hahnemann Medical College and Hospital 230 N. Broad Street, NCB 17802 Philadelphia, Pennsylvania 19102 (215) 448-8342	Screening device for five-year study on independent living senior citizens. How certain behaviorial, cultural, and service variables affect living independently.

* *

Michael A. Garrick Data Collection Supervisor Community Based Care Project Department of Social and Health Services Office of Research Annex PF-11 Olympia, Washington 98504	The Community Based Care Project is a large federally funded three-year research and demonstration project now entering its final year. The purpose of the project is to establish a multidisciplinary team, in each of two demonstration sites, that serves as a centralized screening, assessment, and referral unit for functionally disabled adults "at risk" of institutionalization. Eligibility for participation is determined by Title XIX or Title XX eligibility standards. The major goal of the project is to prevent premature institutionalization by assessing client needs (using the OARS instrument) and to develop an appropriate mix of community services that could maintain the client in the community. The team then acts to facilitate the delivery of these services to the client.

Name, Addresses, and Telephone Number	Purpose

Michael A. Garrick (continued)

The research component of the project is mandated to collect the data required to evaluate the project's success in achieving its goals. Pursuant to this task, research has compiled a large unique data base with potential for secondary analysis directed at related issues. The research design is a separate-sample, multiple-time series design employing data collected from a control community as well as from the two demonstration communities.

Baseline samples were selected from population registers maintained by the state, and data were collected for the six-month period prior to the beginning of the demonstration program. Three additional samples (T_1, T_2, and T_3) were selected during each of the three succeeding six-month intervals. OARS data were collected on the T_1 and T_2 samples. For all persons who were successfully interviewed (response rates varied from 35 percent to 70 percent), data on community services received were collected directly from the agencies providing the service.

In addition to these data, data available from existing state and federal information systems were collected on *all* members of these samples. The research data base contains complete information on cost and units of service provided through Title XIX. Also, data on S.S.I. payments, Food Stamps, and miscellaneous state-funded assistance programs have been collected on all sample members. Using these data, we hope to be able to estimate the total cost of maintaining individuals in community versus institutional settings and

Name, Address, and Telephone Number	Purpose

Michael A. Garrick (continued)

relate these costs to various levels of impairment as measured by the OARS instrument.

* *

John A. Goga
Hospital Improvement Program
Woodville State Hospital
Carnegie, Pennsylvania 15106
(412) 279-2000 x492

Over 3600 patients were administered the OARS MFAQ over a period of several months. The finding indicated that it could differentiate fairly well between geriatric units--e.g., long-term care vs. intermediate-care facilities. Furthermore, the MFAQ has been helpful in assessing significant patient needs and has been administered in a pre-post test fashion following treatment.

The MFAQ is also administered as part of standard procedure upon admission to one of the geriatric units. This information not only provides immediate feedback as to the patient's current level of functioning (on any or all of the five dimensions), but also indicates the degree of orientation to reality. If the symptoms of confusion and disorientation appear significant, the patient is placed into either the basic or advanced reality orientation programs available on the wards.

Finally, arrangements have been made to compare the accumulated data from this institutional population with a community sample in Ohio. It should be noted, however, that these plans have not been finalized.

* *

Anne Haney Gooden
1931 S. 6th Avenue
Tucson, Arizona 85713
(602) 884-9920 x45

Intend to use OARS MFAQ for clinical intake, community survey, and needs survey as an aid to program planning

Name, Address, and Telephone Number	Purpose

D. Richard Greene
Research Specialist
Community Care Evaluation Project
University of Wisconsin-Madison
917 University Avenue
Madison, Wisconsin 53706
(608) 263-5690

There is a dual usage: (1) for the development of case plans for persons who are referred to the Community Care Organization, a home care program for adults; and (2) for research purposes to have baseline data to use for project evaluation.

* *

Virginia Hart
Department of Social and Health
  Services
Office on Aging
OB-43G
Olympia, Washington 98504
(206) 753-2502

The State of Washington has thirteen day-care centers for the aging, which we call day health centers, that are funded through the State Office on Aging. On January 1, 1978, we plan to have day-center staff start using the OARS assessment tool as part of the intake evaluation conducted for each day health applicant. The OARS questionnaire will also be used for periodic assessment of client progress towards treatment plan goals, for discharge planning, and for gathering of data about the day health program.

* *

Sue A. Hartig
Athens Unit
Georgia Retardation Center
850 College Station Road
Athens, Georgia 30605
(404) 542-8970

The University of Georgia was one recipient of the five research grants awarded by the Department of Health, Education and Welfare on the subject of aging and aged developmentally disabled persons (those persons who have mental retardation, cerebral palsy, epilepsy, autism, or severe dyslexia). RPOA's purpose is to define existing services and recommend new service systems which will enable older developmentally disabled persons to remain in a community setting. The main activity of the project is conducting a needs assessment of the target population (age forty-eight and above of developmentally disabled persons). The OARS MFAQ

Sue A. Hartig (continued)

is the assessment instrument utilized, and it is being administered to a sample of 300 persons located in six counties that were selected on demographic criteria as representative of the total forty-six county study area in North Georgia. From the data analysis, a population profile will be developed. With the increased knowledge about older developmentally disabled persons in general and their social service needs in particular the project will compile a comprehensive service delivery design.

* *

Rosemary Hayes, R.N.
7520 Mount Whitney
Dayton, Ohio 45424
(513) 268-6511 x107

I utilized the questionnaire to complete a research project for my Master's Thesis ("A Multidimensional Survey of Health Needs of a Selected Group of Elderly"). I interviewed a total of seventy-four elderly persons living in the community and participating in a Senior Citizens Program or receiving meals at a congregate meal site to identify needs for purposes of developing programs to meet the needs.

I am presently employed in a long-term care institution and plans are being made to utilize the OARS questionnaire for institutional intake and on-going assessment of health status of the residents.

* *

Miriam J. Hirschfield
1539 9th Avenue #3
San Francisco, California 94122
(415) 564-9387

The questionnaire is being used in research on cognitively impaired aged and their families as an assessment tool in addition to a nonstructured interview.

Name, Address, and Telephone Number	Purpose
Susan L. Hughes, CSW 5 Hospital Homebound Elderly Program 541 W Diversey Chicago, Illinois 60614 (312) 549-5822	We are using the questionnaire for dual purposes: (1) as an intake assessment instrument for the 5 Hospital Program; (2) as a research instrument to evaluate program outcomes for clients of the 5 Hosptial Program and outcomes of service for a quasi-equivalent control group. This is being done for my Doctoral Dissertation for Columbia University School of Social Work.

* *

Joan B. Jones Sampson County Department of Social Services P.O. Box 1105 Clinton, North Carolina 28328 (919) 572-7131 x53	The questionnaire is used for protective service cases and used in evaluation of clients that are being considered for rest home placement.

* *

Eleanor S. Kautz Adult Foster Care Program Catholic Social Services 50 South Detroit Street Xenia, Ohio 45385	See Michele J. Foley, above.

* *

Joyce Kwan 105 West North College Street Yellow Springs, Ohio 45387 (513) 767-2301	To sample randomly the population over age sixty in Greene County, Ohio. To use this data generated for planning and prioritizing services, legitimizing funding requests, and educating the general public.

* *

William F. Laurie U.S. General Accounting Office 1240 East 9th Street Cleveland, Ohio 44199 (216) 522-4892	An overview of the effect of federal, state, local, and private programs on older people is needed. To assist the Congress in this regard, GAO developed a two-phase approach: (1) assessing and measuring the overall well-being of a sample of older people in terms of their social and economic

Name, Address, and Telephone Number	Purpose
William F. Laurie (continued)	status, mental and physical health, and ability to do daily tasks, and gathering information on the services and other factors that could affect the well-being of individuals in the sample; (2) updating information about these individuals a year later to identify changes in well-being and attribute them to services and other factors.

* *

Ayeliffe A. Lenihan 46 Shaw Avenue Silver Spring, Maryland 20904 (301) 622-1737	I plan to use the OARS tool on a rural population of elderly women, who are community based, beginning in January 1978. I am interested in sharing information.

* *

Everett Logue Department of Epidemiology School of Public Health University of North Carolina Chapel Hill, North Carolina 27514	Data from OARS Community Survey used in Master's Thesis for an epidemiological evaluation of a small area analysis.

* *

Louise Marzyck 1175 Gribble Richland, Washington 99352 (509) 943-9104 x29 or 51	To help in evaluating the appropriateness of a client's participation in our Geriatric Day Program; determine level of functioning in different areas; and, by making assessment again later, to evaluate progress. We began using the MFAQ for all new clients in June 1977.

* *

J. C. Matthews Memphis Tennessee	Examining impact of home-maker/ home health aide.

Name, Address, and Telephone Number	Purpose
Joyce E. J. Matthews	Ph.D. dissertation, Ohio State University, Home Economics, 1976. Title: Functional assessment of perceived mental and physical health, social and economic resources, activities of daily living, and needed services of elderly participants and nonparticipants of the Columbus, Ohio, congregate meals program.

* *

| Robert G. Matthews, Ph.D. Director, Research and Planning Gateway District Health Department Owingsville, Kentucky 40360 (606) 784-8105 x21 | To determine the existing needs of target population 60 years of age and older in five counties in Northeastern Kentucky. To determine need priority of persons interviewed in the information and referral unit of a health department. To determine the needs of residents of nursing homes in five counties in Northeastern Kentucky. |

* *

| Dr. Lloyd Milligan Neuroscience Laboratory Veterans Administration Hospital Columbia, South Carolina 29201 | The OARS questionnaire is one of several assessment techniques being used to examine patients aged sixty and over, a substantial number of whom are alcoholics who are chronically institutionalized in an acute care hospital. In particular, problems related to discharge and placement are being examined. |

* *

| Jim Moore, M.D. Family Medicine Center 407 Crutchfield Street Durham, North Carolina 27704 (919) 471-2571 | Survey of patient populations in a family medicine residency program. |

Name, Address, and Telephone Number	Purpose
Paul Nelson 105 West North College Street Yellow Springs, Ohio 45387 (513) 767-2301	See Joyce Kwan, above.

* *

Dr. William O'Rourke Mission Towers 180 Water Street Horchill, Massachusetts (617) 372-1124	I do not use the MFAQ regularly. However, I do use the SPMSQ and the SPES. If I can develop a clinical team I will use the MFAQ as an intake tool. I find it very helpful and encourage others to use it.

* *

John Paricer Rehabilitation Institute 3011 Baltimore Kansas City, Missouri 64108 (816) 756-2250	Program evaluation of physical restoration and/or vocational rehabilitation clientel.

* *

Eric Pfeiffer Department of Psychiatry College of Medicine Box 14, University of South Florida 12901 North 30th Street Tampa, Florida 33612 (813) 974-2118	Former Project Director, OARS Program. Experienced teacher of OARS methodology.

* *

Rhey J. Plumley, Surveyor Department of Health 60 Main Street Burlington, Vermont 05753 (802) 862-5701	I am seeking information regard- ing the questionnaire for pos- sible use in Vermont's Nursing Homes, specifically as a social needs assessment tool.

* *

Janet Pudik Easter Seal Society 1545 Wilshire Boulevard, Suite 600 Los Angeles, California 90017 (213) 483-5692	We plan to do the following: (1) to assess clients for pro- grams; (2) to get baseline data as they enter programs; (3) to measure change in clients after their participation in a program.

Name, Address, and Telephone Number	Purpose

Janet Pudik (continued)

The two kinds of programs we intend to begin using the MFAQ in are: Stroke Resocialization Groups, Day Activity Center for Physically Disabled Adults.

* *

Edward N. Pugh
Veterans Administration Hospital
Memorial Drive
Waco, Texas 76703
(817) 752-6581 x316

Fifty randomly selected veterans receiving a regular supplementary cash benefit (Regular Aid and Attendance) are being studied in order to determine whether or not the availability of health care and social services increases the likelihood of continued community residence and decreases the likelihood of institutionalization in this high risk group.

* *

Sarah M. Renda
Luzerne/Wyoming Counties
Office for the Aging
85 E. Union Street
Wilkes-Barre, Pennsylvania
(717) 822-1158

All residents of boarding homes in Luzerne and Wyoming Counties will be interviewed using the OARS questionnaire by the end of 1977 in order to determine the general and specific needs of this population. Survey results will be used for providing services to individuals as well as for planning for services to be used by general population.

* *

Nancy Rhodes
795 North Van Buren
Milwaukee Visiting Nurse Association
Milwaukee, Wisconsin
(414) 276-2295 x293

We attempted to use the OARS instrument for assessment of long-term patients to whom we were providing care to assist them in remaining in their homes. We used it as a supplement to our nursing assessment form to provide increased information about the patient.

We found the OARS tool not adaptable to our situation. We provide direct patient care and found the use of an additional tool to be too time consuming

Nancy Rhodes (continued)

and taxing on our older clients. The information we were able to obtain has been valuable. The OARS instrument also served as an excellent teaching tool for the nurses to use in carefully assessing a long-term client in totality.

* *

Maxeen Roecker
Department of Social and Health
 Services
OB2 MS 41F
Olympia, Washington 98504
(206) 753-0241

Fifteen hundred questionnaires have been administered. This study is being done in conjunction with that of Michael A. Garrick (see above).

* *

Randall Russell
Division of Social Services
West Virginia Department of Welfare
1900 Washington Street, East
Charleston, West Virginia 25305
(304) 348-7980

With some minor modifications the OARS questionnaire is currently being pilot tested by the West Virginia Department of Welfare as part of a research and demonstration project entitled "Measuring the Effectiveness of Social Services." All interviews using this instrument are being conducted by welfare service workers of the agency. All workers performing these interviews were involved in at least one four-hour training session, but, due to training constraints, levels of inter-worker reliability were not established. Staff shortages accounted for low level monitoring of worker activity and various sampling difficulties ensued. Interviews were conducted on intake and review populations of clients classified as aged, blind, and disabled adults living in their own homes. The modified OARS questionnaire is being used as a six-month follow-up instrument and will provide data to assess (1) differences between these two populations and (2)

Name, Address, and Telephone Number	Purpose
Randall Russell (continued)	impact of services over time. Another questionnaire is being completed by clients at time of follow-up to indicate their satisfaction with social services received from the Department of Welfare. Increases in staffing midway through the pilot test have provided an increase in monitoring of worker activity that has improved in response to monitoring procedures.

* *

| Kenneth W. Shirley
Veterans Administration Hospital
Palo Alto, California 94304
(415) 493-5000 x5845 | Survey of health-related needs and problems of older veteran outpatients of Palo Alto VA Hospital. Purposes of planning are to identify: (a) areas in which these types of needs are not being met, (b) extent to which various services or programs are perceived as needed by subjects. General background information on veteran patients in service area, including present functional status (capacity to function independently in the community). |

* *

| Mick Smyer, Ph.D.
College of Human Development
Pennsylvania State University
University Park, Pennsylvania | (1) Development of means of increasing reliability of ratings. (2) Comparison of ICF and home care clients, matched on ADL, to ascertain type of services received and determine impact of setting. It was found that the groups received comparable services, although a greater variety of services were available to ICF clients. Setting appeared to be irrelevant, but a larger service receipt interval is suggested to examine this question properly. Topic formed subject for Ph.D. thesis, Duke University, 1977. |

Name, Address, and Telephone Number	Purpose
Jeffrey R. Solomon, Ph.D. Miami Jewish Home and Hospital for the Aged 151 N.E. 52nd Street Miami, Florida 33137 (305) 751-8626	See Therese Diaz, above.

* *

Mary E. Spencer 5283 58th Avenue, Apartment T-1 Bladensburg, Maryland 20710 (301) 779-0489	The OARS tool will be used this spring for a survey of the rural elderly in southern Prince Georges County, Maryland. Results of the survey will be used in planning services and programs for elderly in this area. In addition, the survey will provide research for a Ph.D. dissertation at the University of Maryland. The dissertation will focus on the black rural elderly in this area.

* *

Cathy Swanson Site Coordinator Wisconsin Community Care Organization Room 315, Tenney Building 110 East Main Street Madison, Wisconsin 53703 (608) 266-7250	After a person (elderly, adult blind, or disabled) is determined eligible for project participation, the OARS questionnaire is used to assess functional status, summarize findings, rate an individual on each scale and on a collective area of functioning scale, and all of this information is used to aid in the development of a service or case plan. We use a variation of the OARS clinic forms in case plan development also. We also use the OARS overall functional rating to compare with a score from a tool we use to determine project eligibility. We hope this will facilitate identifying accurately our target population: those who are very probable of being institutionalized within the next eighteen months or so. Although the OARS instrument was chosen for its use as a program tool, our evaluation, out of the Faye McBeath Institute on Aging and Adult Life (University

Name, Address, and Telephone Number	Purpose

Cathy Swanson (continued)

of Wisconsin, Madison), will also be using the data gathered by the OARS instrument for use in evaluating our pilot project.

* *

Barbara Syzek, M.S.N., Coordinator
Gerontology Center
Otterbein Home
Lebanon, Ohio 45036
(513) 932-2020 x288

Educational purposes with nursing students.

* *

Joyce Tufts
2940 Sixteenth Street #301
San Francisco, California 94115
(415) 864-6470

Research information: to examine and compare the OARS tool with other assessment tools and to determine its applicability to assessment of patients for in-home health and health related services.

* *

Robert E. Wetter
319 S. Limestone Street
Lexington, Kentucky 40508
(606) 233-6551

MED Research will be using a modified version of the Duke OARS questionnaire to help assess current client functioning prior to treatment, six months after treatment, and in multiple follow-ups.

* *

Catherine Wondolowski
Assistant Professor
The Schools of the Health Professions
Hunter College School of Nursing
440 East 26th Street
New York, New York 10010
(212) 686-6800 x219 or 84

Use of the OARS instrument is discussed extensively in class with practice sessions. As a course requirement students apply the instrument to an older adult in the community. In addition, a comprehensive health care plan is developed by the student using the nursing process based upon the assessment data and rating.

* *

Rosalee Yeaworth
University of Cincinnati
Loc. 38
Cincinnati, Ohio 45221
(513) 872-5501

It was used in a thesis study to survey the health needs of a group of elderly to provide data for a community mental health center that needed to expand services for the

Name, Address, and Telephone Number	Purpose

Rosalee Yeaworth (continued)

elderly (see Rosemary Hayes, above). When I attended for the training, I expected to have students using the questionnaire for thesis studies similar to the one listed above.

* *

Bonnie B. Younger
319 South Limestone Street
Lexington, Kentucky 40508
(606) 233-6551

See Robert E. Wetter, above.

* *

D. K. Zinn
West Virginia Department of Welfare
Division of Social Services
1900 Washington Street, East
Charleston, West Virginia 25305
(304) 348-7980

See Randall Russell, above.

* *

<u>Current users at the Center for the Study of Aging and Human Development, Duke University, Durham, North Carolina 27710.</u>

OARS Geriatric Evaluation and Treatment Clinic

Charlene Connolly. R.N.	Clinical application
Jeanette Franklin	Questionnaire administration
Kermit Hamrick, MSW	Clinical application
Alice Myers, ACSW	Clinical application
John Nowlin, M.D.	Clinical and research application
Al Whanger, M.D.	Clinical and research application

Center for the Study of Aging and Human Development

Dan Blazer, M.D.	Research application, program planning
Bill Cleveland, Ph.D.	Statistical analysis
David Dellinger, Ph.D.	Services assessment, theory
Gerda Fillenbaum, Ph.D.	Data analysis, methodology
Linda George, Ph.D.	Public use data preparation
Becky Heron	Training in questionnaire administration
George Maddox, Ph.D.	Theory
Thelma Jernigan	General information

If you have any questions please call Thelma Jernigan (919) 684-4128. If she can't answer them she will direct you to the person who can.